The Face of
Europe

Peter N. Stearns

Carnegie-Mellon University

FORUM PRESS

First Printing March 1977
Second Printing August 1977

Published simultaneously in Canada.

Printed in the United States of America.

Library of Congress Catalog Card Number: 75-44701

ISBN: 0-88273-400-8

Cover design by Donya Melanson Associates—Boston

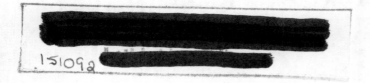

151092

For Carol, a surprise

Preface

THE PURPOSE OF THIS BOOK is to provide something of a profile of the history of western civilization. This will, of necessity, involve personal judgments. Because people do and should hold differing opinions, this book will probably provoke argument, even gentle anger, from those who see things differently. History is not a bland subject to be dished out and swallowed without the possibility of indigestion. I think what follows is quite palatable, although others may differ in their appraisal. Nevertheless, I assume that indigestion is preferable to a loss of appetite through boredom.

There is no pretense that this book will cover all major topics, although an attempt will be made to clarify the principles of selection. We do follow the most common chronology of western civilization studies—that is, from the Greek civilization to the contemporary world. But rather than follow a brief assessment of the Greeks with another of the Romans and then with the medievals, and so on, I propose to view each civilization primarily in terms of what it contributed to the next phase of western development and to what we are today. This involves selectivity; for example, a host of features of Greek society, while fascinating in themselves, simply were not passed on. These elements of Greek society should be studied, but they detract from a sense of history as process, as an explaining of subsequent events. Our concern is with trends that shape who we now are and that even may affect our choices for the future.

There are all sorts of reasons for studying history. Probably most professional historians and most students in history courses, save those who are dragooned into history class by college requirements or an appealing class hour, pursue history because they are fascinated by people and situations from the past. The current trends in education are to prepare a student for gainful employment or specialized study. But in our modern society, most people are presented with an abundance of leisure time—while in school and later in life—and thus have opportunities for pleasurable study of history. Those who find reading history fun should not be ashamed of explaining the reason for their interest. Nor should they dismiss the intellectual importance of studying history.

History teaches us about human behavior. For students who are trying to define their own values and priorities, a knowledge of history can provide a needed prospective in assessing one's values and personal growth. By examining choices made by individuals and groups even in quite different past cultures, we can firm up our own sense of what is practical and moral if we should face situations even remotely comparable. This use of historical example, however, must be subtle, for history does not repeat itself exactly even in very similar situations. But for personal development and political development, history, if properly understood, does provide the most realistic human laboratory.

Finally, history, more than any other subject, teaches us where we are now—what is new and what is not. For example, by examining the origins of past religions and the acts of churches and religious persons, we can understand the position of religion today, and perhaps make personal decisions about what religion should mean to us as individuals. Historical analysis can explain a cultural phenomenon or propose remedies based on an understanding of the roots and evolution of the concept. Everyday judgments, tossed about by eminent social scientists and journalists alike, are in fact historical. The modern family, for example, is judged by the standards of the past, whether real or imagined, and often is criticized on these grounds. In sum, history teaches both trends and breaks in trends; only through both these processes can we understand where we are now and where we as a human society are likely to go.

Thus we are consciously seeking both continuities and points at which new elements that will prove durable enter the scene. We may wish that certain aspects of, say, Athenian culture had persisted more fully than they have, so that our masses would be flocking to hear a modern Aristophanes instead of flocking to the more Roman pursuits of spectator sports. Some past glories have been romanticized beyond much resemblance with reality; other glories, gone forever, would be welcomed back indeed. What is important is to see where we are, not to reflect on what we might have been. This is how, even in a survey of as long a period of time as the development of western civilization, history can be used to tell us much about who we are and who we are becoming.

I wish to thank these people for their critical reading of this book: Frederic A. Youngs, Jr., Louisiana State University; Myron Marty, St. Louis Community College—Florissant Valley; and Karl Roider, Louisiana State University.

The Origins of Western Civilization

THE DEVELOPMENT OF MOST of western history occurred within a context shared by many other cultures: an economy and society based on agricultural production. Within this broad framework of agricultural society a host of differences might develop. In political organization, for example, it has been argued that where agriculture depends on irrigation, which in turn involves close coordination of human effort, authoritarian political systems are particularly likely—e.g., ancient Egypt or China. Religions could vary widely. But there are certain broad similarities within all societies dependent on agriculture, and before turning to the western variants it is well to outline the basic context. Furthermore, since the first breakthrough in agricultural society occurred in the West with industrialization, an understanding of some of the normal limitations of agriculture gives us a realistic goal in an overview of the later evolution of western civilization. What particular set of quirks and values, for example, led the West into replacing agriculture and the countryside with industry and the city as the normal environment for human life?

Agricultural Societies

The basic points about agricultural society may seem obvious, but we rarely examine their complex impact in forming an idea of what that society actually was. First, most people worked the land and did not live in cities. Civilizations around the Mediterranean, including ancient Greek and Roman but also recent Italian cultures, were more highly urbanized than most, for many farmers lived in towns and traveled out to their fields. They might thus maintain urban values. But as a general rule no more than twenty percent of a population in an agricultural society lived in cities, and the percentage was usually less than this.

Civilization, however, has an urban bias; the word derives from the ancient designation for the city. But here we face a dichotomy, which is our second main point about agricultural societies. The cities lived off the countryside economically, but the farmers were often remote from urban culture and might be regarded as positively uncivilized. This is not a fair judgment, though it is true that many key ideas began in cities and spread only slowly to the rural majority. A totally rural society had neither leisure nor enough diversity to produce the high culture we most readily identify with civilization—polished music, formal drama, and so on. So what we regard most readily as "civilized" typifies the minority. It may be more interesting and important to determine what the values of the rural majority were. Urban concepts rarely were adapted without some distinctively rural twists.

Agricultural society is also inherently poor by contemporary western standards which has tagged the phrase, "subsistence economy," to agricultural societies in premodern Europe as well as in modern Asia and Latin America. Agricultural societies that produced civilizations also produced a real margin above subsistence which was enjoyed primarily by the ruling minority. Governments depended on this margin as they taxed the farmers. Churches, which provided the bulk of intellectual life, depended on this margin, as they tithed farmers or persuaded the state to turn over some tax money directly. Other economic activity also resulted from this margin above subsistence, as we shall see. For every eight or nine people working directly in agriculture, a vibrant agricultural society could support one person living apart from the land—governing, teaching and writing, or specializing in making stylish shoes. But while a few state officials and churchmen might make huge fortunes and create an opulent, eye-catching lifestyle, it is vitally important to remember that most people in the cities and most in the countryside whose surplus was taken to support the cities, really did not live much above a subsistence level.

But the narrow material margins typical of agricultural life created for most people many crucial differences from our own style of life. There were more deaths, for example. In most agricultural societies over any extended period of time, about half of all babies born died before reaching the age of two. This cycle was broken in Europe only in the eighteenth century; in India only in the twentieth, and still there was much death that a modern westerner would regard as premature. In America the pattern was broken in the seventeenth century; by the eighteenth century, American rates were rising to near-traditional levels. There was no time, no extra food, and obviously no widespread medical knowledge to care for the weak, particularly the newborn. Rapid population growth did occur, as we shall see, though agricultural societies until recent centuries typically expanded rather slowly. But death was common. Though cultures might vary, they all had to deal with the omnipresence of death, which is why most tried to make death explainable and to reduce its terror through religious rituals and doctrines.

The agricultural economy was also highly uncertain. For pre-modern Europe it has been estimated that in one year out of four some crop failure occurred in a given locality, and periodically more widespread failures would decimate a whole subcontinent. Plagues were another recurrent, unavoidable catastrophe. This of course is one explanation for a high death rate. Uncertainty also contributed to distinctive cultural features shared by most agricultural societies. First, most were tightly communitarian. Whatever the political system, peasants and other common people tended to band together at the family level and often beyond, to help each other in times of trouble. This meant no matter what official values were advocated, the culture of the common people was nonindividualistic, which is of crucial importance in the West where individualism has been touted as a distinctive characteristic. Community advice and assistance were too vital, given the inability to control weather, crop diseases, and plagues, to be replaced by individualism. But assistance did mean control; most of the common people in an agricultural society lived in small, tightly-bound units that discouraged eccentric behavior and might punish severely for it.

Even strict standards and mutual cooperation were not enough to bring stability to economic life. The culture of agricultural people had to mitigate the effects of changes and uncertainties that were beyond human control. They tended therefore to be conservative; it was too risky to innovate, and what had been done in the past seemed best. Furthermore, unpredictability was usually countered by values that preached the existence of a more ordered life after death. Religion, despite its extremely varied forms, was a vital ingredient of agricultural life because of this central function. It was impossible to hope for stability on this earth, so life had to be given some greater meaning, which usually involved belief in some form of heaven or in the preservation of the meaning of human existence by venerating one's ancestors, whose earthly struggle deserved at least this reward.

Poverty and uncertainty interwoven with a rich culture which ranged from festivals to formal religion were the hallmarks of an agricultural society. But poverty, recurrent death, and a battle over scarce resources could poison the most intimate family relationships. All of these contradictory impressions influence our overall judgment of agricultural existence.

Social Structure

Agricultural society gains its basic coherence from its economic foundation and the limitations and problems this imposes; which means in turn that ordinary people, the mass of the population, had the most in common, for they were closest to the soil. But we can go a bit further with our definition of agricultural society, while noting that the privileged minority living on the margin produced by the peasants could afford much greater diversity. One way to understand what the key elements of an agricultural society had in common is to project the social structure valued in most such societies, the one that received normal official sanction.

Most philosophers—Plato, for example, or medieval Christian thinkers like Thomas Aquinas and others from the western world—regarded society as consisting of three basic groups, differing in size and function. At the top were the two leadership categories: military men and priests or philosophers. Here there were two basic questions. Obviously it was vital to know if the class whose primary function it was to think also had the duty to pray; that is, whether they were philosophers alone or priests as well. Different societies would answer this question quite differently. Within the West, the more ancient civilizations leaned more toward philosophers than priests. On the whole, the West traditionally tended to give religious significance and special religious functions and sanction to its thinkers—particularly from the Middle Ages until the industrial revolution. This tradition has left some problems for intellectuals—the modern equivalent, one might say, of philosophers—now that even western society is largely secular.

A more crucial question in the traditional lineup of groups at the top was the relationship between priests, philosophers, and soldiers. Which was to be supreme? China long maintained the supremacy of non-military rulers, though the military played a vital role in times when defense against outside attack was essential. India, though varying somewhat from one region to the next, clearly played down the importance of the military group. Within ancient Greece, Sparta was run indisputably by the soldiers. There was little intellectual life at all, though there were priestly religious functions. But Athens, though boasting that its military was kept under control, waged a seesaw battle between military and political rulers, and in crises always turned to the former. On the whole, the West has opted for military preponderance in leadership, though not as clearly as, say, the Japanese during the rule of the *samurai*. It may be, indeed, that the tension between military and religious-political leaders is the most important feature of western civilization in this whole matter, but the ongoing force of military values cannot be ignored.

The third group in any traditional society was the peasants, the workers. All the political theorists recognized that this was the largest group, and they argued it was just as important as the other two. And it was, in an economic sense but not in a political sense. Rarely in an agricultural society was this group given any direct access to power. The medieval philosopher John of Salisbury put the situation clearly, combining both Christian thought and classical political theory: peasants and workers were the feet of society, without which it could not stand; soldiers were the arms; priests were the soul (this put them above soldiers); and the king was the head. This elaborate metaphor is charming, for it is true that the body needs feet to stand on. But feet are feet, the lowest part of the body, and they are given less attention than, say, soul or arms. This general view of the inferiority of the ordinary worker was shared whatever the vital distinctions at the top within and among priests and soldiers.

None of these definitions provided for a fourth group, which all advanced agricultural societies required in some form. This was a trading class, whose function it was to convey the goods produced by the mass of peasants and workers. At the least this meant arranging transportation, but in any elaborate society more was involved. Greece, for example, began early to specialize in an agriculture of olives and grapes. This meant that more distant areas had to produce the wheat needed for ordinary starch, whether for peasant or priest. In the case of Athens, wheat was imported from Sicily and the Near East (what is now Turkey). But again, somebody had to arrange for this and presumably he wouldn't do it for free. The same applied to the sale of pottery produced by artisans, metal work, and so on. China faced similar problems, for in this vast land the transport of goods was supplemented by elaborate trade with regions as distant as the eastern coast of Arabia. Who was to manage trade, and what was to be their status? In eighteenth-century Russia, a classic agricultural society, some uppity peasants began to act like merchants, transporting not only food but also goods, like cloth manufactured in rural homes, and hoping to make a good profit in the process. Nobles, seeing the threat to the traditional order, quickly ended this activity, retarding Russia's economic progress. But most societies—and even Russia at the time—needed some mercantile activity. They could rely primarily on foreigners, which is what Athens did to a substantial degree, letting *metics* (a foreign element, about ten percent of the adult male population) handle most of the trade. Rome relied even more on foreigners for commerce. China produced her own merchants, and to this day they prove a thriving and enterprising breed. But China never let the merchant group upset the basic order of things.

For in most agricultural societies, because of the fundamental structure that was assumed, people who handled money were a bit shady. Aristocrats and priests feared wealthy merchants as rivals, and even peasants distrusted people who did not produce but who took their goods and made a profit on them. Hence the belief that commerce was somehow tainted, which we find in so many different times and places. Merchants might rise but only because money talked even two thousand years ago. For many merchants, the best way to achieve respectability was to use their money to get out of commerce once they had established a modest fortune on which they could live comfortably. In China, a common pattern, persisting well into modern times, was for the man with some wealth to retire and direct his sons into other activity; the best possible choice was a life of scholarship. Medieval Europe would be faced with the same dilemma and initially would seem to solve it similarly. Merchants were scorned; thus some merchants retired to a life of religion, or gave their sons or daughters to monasteries and convents. But western merchants proved more tenacious and ultimately more venturesome than even their Chinese counterparts. They could begin to construct a culture of their own that eventually cast aside the old hierarchy of priests and soldiers. Why the West did this is one of the questions we must try to answer as we deal with the vital comparative issue of why the West became such a distinctive culture.

But we are ahead of ourselves. The Athenian would easily have recognized the Chinese attitude toward the merchant as one of grudging recognition of his social service but scorn for his actual job. There was a common cast to agricultural society, from its peasant base to its typical reverence for priests or intellectuals and, usually, for men of unusual military skill. This raises three issues. First how, if at all, did the West differ from other advanced societies during its long period in the agricultural era? Sometimes, indeed, it was barely advanced at all, and we must note this inferiority because other cultures have not forgotten that we were once barbarians. Second, why did the West break through the agricultural barriers, what special combination of cultural distinctions—soldier-priest relations, merchant position, even peasant values or sheer historical accident—let it defy the pervasive outlines of agricultural society to become something else. Third, what sort of civilization did we become, and what relation did our innovations bear to still largely agricultural world?

The Background to Greece and Rome

Greece and Rome did not arise spontaneously. Rome, as we will see, was able to copy elements of politics and culture from Greece. More importantly, Greece was able to copy some elements from previous civilizations. The alphabet is a case in point. The Greeks did not have to invent the idea of alphabet; they had the example of an alphabet which they could adapt to form their own. The transcendent fact was that both Greece and Rome were agricultural societies, yet neither had to invent agriculture. On both the Greek and the Roman peninsulas people had been farming for centuries before the more formal civilizations we label Greek and Roman developed. So we need a word about precedents, starting with the rise of agriculture and turning to civilizations from which Greece and Rome could draw, notably the societies of Mesopotamia and Egypt. We have already noted that the rise of agriculture was not specifically western. Mesopotamian and Egyptian civilizations were not western either. We briefly survey them here to indicate what the Greeks and the Romans did *not* have to do, what already had been devised and needed only to be adapted to local conditions. Then we can confront the more important question of how and when specifically western elements developed from this common core, a core which by the time of the early Greeks was not merely agricultural, but had proved capable of creating civilizations with advanced art, science, and political structures.

The Neolithic revolution that launched human civilization is shrouded in mystery. We know roughly what happened and when—it was a gradual revolution—but we do not fully know the human motives involved. What basically occurred is that man switched from hunting to settled agriculture as his principal source of food and clothing. Obviously many peoples, such as the North American Indians, combined the two approaches well into recent times; the break did not have to be complete. Reversion was also possible. Many prospectors and trappers in North America, mainly those of English and French origin, reverted in the eighteenth and nineteenth centuries to a hunting style of life. This meant not only a reliance on game killing and animal foods, but other distinctive habits. Human hunters, like their carnivorous animal counterparts, typically gorged themselves after a kill to the point of nausea, slept, gorged again until the food was gone, and then went three days or more without food.

More interesting than reversions or incomplete transformations is the hold that the hunting instinct still may have held over man when the Neolithic revolution was complete. Indeed, the ease with which people can revert might suggest how close to the surface the hunting instinct still is. A case in point is the aristocracy in western society, where hunting played a large role, partly to provide food—for the aristocracy long used hunting to achieve a better diet than the grain-eating common people—but also to convey a distinctive male prowess. Does a frustrated hunting instinct also enter our human proclivity for aggression and wars? Possibly—but if so we must recognize that over the last ten centuries, some peoples such as the Europeans seem to be closer to that instinct than others such as the Chinese.

The Neolithic revolution produced a number of definable results, visible in some areas about 7,000 years before Christ. The turn to agriculture (supplemented, of course, by hunting where possible) increased the food supply, and in turn caused a dramatic rise in the number of humans populating the globe. Agriculture meant domestication of animals for use as aids to human work, as well as more predictable sources of meat, and above all, for the cultivation of grains. Assured meat supplies, however, were less important than the fact that grain proved a much more productive and reliable supplier of calories and low-grade protein than the hunting economy had ever produced. Between 6000 and 3000 B.C. tools were developed, such as the hoe and a primitive plow, which of course further encouraged the conversion. By 3000 B.C. the wheel had been invented, horses and other animals were harnessed to vehicles, and related discoveries such as the potter's wheel suggested aids that could be translated into advanced artistic forms.

We do not know how much the population increased as a result of this first great productive revolution. Hunting societies had been characterized by high birth rates but the vast majority of children died early. Agricultural societies, with more predictable food supplies, began to move toward their characteristic pattern of about one child dying before age two for every two born—a horrific pattern by modern standards but a great improvement by earlier ones. Before the Neolithic revolution there were no more than 20 million people covering the entire globe, and possibly as few as two million. By 3000 B.C., when the new agricultural patterns had spread to many parts of the globe, the human population probably had increased to at least 100 million and perhaps more.

Equally important was the fact that agriculture compelled and permitted larger human settlements and more regular human interaction. Hunters had worked together and on occasion they had formed communities. The largest thus far uncovered numbered no more than 300 persons, and this was unusual; indeed it resembled a war camp more than a permanent settlement. With agriculture came the need for more careful year-round supervision and coordination of the members of a residential unit. Planting and harvest time, particularly, imposed tasks that often surpassed the abilities of a single individual or even a small family. Because people had to work together they needed a more developed government. Domesticated animals, vital to the new economy, were often in short supply; sharing again involved some kind of local government. New tools were often made by individual families, but it was realized early that some specialization was desirable so that talented individuals might concentrate on pottery making or metal work, and exchange their products for the food produced by others.

Although fairly obvious, these implications of the new economy are nonetheless important. Civilization was now possible, as it involved politics, economic specialization, and probably some social differentiation. The position of women may have improved, for women now had more clearly productive roles in agriculture. Above all, as we have seen, agricultural society produced economic surpluses. Although still vulerable to crisis—crop failure—agricultural society was far less vulnerable than the hunting society had been, and in normal years could create yields greater than the subsistence needs of a family plus the seed needed for next year's planting. Here was basis for the formation of cities, albeit fairly small ones, for upper classes who could specialize in government, religion, and military affairs (or combinations of all of these) at a level above that of a single locality. As agriculture became more sophisticated in some areas, irrigation imposed the necessity of larger units of government, for a locality could not successfully manipulate the vagaries of a river like the Nile.

All of this is, of course, quite general, though we must remember it created a type of civilization that was to last for 10,000 years. Agricultural societies sprang up in many parts of the world. Primitive farmers reached the southern coast of England between 2000 and 1500 B.C.—that is, well before any contact with the famous classical sources of western civilization. They had seed grains, domesticated animals, bows and arrows, hoes, fire-making materials and so on. They easily subjugated the small hunting population that previously had been scattered about the island. Farming communities in Switzerland and Germany date even earlier. By 1500 B.C. the only parts of Europe left to a largely hunting economy were in Scandanavia. This latter fact proved important, as populations were to pour out of Scandanavia some 2,000 years later to help create the strange mix we call western civilization. But it is equally important to realize that quietly, without producing great masterpieces or an elaborate formal culture, most of Europe was civilized in the sense of having converted to agriculture and settled communities, before the birth of more specifically western civilization.

Middle-Eastern Civilizations

But the inception of the agricultural economy was in the Mediterranean basin, not Europe, and it was here that societies used agriculture to produce more advanced structures of civiliza-

tion. Some groups in the Near East practiced agriculture and had
domesticated some animals as early as 7000 B.C. Excavations at
Jericho, in the Palestinian Dead Sea, have revealed an ancient farming village of that date; beneath it was an older hunting village
which had been replaced. Agricultural villages almost as old have
been found in what are now Iraq and Iran; 1,000 years later there
are similar developments in southern Turkey and in other areas of
Iran, around the Caspian Sea. Still later, agricultural villages arose
between 3500 and 2500 B.C. in Peru, Mexico, and elsewhere in
Central and South America. They do not enter our story directly,
except on the basis of their cultivation of corn (maize) and subsequently the potato, which ironically, over 4,000 years later, would
help produce a new economic revolution in Europe. The development of agriculture in the Far East resulted in part from cultural
diffusion; that is, from the spread of techniques first developed in
the Near East. This seems certainly true of eastern India, where
agricultural villages arose by 3300 B.C. In China, the Neolithic
revolution occurred sometime after 5000 B.C., and we simply do not
know whether this was an independent development or brought by
migrants from the more advanced areas of the Near East.

This text promised not to start with the caves, and most people
have been taken out of them as the basis for our consideration of the
foundation of civilization—any civilization, western included. Yet,
from the standpoint of western civilization, we must recall the obvious geographical point: that the new economy arose first not in
Europe but near it, in the Middle East, an area with which Europe
would come to have permanent interaction. Why there? The soil
was good—the desert that now characterizes the area had not yet
been created; it has been speculated that overcultivation and
overgrazing helped cause that. Previous hunting possibilities had
been favorable, which may have given an extra margin for experimentation with new economic means. The question is
fascinating, not fully resolved and perhaps unresolvable. But we
can take it as given: Not only did early, scattered agricultural
villages first emerge in the Mediterranean region but so did more
advanced regional civilizations, notably those of the Tigris-
Euphrates valley and of Egypt. Here the basic geographical advantage is clear, for good soil and favorable weather were supplemented
by the presence of rivers useful for transport and, above all, for
irrigation. This latter inevitably impelled more advanced and
regionally extensive governmental forms; allowed greater produc-

tivity; and created greater concentrations of people and a larger margin for non-agricultural activities such as religion and intellectual inquiry. The same basic phenomenon occurred in China during the same period, though it did not influence western civilization until much later.

The two main Near Eastern cultures demand serious comment. The Tigris-Euphrates civilization—Mesopotamian and Babylonian—produced cities. In the cities crafts turned out goods that might be used in agriculture or by the urban upper class; in the latter category craft could easily merge with art. Formal architecture, sculpture, and painted frescoes adorned buildings by 3000 B.C. Science also evolved from practical roots. With economic division of labor, trading was needed, and for trading one needed units of calculation—hence mathematics. The Babylonians commonly (though not always) used numerical units based on 10, 60, and 360, which we still use in dividing the hour and measuring the degrees of a circle. Babylonian astronomy, the first ever developed, produced charts of the major constellations which serve as basis for our own. And of course writing proved essential. The alphabetic symbols derived from Babylon were used for thousands of years in the Near East, most importantly in the development of Persian writing.

Babylonian civilization had an elaborate religion relating primarily to nature. But there were also gods protecting the major crafts. As life was harsh in a society where nature still was largely uncontrolled, so the gods were violent and angry, though they could be propitiated by sacrifices from mortal man. Basic to Babylonian religion was the idea that the world was created by divine action for divine purposes. This idea, plus a host of specific "myths" about the actions of the gods (including the idea of a purifying flood) were to pass to other peoples, including the Hebrews, and form some of the bases for both the underlying theme and many specific details in the Book of Genesis.

Babylon also produced government. By 3000 B.C. the Mesopotamian valley was divided into fourteen small, warring kingdoms; these were united only gradually. Not only a large unit of government but also a clear code of law, setting forth specifications of what crime was and what the rights of all classes were, resulted from political sophistication. The code of Hammurabi (c. 1950 B.C.) was the most famous of these sets of laws.

Yet, for all its progress and the fascination of its history, Babylon was not to yield much to western civilization.

Overwhelmed by 1600 B.C. by invaders who spoke an Indo-European language, Sanskrit, the major Babylonian heritage passed eastward to the resulting civilization of India. We pointed to some religious legacy passed on via the Hebrews, but this only affected western civilization after the classical period; it had no direct bearing on the religions of Greece and Rome. We can definitely note the mathematical and astronomical guidelines which were to be inherited more directly. But that's about it, which, without minimizing these legacies, goes to show that just because there is a civilization in the general vicinity of a later civilization does not mean it has much influence.

More important for our background was the rise of civilization along the Nile. Egyptian civilization was almost as old as Babylonian, though it may have borrowed a few elements for its early development. The idea of writing, for example, may have been copied, though Egyptian hieroglyphics, their specific form of writing, was a native invention. Egypt was unified by about 3100 B.C., and developed a highly centralized structure ruled by a king and a staff of highly qualified bureaucrats. Egyptian irrigation, the basis of its agriculture, is indeed a classic case of technical necessity producing elaborate political forms. Art, sculpture, furniture making—all were highly developed as well. Both techniques and a graceful style were cultivated and later were passed on to Greece. On the other hand, firmly ruled by a king, the Egyptians did not produce elaborate law codes, political thought, or even epics and myths such as Babylon transmitted to the peoples of the East. Mathematics was less advanced, though the division of the day into twenty-four hours is an Egyptian concept, while the subordinate units of sixty (minutes per hour, seconds per minute) are of Mesopotamian origin.

Transmission of Cultures

Western civilization did not emerge neatly from either Egypt or Babylon, although it was to be influenced by both. Vital elements of both early cultures were not transmitted. Egypt's god-king, for example, was not duplicated in Greece. The concept may have had some influence on imperial Rome, which ruled Egypt directly and whose emperors fancied themselves as virtual gods, but for all the megalomaniacs who emerge as rulers in western civilization, godship has been claimed by few. Law codes were to be a vital classical legacy to the West, but there is no sign that

Babylon's precedent had anything to do with them. So we do not go neatly from the first major civilizations in the Mediterranean basin to the next, Greece and Rome.

By 2000 B.C., however, the major civilizations were beginning to influence surrounding areas, such as the island of Crete and areas of Asia Minor that are now part of Syria and Turkey. Classes of priests, warriors, and traders gradually emerged as governments became more complex. About the same time the people on the northern fringes of the civilized areas, who already had moved from a pure hunting economy to the grazing of domesticated animals—sort of a migratory way station between caves and settled agriculture—began to push toward the south. These people were Indo-Europeans organized in patriarchal clans. Their distinctive feature was their language, for similarity of words from German and Celtic in the North, to Greek and Sanskrit derive from the Indo-European base. Although hardly civilized by Egyptian and Babylonian standards, the Indo-European languages are characterized by rather elaborate sentence structure, such as the use of subordinate clauses. It has been suggested that compared to some other languages, such as the Semitic languages that spread over the Middle East proper as the older civilizations collapsed, the Indo-European tongues are better adapted to synthesizing and organizing thought. They also are relatively specific in their naming of material objects. If this is so, it might set some background for ultimate developments in western civilization, especially in the areas of technology and applied science, not only among the great thinkers, but, in terms of accepting such notions, among common people as well. Thus the Indo-European languages helped to set the West off from some other parts of the world. Lest this be taken as a culturally-biased speculation—and speculation it is—it must be noted first, that India, where Indo-European languages spread widely, did not produce a western civilization. A host of other factors were needed. Second, technology and applied science may not produce an optimal civilization, for along with possible strengths of Indo-European languages were weaknesses. The Semitic languages, for example, adapt themselves better to poetry and other forms of literature. But maybe the language base offers one vague clue to what was to become distinctively western.

Pressed by Indo-Europeans from the North (one group of which pushed directly into Babylonia), by Semitic invaders from the southern part of the Arabian peninsula, and by internal divisions, the great Mediterranean civilizations collapsed or, like Egypt, entered long periods of stagnation. Collapse and stagnation can make life easier for the historian and student; in this case they allow us to jump to about 600 B.C. with the simple statement that not much happened. Important small states developed, such as Phoenicia which began to extend its trading operations. Based north of Israel along the sea, the Phoenicians long had traded with Egypt. They simplified the Egyptian alphabet by 1300 B.C., and this ultimately was taken over by the Greeks, who added vowels, and thus serves as the basis of our own alphabet as further transmitted by the Romans.

The small Hebrew state in Israel, one of the products of the Semitic invasions, left a far greater legacy to the West. Politically, the state meant very little, and proved easily overrun by outsiders. But the Jews had an unusual sense of cohesion, based particularly on a peculiar kind of religion. Instead of the common practice, which would be carried on in Greece and Rome, of multiple deities related to the functions of nature (Apollo riding his chariot to deliver the sun daily, rather like a celestial milkman) the Jews singled out one god, Jehovah. This was the first monotheistic religion in the Mediterranean world. For the leading civilizations of the time, it had little impact, but it was to have tremendous influence. For the Jewish god, though a creator of nature, was much more remote from nature and from human activities than the typical Mediterranean gods. For the Jews there were no special gods for hunting, for the rising of the sun; there was one god, though in some cases a rather nasty one. Monotheism gave the Jews an enduring sense of cohesion; they found it easier to focus on one god than a multitude. It was also to contribute a distinctive element to western civilization, when adapted through Christianity and the dispersal of Jews themselves. The belief in nature as divine was less important in the Hebrew religion than in most classical religions. Man operated under a single god, possibly harsh, but not connected with the sanctity of trees or even the sun. So man could exploit nature. This was for the future, for the Jewish state long remained small and self-contained; but it would prove a vital contribution to the ultimate development of western civilization.

In the sixth century B.C. (559 B.C. is an acceptable beginning date) the Near East was unified on an unprecedented scale under the Persians. The Persian Empire enters our story only indirectly. It constantly posed a threat to Greece, and some bitter wars were fought between the two. More enduringly important is the fact that the Persians created the kind of peace and relative prosperity within the Near East itself which allowed further advances in Babylonian science. Astronomy became more precisely mathematical, arithmetic advanced. These gains were to be passed on to India and then back to the Arabic world, from which western Europe would acquire them many centuries later.

Thus, advanced civilizations had been created, elements of which were to be transmitted. Some of the transmission was late, slow, and indirect. Some played only a minor role in the period itself. As noted, the Jews were developing a religion unprecedentedly based on the concept of one God and were hammering out an elaborate set of ethics; this would become the root of both Christianity and Islam. Israel was a theocratic state ruled by priests and prophets. On this basis it rejected political autocracy of the Egyptian sort. But its prophets did not renounce the world and the importance of human action; in this they differed mightily from the religions of India which took shape during the same centuries. Jewish religious leaders increasingly insisted that God dealt with each individual alone, even if often in anger. All these traits would have immense implications for western civilization. But Israel was a tiny state, not in the mainstream of the great civilizations we have discussed despite the contact with Egypt and the imitation of some aspects of Babylonian religion.

From the standpoint of western civilization we can view the Mediterranean fringes by around 500 B.C. as heirs to a diverse and rich cultural past. Elements had been created in religion, art, and science that were to prove durably useful. But western civilization itself did not yet exist. For it to emerge a change of locale was needed, a different kind of synthesis of the heritage of the past, and some distinctively new features as well. Greek culture certainly can claim this accomplishment. It created the first civilization on the European continent that could pretend to rival contemporary Persia or India or China in any major respect. In its rivalry it did best in terms of philosophy and art and, to a limited extent, in science and technology. It stood its ground militarily for a time. It did less well in politics, though it may have created political values that, applied in a different context, were distinctive and viable. In any event, we must obviously turn to Greece for the first effort to find a western element, in more than a geographical sense, among the welter of powerful civilizations that by now had been spawned from the Mediterranean to China.

Ancient Greece

IDENTIFIABLE GREEK CIVILIZATION emerged about 700 B.C., reaching its high point two or three centuries later. There is, of course, a Greek prehistory; nothing ever starts neatly anywhere. The peninsula had long since been taken over by the Indo-Europeans from whom the Greek language derived. Greece gained cultural stimulus also from Crete, which the Greeks themselves indirectly recorded in the legends of the minotaur and the fabulous wealth of Croesus, one of the kings of Crete. Cretan civilization derived from the Egyptian but in artistic forms was no mere copy. About 1600 B.C. the primitive agricultural leaders on the Greek mainland, with whom the Cretans traded occasionally, began to take an interest in Cretan art and to copy it in their homes. As so often would happen with cultural contacts of this sort, interest led to envy and by 1400 B.C. the Greeks had conquered the island. There followed a period called the Mycenaen age, based on the rule of the fortress city of Mycenae. Yet Cretan civilization was not to be matched in artistic splendor or in trade, for this period had a distinctly militaristic cast. Ironically it was swept away by a second-wave Indo-European invasion after 1200, and again we can note a period, the Greek Dark Ages, in which little seems to happen, although agricultural and manufacturing methods improved and the adaptation of the Phoenician alphabet occurred. But, to confound historians who have been able to discover very little about this 500-year period, the *Iliad* and the *Odyssey,* Greece's two great epic poems, emerged in this period, probably written about the eighth century B.C. and probably by different authors despite their attribution to the poet Homer.

Homer's epics, referring to the Mycenaen age and a war with Troy (a city in what is now Turkey) that probably did occur about 1200 B.C. although not in the form recounted by Homer, reflect something of an enduring Greek spirit. And insofar as the poems were revived and celebrated in later western civilization, they may reveal something of a western spirit as well. Homer's people, almost all heroes, are strongly etched individuals barely able to cooperate in a common cause. As warriors they obviously are strongly militaristic. Their gods, often petty and quarrelsome, mirror the traits of the men themselves. These were no superhuman characters, which meant that the Greeks, though religious and eager to propitiate a god or goddess who might be of help, also could feel that their world was theirs to run. This was a world of human beings, and the gods, while important, were simply on a slightly larger scale. So Greece's Dark Ages somehow produced a spirit of human-centeredness with great range for individual ambition and passions. It produced, as both the *Iliad* and *Odyssey* reveal, a taste for beauty and for bloodthirsty ferocity. Pottery was one of the few other artistic forms perpetuated in the Dark Ages, and the vases were decorated with careful geometric designs, suggesting the attention to balance and proportion that would again endure in Greece. The language forged in this era was rich, with an ample vocabulary and complex sentence construction, able to express shades of emotion and ideas clearly and briefly, and above all to deal with complex concepts and abstractions in a single phrase. In all this there was rich promise for the future. But this was also an unsettled age, with the waves of invasion and the lack of solid political structures. This age left a legacy of political instability and an association of glory with military prowess that would mark Greece and may linger even now in the West.

Formal Greek civilization, prepared in these centuries that have left so little direct record, advanced with great speed after 700 B.C. Let us briefly capture the narrative of Greece's rise and fall, and then turn to the more important questions of what the Greek achievement was and what it means for us.

The Greek Narrative

Politically Greece was organized as a series of city-states or *poleis* (singular: *polis*). These might combine for certain purposes, as to repel a Persian invasion, but more commonly they quarreled. A definite cultural unity was expressed in all-Greek events such as the Olympic games, where athletes competed as individuals from all over the peninsula, but political unity was never achieved. The city-state included a central city with a fortress, temples, and cultural facilities. To varying degrees the city served as a trading center. Here sat the government, including the major courts of law. Around it were the majority of people, farmers. Few city-states were large; Athens was one of the biggest, eventually embracing 1,000 square miles. The typical city-state—and given the number and variety of *poleis* it is difficult to generalize—was ruled by an aristocracy, but some were governed by a dictator or king and one, Athens, made a pretense at democracy which we must analyze later. In no city-state, not even Athens, were most residents citizens, that is, people with full rights of political participation or even full civil rights. Women had no civil rights; this was a heavily male culture, at least at the official level. Most city-states, including Athens, depended heavily on slave labor, and slaves were obviously not free. Foreign-born people, though they might be tolerated, could rarely attain citizenship, although they might, as in Athens, serve such important economic functions as craftsmen and particularly merchants. That minority of the population that did have citizenship, partly because of its small size and exclusiveness, sometimes developed intense political consciousness and local loyalty. This is why we get a common picture of the Greek city, particularly Athens, as a hothouse of cultural and political activity, often disputatious but always vigorous. This picture is not entirely inaccurate *if* we remember three things:

One, there was great variety, not only among city-states but also within the same state. Examples: Sparta had a small citizenry, a true aristocracy; but most residents were slaves, called *helots*, who did the farming while the aristocrats did the fighting. Even the aristocrats lacked regular political participation, for Sparta was ruled by an unusual combination of two kings. Athens, on the other hand, had a wider citizenry and at times much broader political participation. Between 700 and 450 B.C., however, Athens itself was often ruled by a dictator or an aristocratic oligarchy.

Two, even when Athens offered broad citizen participation we must remember the small citizen base. Only forty percent of Athens' adult males were citizens. They had long periods of democratic rule and certainly fervent participation in the rich cultural activities of the city, but this was not democracy in the modern sense because of the limitations on the privilege of citizenship.

Three, a point easily forgotten is that even Athens was largely rural. City-state draws our attention to the metropolis, but most people, even most citizens, had to live in the countryside, for the economy could not function on a primarily urban base. Many of these people rarely could get to the city and did not participate regularly in the activities for which the city is justly famous. Rates of participation in assemblies, by eligible citizens, were rarely over forty percent even for the most vital issues. None of this is to downgrade the dynamism of urban life, but it should remind us that most life could not, economically, be urban.

Whatever its organization, the city-state suffered most from its small size. This is revealed dramatically in the brief duration of Greek civilization at its height—three centuries of glory. Here is a tribute to the vitality of the Greeks, who could make such a mark in such a brief span of time, but also the most telling comment on the weakness of Greek political structure. Yet the peninsula had a long moment of political and military achievement which is a part of its contribution to western civilization. Its achievement in this sense was twofold: It kept the Persians out of the West and it provided the first example of western imperialism.

By any rational standard, the Greeks were no match for the Persians, whose peaceful empire extended farther than any the world had yet known. Under emperor Darius I in the sixth century B.C., the Persians ventured to extend their holdings. Their object was not just Greece but southern Russia, although the Greeks had provided their share of provocation. The stronger Greek city-states were active in trading and seamanship and provided serious competition to the peoples under Persian rule along the Mediterranean coast. Greek communities had been set up in Asia Minor, particularly along the coast of what is now Turkey, and although they were initially loyal to Persian rule they became increasingly restive. When the Persians were defeated in Russia, the Greek cities in Asia rose in rebellion, which caused Darius to attack European Greece directly. He easily conquered the Greek islands and, in 490 B.C., moved on Athens with a huge fleet of ships. The expedition landed at Marathon, north of Athens. But the Greeks were ready. Despite the rivalries among the city-states, this outside force compelled temporary unity. Sparta and other states joined Athens in defense, for after all, non-Greeks of any sort, even the Persians, were deemed barbarians in the Greek judgment, and no part of Greece could be left to their rule. The Athenians bore the brunt of the fighting and the Persians were defeated. Persia tried again a few years later, and this time it was a largely Spartan force that faced their much larger army. This battle and the success of the Greek navy in defeating Persian vessels and cutting off supplies ended the Persian threat. Not only was Greece safe, but most of the Greek cities in Asia became free states.

This, of course, is part of the tale of an opportunity missed. Successful when unified against a much more powerful foe, what might the Greeks have accomplished had they devised some form of government transcending the local level? This was not to be. It is vital to note, however, the negative achievement of the Persians' defeat. Had Persia overtaken Greece there is little doubt that western civilization would not have developed, certainly not in its present form. There would have been no barrier to Persian expansion further west, and while this doubtless would not have been permanent, it would have provided quite a different background in terms of cultural and political values.

The Greek legacy was expansionist, of course, not defensive. Even before the Persian attack, as the Greek city-states stabilized, the Greeks had proved to be actively interested in spreading trade and people to other areas. Rapid population growth at home was one spur, economics was another. Greek soil is not very fertile, and communications within the peninsula are difficult because of the mountainous terrain. But with relative political calm and growing wealth, it proved possible for Greek farmers to specialize in olives and grapes which did well in the hot Mediterranean sun. This required some capital, for neither crop produces quickly; a farmer had to be willing to wait a few years to realize a return on his investment. In broader terms, the conversion required a search for sources of grain which was still the basic staple. This was a major reason for Greek expansion to the Asiatic coast where there was access to the grain trade of the fertile Black Sea area. By 700 B.C. adventurous Greeks had made their way to Sicily and southern Italy and even to southern France, establishing the city of Marseilles. In southern Italy Greece found an abundant source of grain.

The Greek advantage in colonization was their coherent political organization and military skill. The Greeks fought in massed bodies of men—the group was called the phalanx—that was difficult to penetrate as it advanced on a less-organized foe. So a Greater Greece was formed. Some of the colonized areas were independent city-states. Others were ruled from a city on the mainland and were deprived of ordinary civil rights. This was true of many Athenian colonies whose inhabitants could not obtain citizenship and who were ruled with a harsh hand.

Greek imperialism was important for two reasons. First, it helped to corrupt Greece itself. Growing wealth enhanced greed. The established upper classes increased their interest in life's material pleasures. A merchant class, obviously essential for what was now a trading empire, arose and beneath it were artisans, sailors, and others. This would be a disruptive element in a Greek political structure that had been based on a fairly stable aristocracy. All in all, growing wealth allowed leading political and economic groups to indulge in personal ambitions and rivalries which, although not new—recall the tensions already suggested by Homer—became harder to subdue in the common interest. On a larger scale, city-states increasingly clashed in their imperialistic efforts. What slight chance there had been for Greek unity was shattered. As always with imperialist rivalry, the temptation was to apply competition to the mainland itself. But imperialism was corruptive in another sense, particularly in Athens. To rule foreigners without granting them the political rights accepted at home is a dangerous game, not only because the colonized peoples may rebel, which they did, and force a more militaristic regime to respond to rebellion, but also because ambitious leaders at home might be tempted to withdraw rights from citizens of their own state to enhance their own power.

All of this can be read and has been read as the inevitable fate of empires and civilizations. We will return to this topic with the more spectacular collapse of Rome. It has been easy to point to the fall of Greece as an example of what happens when vitality spills over into conquest, conquest into greater wealth and the corruption of primitive virtues—resulting in the inability to defend against less-civilized opponents. Interpret this as you will. But for Greece at least, two cautions: First, the peculiar disunity of Greece itself might have doomed the peninsula to internecine warfare and self-destruction whether "primitive virtue" was preserved or not. One of the main instruments of the Greek collapse, Sparta, had not engaged in the imperialist game and had preserved, most Greeks would have agreed, the virtues of the original city-state, if virtues these were. These included an ascetic life, abnegation of the individual to the interests of the state, avoidance of wealth—Spartan money, for example, was made so large and heavy that it could not be easily carried or used—and minimal cultural activities beyond Spartan religious ceremonies. Yet all of this did not prevent Sparta from tearing up the Greek mainland when its time came. And, turning directly to the imperialist city-states, "corruption" can also in part be regarded as "culture." Empire and wealth brought economic innovation—the invention of coinage, improvements in agricultural methods, and so on. It also provided the basis for elaborate developments in the arts and science, the most enduring heritage of Greece's brief moment in history.

Greek expansion into other areas also helped spread this very culture, a dissemination that would continue even after the collapse of Greek political structure. Without this, Greece, a tiny peninsula, could not have made such a mark on history and doubtless would be dismissed in a paragraph in any discussion of the bases of western civilization.

In all this talk of Greek expansion and economic vitality, it is important to note a few things the Greeks did *not* do. Most notably, they did not build a civilization dependent on advancing technology. A few agricultural advances and some improvements in ships can be noted, but the Greek manufacturing base rested on artisans and slaves. Artisans in Athens, most of them citizens, turned out pottery and metal products, often of great beauty, by traditional manual methods. Slaves worked the mines for iron and precious metals, again with no thought to technical improvements. All of this is negative history, but it is important to realize that a major civilization was based on scant interest in technology and no ethic of improvement in the productive process. In a sense this was why Greece proved so dependent on colonies, for her expanding population and her need for materials could be provided in no other way.

The Collapse of Greece

It seems a pity to evoke the rise of a vigorous civilization and then turn so quickly to its fall. Indeed, we have yet to capture the essential achievements of Greek culture, which obviously outlasted Greece itself. But some of the greatest Greek achievements postdated Greece's political decline, which is one reason to deal with decline first before turning to the evasive essence of Greek culture.

Even during Greece's rise between 700 and the later fifth century B.C., many city-states had experienced periodic political instability. The problem usually involved quarrels within the aristocracy. A majority group would be opposed by an ambitious minority faction, who might enlist the aid of the new business classes. This latter faction could govern only by uniting behind a tyrant, whose rule might be progressive and beneficial economically but who was, nonetheless, bound above all to try to suppress dissent and threats to his complete political control. Athens went through several oscillations of this sort before 500 B.C. It produced a codified set of laws under Solon, defining the rights of citizens, but it also produced two military dictatorships. These latter usually relied for support on the lower classes of citizens and constructed public works to provide employment and diversion. This was not to be the only time in western history when aristocratic rule seemed to offer a clear rule of law, but dictatorship provided more immediate practical benefits.

By 500 B.C. political conditions in Athens seemed to have stabilized. The age of tyrants was past, and major decisions were made by direct citizen participation in large assemblies. To some, this system of government, steadily refined for the next eighty years, represents democracy at its highest point. The very word derives from the Greek *demos,* meaning people. But "the people," in terms of active citizenry, were a minority. In addition to slaves, women, and foreigners were the growing number of city-states that came under Athenian domination without rights of political participation.

Because the Athenian navy was crucial in the final defeat of the Persians, the Athenians seemed the undisputed leaders of Greece during the fifth century. This was enhanced by a cultural explosion—in sculpture, philosophy, and drama—which has made it so easy to confuse Athens with the whole of Greece (which still consisted of about 200 city-states, many of which produced nothing memorable at all). Putting it crudely, Athens developed, in addition to its direct empire, a diplomatic protection agency called the Delian League. Between 478 and 462 B.C. the Athenian navy combined the island city-states which dotted the Aegean Sea to drive the Persian navy away. But once the Persian menace was gone Athens refused to relinquish the leadership of this new combination, refused to let individual states drop out, and exacted heavy taxes from the states without allowing them any say in government affairs. This was a sea-based empire of some two million people, and while subject states might have some autonomy and even an officially democratic structure on the Athenian model. Athens ruled the roost and became ever more dependent on the spoils of imperialism. To maintain power and to keep pirates and Persians out of the Aegean Sea, Athens needed a large navy; a navy needed sailors; sailors, many of them citizens, wanted some personal benefits. This led to a series of demands for higher pay for sailors and more entertainments and a constant temptation to squeeze a bit more out of the subject peoples.

Under the eloquent leader Pericles, who ruled Athens with few interruptions from 461 to 429 B.C., potential problems seemed easy to ignore, although there were satirists aplenty who were already criticizing Athenian greed and softness. Democracy, by Greek standards, seemed complete. As Pericles said, "The administration is in the hands of the many and not of the few. But while the law secures equal justice to all alike in their private disputes, the claim of excellence is also recognized; and when a citizen is in any way distinguished he is preferred to the public service, not as a matter of privilege but as the reward of merit. Neither is poverty a bar, but a man may benefit his country whatever be the obscurity of his condition."

There was a bit of gobbledegook in this statement, but it accurately summed up the two goals Athens was trying to achieve. First, citizens did have a voice. The sovereign body was the Assembly of all male citizens convening on a rocky hillside about every ten days. The Assembly could decide whatever it wanted. Usually only five or six thousand of the forty-three thousand male citizens attended, but even this constituted a massive legislature. To carry on the democratic spirit the executive committee of the Assembly, charged with preparing business and carrying out decisions, was chosen by lot to serve for one year. For day-to-day operations magistrates also were chosen by lot and at the end of their year of office were investigated by the Law Courts; if they had served badly they could be punished (the Law Courts themselves derived from the Assembly).

But Pericles also mentioned excellence. Pericles was himself an aristocrat; so were most of the other major leaders of Athens during the democratic period, and some provided wise leadership indeed. If a person were unusually eloquent in the Assembly

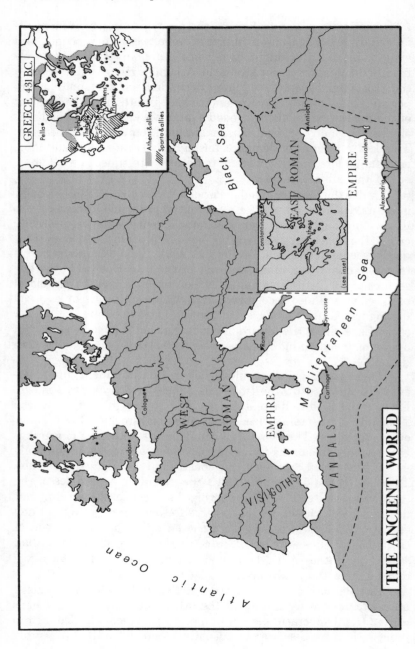

THE ANCIENT WORLD

he might in effect rule without formal office. For military matters a board of ten generals, usually headed by Pericles, was elected; here the principle of choosing by lot, which risked the chance election of someone incompetent—although it was implied that all citizens were capable to rule—was not ventured.

This was, then, a distinctive form of democracy. It included, given its short life, a great deal of deference to traditional, well-born leaders who had the wealth and education to speak well and devote themselves to politics. It was a system with a hosts of merits, not the least of which was the opportunity for thousands of people to become actively acquainted with politics and to feel themselves part of the system in a way that larger scale democracies have never achieved. But let us remember that this was *not* a modern democracy, though it shared some of the same ideals. One may argue that it was preferable or one may argue the reverse. But the distinctions must be kept in mind when we turn to the inescapable fact that this form of democracy broke down when first faced with serious trouble and that it brought some of the trouble upon itself. Some would pronounce this a judgment on democracy's ability to respond to crisis. It may be more sensible, however, to see it as the product of the limitations of Athenian democracy and the newness of the system.

The political downfall of Greece began with the downfall of Athens. Belief in the independence of the city-state was far stronger than any democratic spirit in Greece. Athens had violated this with her manipulation of the Delian League. She also had antagonized city-states like Sparta who resented Athens' growing power and prosperity. So Athens faced rebellions within the empire, some of which were put down brutally with massacres of thousands of people. And Sparta found it easy to form an alliance of other city-states to resist Athenian aggression. The result was the Peloponnesian War which dragged on from 431 to 404 B.C. The war was complicated by various factors. A brutal plague struck Athens and the Greek population began to decline, robbing the peninsula (and Athens particularly) of a major source of vitality. It is always difficult to say whether populations decline because a civilization is fading or whether their decline causes the civilization to fade; but the fact is that something was fundamentally wrong, and the war was only part of the problem.

Long before its end, the war destroyed Athenian democracy. Pericles was there at its inception to urge Athens to unite in defending a free, democratic, cultivated way of life against the militaristic, narrow-minded Spartans. But after the death of Pericles during the first plague, Athens increasingly divided into democratic and aristocratic factions, though a few ambitious aristocrats cast their lot with the people. The people thirsted for war. Under their leadership Athens sent an expedition to Sicily to try to defend her colonies there and to bring back booty for the sailors and other commoners. This was not the peoples' finest hour, for war to them meant jobs and plunder, and by failing to focus on the central Spartan threat they had not conducted the war sensibly. The Sicilian expedition was a disaster, costing many lives and ships. The aristocrats wanted peace. They rather admired the Spartan system, which recalled older Greek virtues such as rule by the aristocracy. They were selfish, but in retrospect their selfishness seems wise. Persia put her oar in by backing Sparta; this allowed her to take over the Greek cities in Asia. So Sparta won and tried to set up a hegemony in Greece. This was resented just as much as Athens' pretensions had been; national unity was impossible. Soon Sparta was replaced by Thebes, another large city-state, and it appeared that Greece was in for an endless succession of internecine wars.

The next effort at supremacy came not from a city-state but from a kingdom to the north of Greece—Macedon. It was a backward state whose inhabitants were not even regarded as Greeks. In 359 B.C., a new king, Philip, consolidated control over his kingdom and began to conquer the Greek states, beating Thebes and Athens in 338. His son, Alexander, went on to conquer most of the Persian Empire and Egypt—the bulk of the civilized world as the Greeks would have defined it. Ultimately Alexander overextended himself by trying to penetrate India, but not before he had spread elements of Greek culture throughout most of the eastern Mediterranean. For Alexander was steeped in Greek learning, tutored by Aristotle, and eager to use Greeks to administer his conquered lands. He was a military genius whose career was cut short by death at age 33; but his cultural contributions, however indirect, are important.

Hellenism

Following Alexander, a period known as the Hellenistic Age ensued, in which Greek influence spread even though Greece was no longer a political reality. Indeed, Greek learning continued to develop outside the peninsula, as in medical advances made in the city of Alexandria, founded and named by Alexander in northern Egypt. Greek trading practices, including a standardized currency that Alexander had introduced, spread widely in the Middle East and eastern Mediterranean. But after Alexander's death there was no political unity. Rival kings replaced him and individual cities soon asserted their rights to self-rule. In Greece itself the conflict between aristocrats and commoners periodically flared in bitter clashes. The Hellenistic Age is noteworthy primarily for its continued diffusion of Greek artistic and philosophic values—although the quality of art and drama deteriorated somewhat—and more remarkable, innovative developments in philosophy and science. Greek influence extended east to India, even to China, affecting artistic styles and in some cases politics. More to our purpose is the importance of the vague Hellenistic unity in spreading Greek values westward where they could be picked up by the Romans. Hellenism set the basis for Greek influence in the Middle East that would last for centuries, even when overlaid by Roman rule. Here was something of a prototype for the Byzantine Empire, which succeeded Rome in this area and lasted until the Moslem conquest, terminating in the fifteenth century A.D. From Byzantium, cultural artifacts and values, such as the form of the alphabet and the nature of government, spread northward to Russia, giving Russia more a Greek than a western heritage. More immediately, the Hellenistic world with its lack of political cohesion openly invited a dynamic power to convert cultural and economic ties into political unity, to form the more enduring empire of which Alexander had dreamed. This new power was to be Rome. Although Rome could not claim all of Alexander's lands, it would move in different, more European directions. But Rome, as noted, would be touched by Hellenistic culture, forming a link between its own political success and Greece's more obvious intellectual and artistic achievements. Without Alexander and the gradual expansion of Rome, Greek civilization might have perished amid political chaos or simply have moved eastward. Rome provided the sword that allowed the works of the pen to survive for western civilization.

The Greek Heritage

When we speak of Greek heritage we must recognize the need to deal with two elements: what Greek culture was and how it later was interpreted. Sometimes the two are very close, as in the case of science. The Greeks created a new scientific approach to the study of man and his environment which had only been suggested by Egyptian medical research or Babylonian astronomy. The Greeks provided discoveries, but above all they developed a manner of thinking which was not carried on by the Romans and their successors. When science was revived, beginning in the Middle Ages, it often was abused, for the Greek discoveries were taken as sacrosanct and the spirit of inquiry was repressed. But ultimately there was a certain mesh, and what the Greeks intended and what western scientists later achieved have a genuine relationship.

Let us begin, briefly, at the opposite pole where Greek intentions and the subsequent use of them differ rather sharply. The case is politics, which we have touched upon already in our summary. Subsequent observers, reviving the classics, could find virtually anything they wanted in Greek political culture. Rousseau, in eighteenth-century France, held that Greece had proved that democracy was possible only in the confines of a city-state where everyone could participate. He was of course not talking about all of Greece but about Athens and a few other states. Jefferson referred to the Greek democratic tradition, although he was willing to see it applied beyond the city-state framework.

Let us suggest two major points about the Greek political heritage. First, little of the political system was incorporated by succeeding cultures. The tradition of small units of government antedated the Greeks and followed from the difficulties of early agricultural societies in establishing large governmental units. It was compounded in Greece by the mountainous divisions which impeded unity and regular communication. It would continue after Greece—Rome began as a city-state—but not because of direct Greek influence. Later democracies might invoke Greece but Greek ideals did not shape the political views of these countries, which simply found it convenient, given the prestige of Greece, to reach back for examples. Greek political theory was almost entirely antidemocratic, and the Athenian example during the Peloponnesian War confirmed this tradition. Only when courses in western civilization were created, and there was an impelling need to reach back for a common core of political values, was Greece made into a democracy. Greek politics failed and there was no reason to copy them. And this leads to the second point: If there was a Greek political heritage, among the chaos of city-states, it was on the whole absolutist, even totalitarian. Sparta is the prime example, but Athens had its absolutist strain too. Even in Athens the citizen owed his being to the collectivity. Socrates, a free thinker who defied public norms by criticizing existing policies and encouraging skepticism, acknowledged this concept when he accepted the justice of the verdict against him and preferred suicide to exile. The collectivity, the state, was supreme.

There was no definition, however debased, of individual rights. Admittedly, there was tension, at least in Athens, as there must be in any state that allows individualism at all. Pericles, speaking to inspire his fellow citizens in the early stages of the war, put it this way, contrasting Athens with Sparta; "While we are . . . unconstrained in our private intercourse, a spirit of reverence pervades our public acts; we are prevented from doing wrong by respect for authority and for the laws. . . . An Athenian citizen does not neglect the state because he takes care of his own household." The Greeks admired heroes, both in legend and in competitions to determine the best athletes, the best singers. A strain of individualism was present—expressed, for example, by the opportunity for free speech in the Athenian Assembly. But the sense of devotion to a greater whole predominated, combined with the careful distinction between the minority of people who could benefit from civic freedoms and the excluded majority.

If Greece passed anything on to later political culture, it was toward the collectivist end of the spectrum. But more probably, despite the use and abuse to which Greek tradition later was put, it passed on little at all, save in the realm of political theory where aristocratic opponents of democracy, like Plato, devised elaborate hierarchies of orders of people that were copied in the Middle Ages and Renaissance. This leaves us with three related areas of Greek influence: art, philosophy, and science.

Art

Greek artistic forms, copied by the Romans and largely abandoned in Europe (but not in Byzantium) after the Roman era, were revived in the Renaissance and have influenced western art ever since. Architecture gives us the clearest example. The Greeks devised three embellishments for the tops of columns supporting massive buildings: the Doric, Ionic, and Corinthian styles. These three developed chronologically, with increasing ornateness, which may have been a sign of greater artistic genius or of a decadent sense of clutter. All were employed in the structure of massive buildings, particularly temples honoring the gods. Any downtown area in a large city has older banks and government buildings which reflect this Greek style. For example, in Washington, D.C., the Greeks would recognize the government buildings without much difficulty. Totalitarian governments seem to have a particular fondness for usage of the Greek columnar styles in massive public buildings. Hence we see a major Greek influence on Russian and East European public architecture in the twentieth century and an even more obvious and ironic influence in Hitler's "Teutonic" monuments. The stadium is a Greek invention. We have slightly enlarged its form but not altered the basic contours. So, although the Greek architectural precedent was interrupted by the Gothic period, and more recently has been challenged by modern architectural forms, its influence cannot be denied.

The other arts are harder to trace. Greek music was important to the culture of the time but leaves almost no direct remnant. The same is true of painting, save for pottery decoration. Greek buildings and statues which we regard as pure stone were, in fact, elaborately painted and decorated. It is amusing that when Europeans copied the Greek art and architecture they copied what remained, not what had been designed. The cold marble of Michelangelo does not reflect the original style of the gaily painted costumes of Phidias, now washed clean by time and weather. But the realism and power of Greek statuary obviously exercised much the same influence as did architecture. In Greek culture the statues were meant to celebrate the heroes of the day—from the winners of the local drama contests to the gods. The same forms were later adapted, to commemorate the Greek heroes, by way of pious recollection, as well as new heroes from popes to Napoleons.

Greek literature, poetry, and particularly drama, left a multifold legacy which was transmitted to the Romans and revived by the Renaissance. Classic French dramatists in the seventeenth century almost literally rewrote Greek plays and themes. *Phèdre,* by Racine, not only had a Greek setting but assigned a Greek god to watch over each major character and conveyed the depth of emotions which the Greek tragedians did so well. The play follows very closely the work of Euripides. Examples of this sort abound. The Greeks also left a set of rules for drama and poetry that were followed until the nineteenth century. Poems were to have regular numbers of syllables, the number depending on the type of verse. Plays, according to Aristotle, should follow a threefold rule: unity of time (a play should convey actions occurring roughly within a twenty-four-hour period); unity of place (since relevant actions cannot happen simultaneously in different places, a play should focus on one spot); and unity of action (a play should follow a coherent plot line, not present a jumble of unrelated events). In setting down these "rules," Aristotle was codifying mainly what previous Greek dramatists, such as Sophocles and Euripides, had practiced. He also expressed the rationalist strain in Greek thought that could apply to art. There should be rules which both author and audience would understand. Aristotle probably did not intend his rules to be taken as absolutes, but subsequent generations, convinced that everything Greek was good, refused to transgress. This would limit the diversity of artistic expression in the West—compared, for example, to India—in the interest of order and consistency of style. A full rebellion against these limits occurred only in the nineteenth century, and it is still possible to argue that western civilization's strength, while hardly devoid of artistic expression, has been mainly in other realms of thought and action, compared to many other civilizations, because art was constantly subjected to rules and values imposed by rationalism.

Another feature of Greek drama was the emphasis on powerful human emotions, designed to stir an audience to ribald laughter or immense sorrow. For instance, Sophocles in *Oedipus Rex* so powerfully probed and portrayed the hero's imperfections and psychological flaws that modern psychology has come to use the term "Oedipus complex." The Greeks preached reason and balance, but they also believed that man could easily overstep both into situations of immense tragedy. Their plays may have been outlets which helped to preserve a sense of balance. Certainly their dramas delineated tensions that would be taken up by later western science and literature. They illustrated human dilemmas that perhaps were not distinctively western; only their explicitness and their dependence on words, within the bounds of certain stylistic conventions, has set them apart from the more ritualistic drama of many Asiatic and African cultures. While far from deficient in music, dance, and art, western civilization still tries to deal with the human dilemma more completely through words than do other cultures.

In sum, art and drama were undeniably more important in Greek than in modern civilization. But they left models and rules that are still copied to some extent and, perhaps, a basic spirit that we still share when we turn to the arts. For Rome, the Renaissance (another artistic age), and even later eras, the arts provided one of the most obvious Greek legacies. Yet philosophy, less important in Greece's heyday, had more influence; and science, almost an afterthought to Greek civilization proper, came close to rivalling it. What a civilization leaves thus does not necessarily correspond to its own set of priorities, which is not to ignore the formidable Greek artistic influence.

Philosophy and Science

Greek philosophy and science belong more to the Hellenistic age than to Greek civilization. There were a number of schools of philosophy, but certain main threads emerge. Philosophy was isolated from other disciplines; few Greek philosophers paid much attention to the gods, who were useful as literary devices and vital to public culture, but were not worthy of great intellectual interest. Greek philosophy, the study of man and his universe, was largely secular. This was an innovation, for religion had been much more predominant in previous Mediterranean civilizations. It posed an enduring challenge for western civilization, as it later unfolded, of whether to approach knowledge through assumption of divine guidance or to deal with it in human terms.

Greek philosophy stressed the ability of human reason to penetrate deeply into the theoretical nature of the world *and* to devise appropriate ethics for human conduct. Socrates, who died for his principles, was primarily a moralist seeking to teach his fellows to probe their own conduct and to reason out what was best for themselves and society. His insistence on moral behavior, in a period when Athens was encountering increasing troubles in the war with Sparta, roused the anger of his fellow citizens and caused his condemnation in court for, ironically, corrupting morality. Socrates urged that the striving for money and property be preceded by the chief human duty, which was "the improvement of the soul." He chose death over exile because his moral code prompted him to force his jury to martyr him to his concept—that man's obligation was to his own soul.

There were other moral philosophers in Greece, though none so self-sacrificing as Socrates. Most Athenian upper class youth were trained by tutors who combined moral lessons with training in rhetoric and other practical lessons useful for political life. More important was the continuation of the interest in moral philosophy through Plato and Aristotle into the Hellenistic age. Aristotle, for example, preached balance and order, perhaps the most typical Greek precept, against a background of recurrent instability; moderation was the key to life. In the fourth century B.C., under Hellenism, Epicurus, using a complicated theory of the material nature of man, urged a simple life, since overindulgence brings pain and avoidance of pain is man's logical goal; even public business should be shunned lest it cause sorrow. This philosophy continued into the Roman era. More durable still was the Stoic approach as advocated by Zeno (335-263 B.C.). Zeno saw the world guided by divine reason. Because a spark of this reason existed in every man, one could understand God's will and lead a virtuous life based on temperance, bravery, and justice. Tribulations of the body were of no importance as long as one preserved one's inner, moral independence. Here was an ethical code that demanded great rigor but could be adapted to a variety of individual needs and to a larger, religious view. Add love of one's fellow man, which the Stoics eschewed because it threatened one's independence, and one comes close to Christian morality. Amid great diversity, Greek and Hellenistic moral philosophers were hammering out a belief that man could control his own actions and be guided by moral principles, whether as part of some divine plan or, as with Epicurus, out of simple self-interest or, with Socrates, for the public good. The unifying themes were rationality and moderation; man had a mind and could use it to control himself. And man was what the world was all about: "Man is the measure of all things." This secular humanism complemented, indeed necessitated, the search for rational ethics.

The second area of Greek philosophic inquiry did not contradict this first major approach, but it was more abstract. No one illustrates it better than Socrates' famous pupil, Plato (429-347 B.C.). Plato certainly was concerned with ethical problems; his contribution to political theory has been briefly noted and was designed to place ethical men, the philosophers, in charge of society. These philosophers would control the licentiousness and liberty that Plato saw about him in Athens—of all the city-states, Plato admired Sparta most—and rigorously control the masses of people. Whatever the merits of the scheme, philosophers have never been invited to assume this role in actual politics in the western world. Plato's most lasting contribution came in his quest for the basic essence of things—the Good, the True, the Beautiful. Somewhere, to simplify this approach, there exists a perfect tree, the essential tree, of which all actual trees are sullied derivations. The philosopher must seek the essential tree in order to understand its nature. He begins by reason, but Plato had what was for the Greeks an unusual mystical side that held that the final vision of truth could be achieved only in a kind of trance. Platonic philosophy, with its approach to perfect prototypes of objects and of abstractions such as beauty, would have many revivals.

Through Plato's time Greek philosophy had not been oriented toward the scientific. It prided itself on logic, on setting premises and reasoning from these. But the premises were untested. This approach was compatible with advanced work in mathematics—one of Plato's many interests—because mathematics also starts with premises, not observation. But philosophy could lead to some silly constructs about what the world was like. In 500 B.C. two philosophers, each with equal logic, claimed respectively that everything in the world always changed and that beneath outward appearances nothing basic ever changed.

With Aristotle, a student of Plato, the philosophic tone began to alter. Abstract reasoning was retained; we have seen in Aristotle's principles of drama his desire for clear, rational order. The quest for the perfect form of an object, Plato's guiding passion, remained, but its mystical element was toned down. Aristotle also concentrated on political theory. He summed up previous work on logic in a number of compendia, his pattern of logical thought remaining dominant to the present day. But Aristotle was also an empiricist, carrying out wide observations and collecting factual material prior to logical analysis. His own work led to concepts in both physics and biology, many of which remained dominant through the Renaissance.

Scientific work was carried on in the Hellenistic Age, particularly in Alexandria. There was great attention to astronomy, heralding new information on the orbits of the planets; here the modified Greek approach was particularly evident. Astronomers wanted planets to have uniform circular motion since this was logical and rational. Finding that this did not fit observed facts, they rejected the approach. But it was Hellenistic astronomy, completed by Ptolemy in Roman times, that posited the earth as the center of the universe around which planets and sun alike revolved. Scientists also worked with agriculture, but the second principal area of interest was medicine, including the dissection of corpses. Here again the most complete compendium was produced only in

Roman times by the Greek physician Galen, but this summed up a great deal of anatomical knowledge. Mathematics continued its advance with Euclid's text on geometry, probably the most influential mathematical treatise ever written.

The Greek-Hellenistic tradition ended about the first century B.C. The political disruption of the Hellenistic world, under Roman conquest, contributed to this, and the Romans were not interested in science. Scientists also had gone too far for much educated public opinion. Dissection and close study of planetary motion defied both traditional superstitions and a growing religious interest in the century before Christ. Practical application seemed limited, although some scientists did work on war machines and the like. Doctors, for example, found little use for the anatomical discoveries because they saw no connection between these and curing the sick. On the whole the theoretical, rationalistic approach persisted in Hellenistic science; one scholar refused to write a handbook on engineering because "the work of an engineer and everything that ministers to the needs of life is ignoble and vulgar." This left most people, even the educated, in the grip of superstitious views of man and the universe for centuries, not only in Europe but also in the more sophisticated Arab world. When Greek science was revived, what empirical spirit it had developed, as in medical dissection, was missing until well into the nineteenth century. For example, reverence for the past kept most western doctors memorizing Galen instead of studying real health problems or real cadavers.

Science, then, was at best an ambiguous Greek legacy, far less clear than the heritage in artistic forms and principles which were slavishly copied. As with Greek science, Greek artistic achievement seemed so awesome that for a long while no one sought to innovate. But in the arts the Greeks left literature and monuments of great beauty that would set standards in periods in which the secular arts gained new importance. The same holds true for the major Greek philosophical systems. We will see them imitated, with old arguments, sometimes only half-understood, revived—Platonists fighting self-styled Aristotelians. This was no fault of the Greeks, save insofar as they encouraged an attention to logic that might overshadow the quest for empirical fact. It derived more from a learning process, or relearning process, that began in the Middle Ages. The Greeks provided some secular guideposts as interest in philosophy revived; and even before this, their influence would be felt in Christian theology, which embraced many Greek ethical and philosophical concepts. The ultimate Greek contribution, however, was rationality of thought; even drama, expressing powerful emotions, had an underlying rational structure. We have questioned the extent to which Greek politics contributed to, or reflected a belief in rational individualism, but there is no doubt that Greek culture set the basis for a distinctively strong western intellectual belief in the power of man to reason from the inherent rationality of his universe. From the Greeks onward the western intellectual tradition would debate the use of reason. Some Christian mystics might argue that reason is evil and man irrational, and therefore that he has to be guided by simple faith, but they always had to argue, not merely proclaim or assert that man is irrational. Rationalism, the belief that man's mind could order itself and relate him to a larger order about him, was here to stay.

The Other Side of the Greeks

Many historians think that the Greeks reached a pinnacle of human achievement that has never been equalled since—theirs was such an outpouring of creativity in such a short period of time that the bases of a whole civilization were set! This seems an exaggerated view, quite apart from its disregard of the accomplishments of civilizations elsewhere in the world. But it is not an idle exercise to compare Greek values and behavior to our own and assess the relative strengths and weaknesses of each.

Even if one takes something less than a totally adulatory view of the Greeks, however, one major question remains. Having set forth or hinted at so many modern developments—rationalism, science, democracy, totalitarianism, free speech, relative secularism—why couldn't the world or at least the western world have continued from this base? Why were there subsequent centuries of backwardness and stagnation? To answer to this, four factors must be realized. First, the Romans, who conquered much of the Greek world and sincerely admired the Greeks, simply were not interested in many of the problems that had preoccupied Greek leaders. This was partially true in art, but more substantially true in philosophy and science. Rome had a civilization, and we have inherited from it, too, but ironically, it served to play down some of the Greek strengths.

Second, it is obvious that Greece reduced the staying power of its values by a totally inadequate political structure. Alexander helped to some extent, but the Greek world was disorganized, which made even preservation of some key work impossible. And disorganization made the Greek model undesirable in some eyes. The quest for truth might be noble, but perhaps a stable government was better. By failing to establish a durable political structure the Greeks reduced their power to continue, and to persuade others to continue along the lines of rationality and secular ethics that their thinkers had staked out.

Third, and here we enter an undeniable realm of debate, the Greeks were far from modern, and it is not clear that, had their civilization endured and advanced, they would have created a modern world. Lags in science and technology, quite apart from the ambiguities of Greek politics, clearly point this out. This is not to say that the Greek world was bad; it may have been preferable to our own. It is to suggest that, although Greek elements were to become part of western civilization, the Greeks had by no means laid a complete foundation.

Fourth, Greek civilization was largely the business of aristocrats and intellectuals. It did not break through to the common people, and this hampered its ability to endure. One need not be an ardent democrat to suggest that if the common people retain values different from those of the elite, the elite has failed to set the base for the maintenance of its own culture. The common people did not learn democracy, and while they might be obedient, they had little reason to feel the passionate devotion to the civic good preached by Pericles and his counterparts elsewhere. To be sure, absence of political power may be less damaging than it seems on paper. Greek women, for example, were publicly scorned in a highly masculine society. Pericles put it this way: "For a woman not to show more weakness than is natural to her sex is a great glory, and not to be talked about for good or for evil among men." In families with too many children, female babies often were killed at birth (by exposure, leaving them outside on a cold mountain.) But privately, women had more freedom and family influence than formal values might suggest, at least among the wealthier families. One estimate holds that two-fifths of all Athenian property was owned by women.

Yet why should we expect women, slaves, or even free farmers, remote from the bustle of the city, to adopt political and philosophical values that were of little use in their daily lives and with which they had little contact? For all the splendor of its monuments, this was a poor society. Most people had to concentrate on the difficult business of earning a living with enough margin to pay the taxes assessed them by the city. In a peasant economy (whose outline would persist for almost 2,000 years), the whole family worked. Marriages, for example, were based on economic considerations, even among the wealthier classes. A man was to provide support, the woman an ability to work (or direct servants) and bear children, who in turn were put to work at an early age. This does not mean that they lacked values and ideas. The clearest contact between many of the common people and the civic leaders of the city-states was through religion which was so largely ignored in Greek philosophy, some of whose practitioners even attacked the traditional Homeric set of gods as lecherous frauds. There was no powerful priesthood in Greece; to this extent a certain secular spirit might have been possible among even ordinary folk. But the farmer, subject to the vagaries of nature, as were the natives of Egypt or Babylon, looked to a host of gods for aid against disaster and resorted to magical practices to gain their favor. Civic religious festivals, honoring major gods such as Apollo, had a genuinely popular air, mixing a festival atmosphere with the desire to propitiate the powerful god responsible for driving the sun across the sky. Periodically, more mystical, highly ritualistic religions penetrated from Asia Minor, attracting common people to acts of purification. Pilgrimages to Delphi, where priests meted out advice derived from Apollo, drew many troubled souls. More relevant to the farming population was the "mystery" or passion play which was viewed after a preliminary purification. One of the most famous was enacted annually near Athens to celebrate the recovery of Persephone from the lower world of Demeter (Mother Earth) which reflected the yearly cycle of crop-growing and a promise of an afterlife. Mystery cults imported from Egypt and elsewhere spread even more widely as Greece collapsed. Some attention was given to Jewish monotheism, but far more popular was the despairing worship of Fortune or Chance as a deity and the rise of Blind Fate as a force to be propitiated. Astrology was created from Babylonian origins as a means of finding one's destiny and determining what the gods desired.

Greek civilization can be seen as encompassing two worlds not entirely separate but certainly not harmonious. The achievements of the Greeks that we perhaps have exaggerated were those accessible only to a few people at the top of society, and perhaps, to a limited extent, artisans and other common people in the cities proper. Not surprisingly, when these values were revived, they were revived by an elite, and it would be a long time before they spread more widely. What did individualism and rationality mean to the massive slave population? to a struggling farmer? to a colonist eking out a living in Sicily? to the many women shut off from most public events? The average Greek was much like his counterparts among earlier Mediterranean peoples, clinging to religion, farming with methods little changed over the centuries, politically apathetic. This was one reason that the common people later would be far more open to eastern religions, including Christianity, than to the values of formal Greek art and letters, which were not consciously disseminated to the masses and which often were the products of conservative aristocrats profoundly suspicious of mass passions. Even within the Athenian citizenry the tensions showed, as when the Assembly in dealing with Socrates indicated that intellectual inquiry must have its limits. The tensions showed later in the widespread suspicion of the irreligious quality of Hellenistic science.

None of this should lead us to condemn Greece for ignoring modern canons of the proper treatment of the poor. This was a distinctive society, not a modern one, even though it contributed a few elements toward the construction of modern values. We must remember the common people, however, to balance that view of Greece, or at least of Athens, as a paradise of cultural and political zeal. To explain why a highly persuasive value system, modern in many respects, could not readily be carried on, we must remember that the Greek elite failed politically. The Roman elite that replaced it learned something of its interests, but had other concerns. The common people lived out most of their lives in a different orbit.

Suggested Readings

On pre-Greek civilization, G. V. Childe, *What Happened in History* (New York, 1964), *The Prehistory of European Society* (Baltimore, 1958), and C. S. Coon, *The Origin of Races* (New York, 1962).

General histories of Greece and Rome include C. G. Starr. *A History of the Ancient World* (New York, 1965) and A. R. Burn, *Greece and Rome* (Chicago, 1970). On early Greece, C. G. Starr, *Origins of Greek Civilization 1100-650* (New York, 1961) and M. I. Finley, *The World of Odysseus* (New York, 1954).

Two interpretive accounts are M. Smith, *The Ancient Greeks* (1960) and H. D. F. Kitto, *The Greeks* (London, 1951); see also G. L. Dickinson, *The Greek View of Life* (London, 1957). On politics, W. G. Forrest, *Emergence of Greek Democracy* (New York, 1966) and on colonization, A. G. Woodhead, *The Greeks in the West* (New York, 1962). Special studies include J. Boardman, *Greek Art* (New York, 1964) and L. Robin, *Greek Thought and the Origins of the Scientific Spirit* (New York, 1948). On Hellenistic civilization, Max Cary, *History of the Greek World from 323 to 146 B.C.* (New York, 1959) and W. W. Tarn and G. T. Griffith, *Hellenistic Civilization* (London, 1952).

Roman Civilization

ROMAN CIVILIZATION extended from approximately 600 B.C. to 400-500 A.D.; Rome was not, as they say, built in a day. Even its eventual decay, which can be traced from about 200 A.D. was a slow process. The Romans were a stolid people, and what they build they built to last.

Rome's strengths as a civilization and its contributions to later western development were different from those of Greece, but there was one area that overlapped. As their conquests extended to Greece and Hellenistic Egypt, the Romans could not help but become involved with the culture there, and the overlapping consisted essentially of preserving much of what they found. Hence one of the real Roman contributions, however inadvertent, was to provide sufficient interest and political stability to make certain that many precious documents were preserved. In terms of direct activity, however, the Romans lagged well behind the Greeks in art and philosophy. We have already observed that because the Romans had no interest in science, there was no revival or continuation of the promising developments that had lasted into the first century B.C. under Roman rule but Hellenistic cultural inspiration. Even in mathematics the Romans were content to issue educational manuals without taking any major steps forward.

In the arts, particularly poetry and history, the Romans were more creative, even though they tried to follow Greek models too slavishly. For example, Virgil's *Aeneid* was a deliberate attempt to

43

copy Homer and produce the great Roman epic, and although it is not without merit, it is heavy and lifeless by comparison. But as Roman civilization matured, Virgil and others produced elegant poetry, some of it conveying Greek philosophical principles, as in the Stoicism of Lucretius. There was vague interest in the higher reaches of Greek philosophy; Platonism gained a slight revival. More important was the obvious concern of a politically active people for an adequate moral philosophy. Greek precepts were copied, but men such as Cicero, one of the leading moralists of the late Roman Republic, produced their own counsels of moderation and ethical behavior that had wide currency at the time and would be cited repeatedly when classical civilization was revived in the West. Even the Christian Middle Ages felt comfortable with Cicero (as with some of the Greek moral teachings) because of his concern with moderation and self-control as the basis of the good life.

Although in the area of ethics there were few striking Roman innovation, there is one cultural activity in which the Romans were most innovative—architecture. They were practical people, more like us perhaps than were the Greeks in this respect. They could build bigger than the Greeks and more grandiosely, even if they introduced few new basic styles. Their stadiums spread wherever their conquests reached, so massive and durable that they are still used today in many areas, such as in southern France and Spain, for activities ranging from bullfights to outdoor basketball games. Their monuments to gods and emperors were huge. Their road building was justly famous. Using the labor of slaves and soldiers, the Romans built—mainly for military purposes—straight, solid roads all over their empire. Few of these can be used today, but some are still visible, and many a throughway, even in distant Britain, follows the same route laid out by Roman engineers. On an equally practical level the Romans built huge aqueducts to carry water from the mountains into their larger cities. Almost by accident, these were often works of great beauty, with delicately arched contours. In their aqueducts and in some of their smaller temples the Romans frequently used brick, thus moving away from the Greek preoccupation with stone. But no matter what the material used, the Romans built without mortar, arranging their arches so that tightly packed chiseled stones held together by themselves (topped by the vital keystone which kept the tension at the top of the structure). They also built domed structures, thus getting away from the purely rectangular approach of the Greeks, although these were not yet typical. In the main, Rome's achievements in this area were of an engineering rather than an esthetic nature. Greek styles sufficed for decoration of columns, the shape of most temples, the statuary, and so on. The Romans tended to a more ornate, heavy adaptation of Greek art, which is usually less attractive than the original.

Thus we do not look to the Romans for much more than preservation of basic Greek styles in the various arts, often with some loss of quality. However, the engineering achievements should not be neglected, and they were passed on to post-Roman civilization. The building of aqueducts was far too complicated for the heirs of Rome. For centuries Rome's magnificent buildings were torn apart by most people as a source of stone for the constructing of their own modest dwellings. Not until the eighteenth century was a clear new use found, when tourists began to visit sites of Roman ruins in the Mediterranean area and in northwestern Europe. Long before then, however, Roman architectural achievements such as domed buildings were being copied.

The Romans had an active economy but did not carry on the Greeks interest in commerce. They were not avid seafarers for they simply did not like the water. Their boats were much heavier and clumsier than those of the Greeks, and the typical Roman sailor stayed as close to shore as possible. There were sea battles in Rome's military history, but mainly in the early days, against Carthage, and conducted with great reluctance. The Romans were landsmen. Their roads were built to move troops and goods as far from the sea as possible, even though transportation by land was much more expensive and cumbersome. But their armies for a long while had no equal, and this was the basis of many of their other achievements.

However, Rome experienced the typical problem of the agricultural society: what to do with commercial values? Commerce was essential to Rome as it became a wealthy and cosmopolitan civilization. Like the Greeks, the Romans were to specialize in agriculture, drawing grain from more distant regions, such as Sicily, and committing much of the soil of central Italy to olives and grapes. Metal ores were needed, and Rome in turn produced some manufactured products. But Rome's craft tradition, given the size of the empire, was not so widely developed as that of the Greeks, and its attitude toward mercantile activity was not encouraging even though individual merchants advanced in society. Merchants had no clear social standing or political rights in Rome. After Rome's collapse, trading declined still further, simply because of increasing political instability. This was not true in the East, where Greek values still held sway, but in the West, Rome's snobbish disinterest in economic matters may have contributed to the difficulty of reviving mercantile values.

These, then, are areas in which Rome's contribution was minor or even negative. It is obviously vital to realize that Greece and Rome cannot be lumped together as a single civilization. When late medieval and Renaissance figures turned to an interest in the past and tried to draw lessons from it, they tended to merge Greece and Rome into a single classical heritage. This suited their purposes, for they could draw what was useful from each culture—perhaps some support for trading from Greece; an interest in Greek as well as Roman artistic styles; and fascination with Rome's political achievements. But their merger should not confuse us at this stage. Rome copied Greece after having developed her own culture during the many centuries of isolation from Greek influence, and she copied in her own manner.

The Main Accomplishments

None of this should minimize Rome's enduring achievements, precisely because they were of a different order from those of Greece. Engineering has been mentioned; other achievements are in politics, law, and religion. In politics, Rome bequeathed a democratic tradition, but its main contribution was in the development of an unprecedented empire, well organized and, for several centuries, amazingly peaceful. This empire was to awe Europeans for centuries to come, and would inspire some ambitious leaders to attempt a recreation of it. As late as the twentieth century, Mussolini had ideas along this line but lacked the ability to make them become reality. It was also vital that the Roman empire was the first great political structure to extend itself into the heart of Europe, as well as following the more traditional routes of Mediterranean politics into North Africa and the Near East.

In law, closely associated with empire, the Romans provided clear standards for the definition of crime and the treatment of criminals. They were not the first to codify laws, but their effort, an evolutionary process continuing into the third century A.D., was based on the belief that public offenders should have a clear knowledge of rights and punishments. We might judge many provisions of Roman law as being inequitable—for example, the treatment of women—but overall the effort at justice was, by the standards of the time, genuine. The Romans also introduced trial by jury, not the mass jury of Athens which could be swayed so easily by a demagogic orator or by mass passions, but a small group of citizens who could, it was hoped, deliberate calmly. Whatever the merits of the system and its execution, the heritage is clear. Many European states revived Roman law as they advanced in civilization during the Middle Ages; the Catholic Church did the same. There were modifications, of course, but to this day the legal systems of France, Italy, Spain, and the state of Louisiana are based directly on Roman codes—which include the assumption that an accused criminal is guilty until proved innocent. Even in countries such as England, that relied on Germanic law and its evolution into common law, Roman principles would have their influence.

Finally, as to religion, official Roman religion was much like the Greek—indeed there was direct imitation. Jupiter replaced Zeus as the main god, but his functions were much the same. Greek legends about the foibles of the gods were taken over without difficulty. As in Greece, Roman religion was an important part of the civic order. Religious festivals commanded great attention. They were political as well as ceremonial occasions, for just as individuals continued to believe that they could advance their fortunes or assure their health by propitiating the appropriate god, so the Roman state and its officials believed that the gods would support Rome so long as they were properly treated. Elaborate temples and monuments as well as celebrations were needed; the Romans even added a group of priestesses, the Vestal Virgins, to honor the gods. As in Greece, there was no important priestly class, and politicians were not interfered with in their conduct of state affairs.

The importance of Roman religion must not be underestimated, but here is a case in which what was central to a particular culture is less important to us than what came in under the aegis of the Roman attribute of tolerance. As they extended their empire, the Romans encountered a host of religions, and they decided that tolerance of these was the best approach. For example, Jewish religious practices were not interfered with except when they threatened the stability of the state. An example of the latter occurred in the case of a wandering prophet called Jesus Christ. Christ's preachings, designed to reform and purify the Jewish religion, offended Jewish religious leaders. This bothered the Roman rulers of the area, not because they cared about the controversy but because public order might be threatened if the Jewish leaders took matters into their own hands. So, without enthusiasm, they got rid of Christ—or so they thought.

Tolerance allowed the survival of a host of eastern religions that were more dramatic than the official Roman cult. It was possible for these to spread west to Rome itself, as occurred by the second century A.D. Even here officials were not concerned; they might even favor some of the new religions as strengthening the valor and self-sacrifice of the troops. And they often tried to combine elements of the new religions with the official cult. Tolerance was not, as is well known, extended to the initial spread of Christianity. This new religion was lionized (in a literal not figurative sense). But this was not inconsistent with Roman policy. Christians, giving pre-eminence to God, refused to swear primary allegiance to the state. This made them politically subversive, and they were treated accordingly, although persecution varied in intensity from one emperor to the next. But Christianity spread widely and the Roman principle of tolerance, combined with a good sense of the practical, won out. Rome embraced Christianity and gave it the political backing necessary for its spread throughout almost the entire Roman world; it also changed the religion significantly in the process. Thus, religion, specifically Christianity, must be counted as Rome's final contribution to western civilization, even if it was not at all Roman in inception.

Empire, law, religion—this was the Roman legacy. We must now seek to learn how the Romans came to be in the position to pass on this legacy, and then turn to the fascinating question of why the Roman effort finally failed, why the legacy had to be picked up by hands that were not Roman and altered in the process.

Rome from Republic to Empire

Like so many agricultural cultures, Rome began as a city-state about 600 B.C. It was founded by descendants of Indo-European invaders from central Europe who merged with earlier Italian peoples. The Roman language and many basic social patterns were inherited from the local farmers who had populated the region long before the city was founded. But the city itself borrowed from an earlier Italian civilization, the Etruscan, slightly to the north, and to a lesser extent from Greek colonies in the south. This gave form to early Roman religion and also to political structure.

Rome began as a kingdom under Etruscan rule. But about 509 B.C. the Roman aristocracy overthrew the king, and Rome became an aristocratic republic not unlike the Greek city-states. Intense local civic pride was part of this pattern, as in Greece, including a willingness to sacrifice self in the interest of the state. Heroic military action by a few individuals, such as the fabled Horatio holding the bridge over the Tiber river against an Etruscan army, gained Rome increasing independence.

Roman family structure was the basis of this kind of culture. It emphasized obedience to the father, although the mother was honored as well. Even though the aristocrats competed for power, they could unite when loyalty to the state was at stake, because they had been trained to subordinate themselves to the common good, just as children were taught to yield to family interest. Religion was another binding force, as was the consideration with which aristocrats treated the common people of the city. In the early days of the republic there was much social tension, but uprisings gave the citizens of the lower class, whatever their wealth, their own representatives, called tribunes, to oversee their interests in the government. The first law code, the famous Twelve Tables, was introduced about 450 B.C.; this restrained the upper class from arbitrary action. By the third century B.C., citizens of the lower class, called plebeians, could be elected to public office and pass laws.

The Roman city-state was not like the Greek. The Roman people met in assemblies, but the assemblies were called and run by officers. There was no choosing of leaders by lot; two consuls were elected by the people each year to serve as executive and military leaders, and almost always these were aristocrats or wealthy plebeians. The consuls scrutinized each other's activities so that neither could seize power; behind the scenes the aristocracy could usually run the show. Aristocratic power was formalized in the Roman senate which was composed of anyone who had held public office and who then served as senator for life. This group had only advisory powers, but, composed of experienced and prestigious men, its influence was considerable and it lent stability to the state.

What we have just described is the Roman state as it existed at about the middle of the third century B.C. There were to be later changes and new political principles, but this occurred in a period of chaos which ultimately led to the overturning of the republic. The picture of the Roman state around 250 B.C. proved so attractive to many western political theorists long after the republic was gone that it was copied, at least partially, by a host of western political governments. What was particularly appealing about the Roman arrangement was its balance. Underwritten by definite laws which protected the rights of the citizens, the Roman government checked unlimited democracy without yielding to total upper-class rule; and it prevented executive dictatorship. The division between a popular assembly and an upper-class senate was to be imitated many times. Although legislative authority was predominant, there were separate judges and a separate executive; here was a hint of division of powers and it seemed to work well.

Based on political stability, Rome prospered and began a pattern of conquest which none of the Greek city-states had been capable of. Internally, the population increased, which is always a creative factor if properly channeled. Conquest offered the means of distributing the surplus population and of providing wealth for the masses, which helped keep them quiet. Also, Rome was well situated, being in the center of Italy, for once the Etruscans had been beaten and their culture collapsed, there were few powerful rivals surrounding Rome. Finally, the Romans were lenient rulers. They required obedience from the conquered peoples, some land for the surplus population, and a stated number of soldiers for their army. But if all these demands were met, they were quite content to allow local variations in government and customs and even granted citizenship to those conquered peoples who seemed qualified for it. So, gradually, the Romans became masters of all of the Italian peninsula, completing their conquest by 264 B.C.

Roman Expansion and Internal Chaos

Having started so painlessly, the Romans never willingly stopped. The rich island of Sicily was their next logical goal. Rome first worked to gain the western part of the island, where it encountered a powerful foe for the first time. Here dominance had rested with the Phoenician state of Carthage in North Africa. Three wars resulted. In the first, although forced to build a navy, the Romans won western Sicily. In the second, 218-201 B.C., Carthage invaded Italy. The great general Hannibal crossed from Spain into Italy with a huge army, its provisions carried by elephants. He defeated the Romans in one battle after another and ravaged the Italian countryside for fifteen years. But most people remained loyal to Rome, and when his supplies ran short, Hannibal's troops were finally exhausted. Indeed, the Romans threatened a counter-invasion against Carthage, which forced Hannibal to return for defense. Rome had survived her worst trial with sore losses but no damage to her political stability. And with Carthage on the run it was easy to take over the Hellenistic states of eastern Europe and North Africa one by one, for these were too weak internally to offer more than token resistance. Within a century, by 133 B.C., Rome had conquered Macedon, Egypt, and finally Carthage herself, which was completely destroyed in a vicious attack in 146. Rome held the eastern Mediterranean, including Israel; the city states of Greece; the whole of North Africa; the coasts of Spain and southern France, Sicily, Sardinia, and Corsica.

Why did Rome expand beyond Italy? Initially, expansion was not due to conscious policy. A certain momentum existed: once Italy was conquered, why not go on; and once Sicily was conquered it had to be protected by destroying North African rivals, and so on. This is the kind of absent-minded imperialism that we will find later in western history, particularly in the case of Britain; that is, it was not the result of conscious expansionist policy. Most of the Mediterranean world was so politically weak that it constituted a vacuum of power. And, however odd the image, it seems true in western history at least that diplomacy, like nature, abhors a vacuum. Some rulers, such as those of Egypt, actually called the Romans in to resolve internal chaos. Rome at first refrained from ruling the conquered areas, thus showing its lack of clear imperial policy and the influence of statesmen at home who maintained that the republic would be endangered and corrupted by its overseas commitments. (In this they were correct, as events soon provéd.) But soon provinces were formed and tributes of grain and precious metals were exacted. In return, Rome provided some meager amount of government, with protection from invaders and local unrest. The empire was not yet well organized.

As with Athens before, imperialism had its effect on the internal politics of the republic. It brought new wealth and new cultural values, and the old ways were increasingly seen to be inadequate. The basic problem was twofold: a decline in the traditional virtues of the aristocracy, and a change in the nature of the urban poor. The aristocracy, more interested in individual political advancement than in the common good, grew greedy and wealthy from the proceeds of imperialism. They carefully excluded the rising class of businessmen and non-noble citizens, despite the latter's role in the increasing prosperity of the vast new trading area. The wealthy generally took on new airs as they came into contact with Greek art, which offended conservatives defending simple ways. Cato told his son: "If ever these damned Greeks come to pass their literature to us, all is lost." But more Romans were drawn to fashions of the East. Some of them, such as Cicero, at the end of the Roman republican era, conveyed his learning of Greek philosophy; others were more frivolous.

As early as the second century B.C., the poor became poorer, and imperialist greed, distorting the relationship between the upper and lower classes, played a major role in new social tensions. Hannibal's raids dealt a hard blow to the farmers. The upper class, bent on making money, set up big estates and used as slave labor those people captured in the imperial conquests; indeed, the use of slaves in Rome was more extensive than in any society until that in the American South and in parts of Latin America in the eighteenth and nineteenth centuries. Thus, the peasants were forced off the land in great numbers, and many moved to Rome. Here was the origin of a massive urban mob, eligible to vote in the assembly and ready to follow anyone who would help them survive.

What resulted was, first, a democratic flurry under the Gracchus brothers who wanted to solve the problem by redistributing land. They were murdered in 142 by conservatives. There followed a succession of generals who recruited landless men; they depended on sheer force and the ability to distribute spoils to maintain power. Some pretended to be friends of the people, others of the aristocracy, but increasingly all were motivated by personal ambition. Julius and Augustus Caesar came directly out of this tradition. For almost a century, until 33 B.C., Rome was in chaos. This did not prevent significant cultural developments, including the magnificent oratory and moral philosophy of Cicero, who tried in vain as a politician to restore the older ways; he had more success in preaching his ethic of moderation that in later centuries inspired many.

But from a purely political standpoint this era was highlighted by three features. First, coming out of the earlier days of the republic was a populist tradition, a belief by the people that they had a particular stake in their city. This did not constitute a persistent democratic tradition, but there was a sense of people's rights that could be recalled in the Renaissance and again as late as 1848. More directly, of course, because of their sheer numbers and poverty the people were a force to be reckoned with in any solution of Rome's immediate problems.

Second, political dangers in the city made Rome ever more dependent on empire. Taxes rose steadily elsewhere, and private corruption affected the colonial areas still more severely. Oddly, this did not shake the Empire, but clearly some order had to be created. At the same time the whole Roman structure became steadily ever more reliant on expansion in its need for booty and new supplies of slaves.

Finally, the republic itself became unviable. The aristocratic Senate no longer provided consistent wisdom and the populace vied for favors from the rich, particularly the victorious generals. Rome had implicitly chosen between a balanced republic and an empire, in favor of the latter, and this made a military regime inevitable. This regime was inaugurated on a permanent basis by Julius Caesar. His military credentials were excellent. He had conquered the whole of France and part of the Low Countries and Europe, opening up a huge segment of Europe to the influence of Mediterranean civilization. Ironically, this series of victories against the barbarians was his most lasting achievement, for it began to establish what came to be the boundaries of western civilization. But this was far from his mind as he turned his armies back to defeat rival generals and gain control over the Roman state. The control was brief, for Caesar was murdered by aristocratic defenders of senatorial power, but it passed to Caesar's grandnephew, Augustus. By 31 B.C. Augustus had defeated his rivals. The Republic was dead, and the Roman Empire, a political structure governing Rome and all the colonies, was now to be created. The empire turned out to be Rome's major contribution to the western arsenal of political precedents.

The Roman Empire

From Augustus into the second century A.D. the Roman Empire seemed to be a gigantic success story. Solid institutions were created, retaining a few of the forms of the republic but building the state on new bases. Territorial expansion continued without major setback. By the second century the empire included France, Belgium, Holland, Austria, Hungary, Rumania, Switzerland and, at the fringe of the known world, the southern two-thirds of Britain. North Africa was Roman, as well as the whole eastern fringe of the Mediterranean, penetrating deep into Mesopotamia. The empire faced rivals on its borders; fierce Scots prevented further advance in Britain, where the Romans built Hadrian's wall to deter their depredations. Germanic tribes made it difficult to move beyond the Rhine river. But no European opponent was more than a nuisance; none could contemplate attack. The situation was a bit more troublesome in the East. The Persian empire had collapsed, but after an interlude in which most of its area was occupied by Hellenistic city-states loosely united under a king, a tribe of Parthians swooped in to take over the eastern segment of Asia Minor. This was the only "civilized" people known to the Romans who were outside their empire, and because of their military strength the border between the two states saw intermittent fighting and reshuffling. But since the Parthians were pressed by Chinese and other forces to the East, they were content to remain on the defensive.

Rome, then, was an immense empire. Within it peace prevailed, the *pax romana;* Rome could easily quell civil disorders within its boundaries. Central to its success was the extension of earlier policies of imperial rule. Some primitive areas of the empire were organized on a tribal basis, as in Britain; but in the civilized core, city-states formed the unit of local administration. Even in Britain, Rome's advent meant the rise of new cities, although these served mainly as military encampments or resorts and religious centers. The city-states were given great local autonomy, being allowed to continue their own festivals and customs after the Greek pattern. The imperial government watched, through provincial supervisors, only to make sure that the states did not engage in squabbles or tolerate internal social tensions. In other words, the empire had a central bureaucracy but a small one, designed mainly to keep an eye on local activities and, of course, to collect taxes. The stationing of military forces was not even a regular necessity, although, of course, troops would be brought into any troubled province. Finally, starting with Julius Caesar, the right of direct Roman citizenship was extended to members of the upper classes and others who performed unusual service for the empire, well beyond the bounds of Italy. One of the apostle Paul's proudest boasts, and one of his most useful assets in spreading Christianity through the exercise of his legal rights, was his Roman citizenship: *Civus romanus sum.* Thus, for the elite, local autonomy was combined with pride in membership in what was obviously the greatest political structure ever created.

For ordinary folk, these details did not matter much. More people lived in cities than ever before, but still the majority had to engage in farming. They had no rights of rule. Not only were they denied Roman citizenship, but they did not even participate in the city-state government, which controlled rural territory as far as sixty miles from the city itself. Yet this situation was not new, and the fact that Rome brought peace and minimum interference with the daily struggle for survival made them content for at least two centuries. The common people learned little from Rome, save perhaps a vague sense that they were a part of a great political enterprise, something that might be remembered later. There were few improvements in agricultural techniques, for Rome was even less interested than Greece in technological change. The common people were on the verge of great upheaval, but for the present they remained much like their agricultural ancestors in Greece.

As in Greece women were officially considered inferior, and since Roman law was later revived, this is a topic of continuing importance. "The husband is the judge of his wife. If she commits a fault, he punishes her; if she has drunk wine, he condemns her; if she has been guilty of adultry, he kills her." (This latter, however, was controlled by the necessity of approval by a family court composed of members of both families.) So said the laws of the Republic, which gave women no legal rights as either plaintiffs or defendants in court and allowed only husbands to initiate divorce. On the other hand, Roman society was for a long while more family-centered than that of Greece, which allowed women more private influence. Under the empire, the family was encouraged, and single men and women were penalized; widows, for example, were given only two years to remarry. This encouragement of family life was also due to a need for progeny who could replenish the ranks of the military. A woman who had three or more children could own property. On the other hand, legal inferiority remained; if divorced because of adultery, a wife lost to her husband half of the dowry she had provided on marriage and a third of any property she had. She was also required to wear special dress that set her apart like a prostitute.

As with the peasants, then, women had little special reason to welcome the empire, and in this case a legal culture was established that reappeared wherever Roman law was revived and is with us still to some extent. But for peasants and women alike, this situation was essentially customary, so that the empire gave them no new reasons to complain.

At the very bottom of the social order was the mass of slaves on which Rome depended for much agricultural work and for the more brutal industrial jobs, notably mining. Most of the slaves were acquired in Roman conquests, so that a mining crew mixed fair-haired Celts from England with blacks from Saharan Africa.

All of this complex geographical and social structure was ruled in the final analysis by the emperor himself. Theoretically elected by the citizen assembly of Rome, a ritualistic remnant of republican days, the emperor was usually chosen by his predecessor. In some cases, as in the fifty years after Augustus, the emperor selected his own son, but usually the new ruler came from a separate family and was chosen for his abilities, or through intrigue and popularity with the army. The result was corruption and assassination at the top, but its worst effects would not be felt until other defects in the empire became apparent. Some early emperors, such as the infamous Nero, were openly autocratic, tolerating no interference with their whims; but sensible emperors, of which there were many, conciliated the Roman aristocracy (the Senate still met, although it was essentially powerless); the Roman people, by offering them provisions in bad times and entertainment in good (the famous bread and circuses approach); and, of course, the army.

Augustus made the army the real cement of the empire, a standing, professional force directly loyal to himself, with officers appointed explicitly by him. The ability of the army to prevent civil war, except in two cases in which it rose against an emperor, and its success in steadily pushing the boundaries of empire outward made the empire function without serious difficulty for over two centuries.

Weaknesses in the Empire

But problems were built into this structure. There was no assurance that the emperors would be men of quality. Added to this was the fact that the great power which they wielded was a source of temptation, so that they became more and more autocratic as time erased any memory of republican traditions and restraints. Incompetents wielding absolute authority became distressingly common after the second century. Dependence on the army was dangerous as the republican spirit waned. With growing wealth and entertainment, many people, particularly those in Rome and Italy, lost their military spirit: Why risk one's life in some far-off camp when there was so much fun to be had at home? Thus, increasingly the army was recruited from sons of soldiers, inhabitants of the frontier areas of the empire who had not yet tasted the good life, and even "barbarians," such as Germans, from outside the empire altogether. The army was stretched very thin—300,000 to 500,000 men from a population of fifty million, a lower ratio than would prevail in seventeenth-century Europe where over one percent of the population was under arms—guarding thousands of miles of frontier. Small wonder that by the early second century, under the emperor Hadrian, Rome gave up its policy of expansion and turned to a defense of what it had. But without expansion, the key to Roman vitality for so many centuries, could the empire last? For up to this point stability and expansion provided the opportunity for trade and prosperity, even though the upper classes were the recipients of most of the latter. An eighteenth-century historian called the high point of empire (96-180 A.D.) the period in human history "during which the condition of the human race was most happy and prosperous." Certainly aristocrats and businessmen with their villas in summer resorts like Pompeii, their baths, and their servants, would have agreed.

However, Roman industry was more backward than Greek. Many areas, particularly in Europe proper, had to maintain an essentially local economy, not only growing their own crops but making their own pottery and metal goods. The eastern part of the empire, with its Greek heritage, quickly seized industrial superiority, but this involved no new techniques of manufacture and it seriously threatened the political balance of the empire. Essentially, Rome had political power but the East had economic power, and the two forces clashed. None of this is meant to minimize prosperity or the possibility that individuals could rise from a humble state to great wealth and prestige through trade or cultural achievements, but economically this was not an innovative civilization.

Lack of economic dynamism meant, in turn, that once booty from expanding empire dried up, and with the new defensive policy, the empire could survive only by raising taxes. Here we return to the huge groups whose conditions the empire had not previously greatly changed. Nothing could make life worse for the slaves; periodic slave revolts were inevitable, but they were brutally put down. Women remained in their family roles, and in the upper classes, of course, they actively shared in prosperity and the growing interest in the material pleasures of life. But the peasants faced outright ruin. By the second century farmers were conducting strikes against taxes, and some subjects, such as the Jews, conducted revolts even in the cities.

Thus there were chinks in the empire, but even if we can trace the beginnings of Rome's fall to the second century, the empire still had three centuries to go and great achievements to mark periods of its final phase. It had inspired loyalty, and not only from Romans and Italians. The emperor himself was constantly praised as a godlike figure, and although some of this was sycophancy, there were real spiritual as well as economic and political bonds for the middle and upper classes in the empire. The emperor was father, his powers derived from the gods, and he was in a sense divine himself. It was a Greek who said "All the civilized world raises with one voice that prayer that your Empire may endure in eternity.... As if summoned to a feast, all the civilized world has laid down the burden of its arms and has turned to decorate itself and to enjoy the delights of peace."

Roman Culture and the Roman Heritage

Not surprisingly, given the major Roman interests, formal culture remained limited until the last century of the republic, when Greek models were copied and Greek artists and writers, some of them slaves, worked directly for Roman patrons. The Romans did not blindly copy; their painting, for example, differed from what we know of the Greek, showing more realistic portrayals of nature and the human form. Hence, Roman statuary, often busts of the great men of the day, reflects attention to individual facial traits more than the stylized approach of the Greeks. However, the central cultural contribution was to spread a Greco-Roman art and literature to the vast empire and particularly to Western Europe, where such products had never before been known. This dissemination involved building monuments and erecting statues in what we now call the classical style all over the Mediterranean world. It involved the work of important writers who perpetuated Greek philosophies, such as Stoicism, and also interests ranging from satire to serious history. It also involved the production of textbooks for teaching subjects such as writing but also science and mathematics, where nothing new was achieved in basic knowledge. Textbook writing, increasingly important as Roman creativity waned in the later empire, helped preserve the rudiments of learning not only for the Romans themselves but for later ages.

So we stress Rome's role in spreading ideas more than creating them. But we must add that the spreading was accomplished in Europe through the Latin language, not the Greek, and that the Romans not only had a different language and alphabet (the latter, of course, still in use), but also worked during their culturally creative period to polish their language. Here, Cicero, the abortive defender of republican virtue, played a key role. His speeches were models of classical Latin style—clear, rhythmical, expressing calm reasoning or deep emotion. His essays in many of fields, including the art of speech, were legitimate prototypes for anyone who sought to learn Latin, and he added to the language a philosophical vocabulary that made it as serviceable as Greek for expressing the whole of classical culture. In his own work and in the textbook imitations he inspired, Cicero aroused great interest in linguistic precision and gave to Latin a prestige that would color western civilization until our own century.

Finally, in terms of strictly Roman achievements, there was the law. Early republican law, already codified, now had to cover the more complex social relationships of the whole Mediterranean world. The result commanded a tremendous amount of intellectual creativity, systematizing legal precedents and decisions into ever more comprehensive handbooks. What resulted was a full set of reasonable (that is, practical, clear, and widely applicable) principles for the conduct of business and civic affairs. Even under the empire it spelled out rights as well as duties for citizens. And as we have noted, it was to have a long future. The creative period of its development ended, however, with the early third century, partly because the legal corpus worked so well, but partly as a concomitant to the decline of the vitality of the empire in general. But the notion of a system of law equally applicable to all men independent of place of birth or, to some degree, personal status, and the Roman idea that human law reflected a basic "natural law" mirroring the order of the universe, would be revived, along with specific Roman legal strictures.

Christianity

For those who like their history tidy, it is unfortunate that Rome did not fall before Christianity arose. In fact, however, the two cultures are inextricably intertwined chronologically and ultimately in political institutions and social values. Rome had little or nothing to do with the inception of Christianity, which had local roots. But the existence of a vast, stable empire was almost surely the basic reason that the new religion was able to spread so widely. Some would argue, of course, that God would have guided Christianity's development in any event. At the time, in a more subtle version of this approach, theologians claimed that God created the Roman empire directly so that Christianity could spread. Here it is left to the reader to select the degree of divine guidance found in history. It matters not whether one regards Christianity as a final Roman legacy to the world or as a separate development that conquered Rome; what is clear is that the heirs of Roman civilization as it collapsed, both the barbarians in Europe and the new Byzantine empire centered in Turkey and Greece, inherited classical culture, Roman political structures, and the new religion.

There is one final conundrum to which we will return; some have argued that Christianity played a role in Rome's fall by undermining its military virtues in the name of peace and gentleness. This we must assess when we turn directly to the empire's collapse. It is also possible to claim that Christianity gave cohesion to an empire that otherwise would have collapsed earlier and/or that collapse was inevitable. Whatever one's position, the fusion of Christianity and classical culture began well before Rome was in its final death throes and, without question, had more impact on people at the time and on later generations than classical culture itself had ever had.

We must recall that Christianity began in an outlying area of the empire with little link to the great political and cultural events of the day. It was related to two developments already noted: to the distinctive, monotheistic Jewish religion; and to the growing religious fervor that had been building up in the eastern Mediterranean, particularly among the common people, as the Hellenistic world became less stable.

Christian Values

Christianity spread a set of values radically different from those of Greece or Rome. Not only did Christians worship one God, but they were ordered to love their neighbors as themselves. They were enjoined to see this world as a testing place at best, at worst a place of sorrows, and to pin their faith on life after death, for Christ had sacrificed himself to redeem mankind from the original sin that previously had prevented salvation because of God's just wrath. Love of neighbors and otherworldliness were new to Greece and Rome. Christianity also stated a new kind of individualism. Each person had a soul of his own and it was partly up to him what he would do with it, whether he would seek salvation or not. In this sense Christianity preached not only individualism but a potential equality; Greeks had believed in individual achievement, for example, but also in a rigid social hierarchy that made a mockery of any active belief that all men possessed some common potential. But Christians, like the Greeks and Romans, surrounded individualism with an obvious tension. For the Greeks, as we have seen, individualism could easily be buried in the obligation of loyalty to the collectivity of the state. For Christians, a person might have an individual soul but he was also under God's firm guidance; one of the problems Christian thinkers would constantly grapple with was how man could be free and yet be obedient to an omnipotent God.

How did these innovations come about? Judaism provided the obvious basis. Jewish religious thought and institutions had been in ferment during the two centuries before Jesus' birth. The official priesthood had become rigid, unimaginative, and, as Jesus would claim, often more interested in position and wealth than in religious values. A host of radical sects grew up, preaching the coming of a Messiah or savior who would bring a Last Judgment to mankind. Other, more moderate sects sought a true belief away from the formal rituals of the temples at Jerusalem, preaching brotherly love and—a new element for Judaism—the possibility of life after death for the virtuous.

Here we treat Jesus as a historical figure. Christians believe that he was the son of God, sent to earth to live a sinless life yet die as a mortal, thus sacrificing his human body to purge men of sins for which they could never atone. The explanation for Christianity's origins and rise is thus a matter of God's will. The Christian explanation is important, but it must be stressed that it is compatible also with a more secular historical approach.

Jesus obviously combined extraordinary gentleness of spirit with amazing charisma. As he began his preaching he gathered around him a group of devoted disciples who believed that here was the prophesied Messiah who would return. None of this group initially wanted to start a new religion. They hoped to reform Judaism before it was too late and, after Jesus' death and what was believed to be his ascension to heaven, they expected his imminent return and the end of the world (an apocalyptic element in Christianity that is still extant today). But it was impossible for the disciples to remain in the Jewish faith. They were persecuted, and the Jews for the most part had no reason to abandon their traditional religion or to believe that Jesus was anything more than, at best, another prophet or, at worst, a fraud. From the small groups of devoted believers living a simple communal life while waiting for the final coming, Christianity became a religion. Initially this meant recruiting new believers who had not known Jesus, many of them non-Jews attracted to the ethical purity and monotheism of this new religion; soon it meant setting up institutional structures to keep this growing band together.

The Spread of Christianity

So the disciples and other converts spread out into all parts of the Roman empire with varying success. During the first three centuries A.D., before the institutionalization of the church was even near completion, they benefited from a number of factors. We have stressed already a yearning of the common people for a religion that would be less formal, more emotionally satisfying than that centered about the classical gods. Eastern religions which had gained popularity in the waning days of Greece spread widely and diversely under Rome. The cult of Isis, a featuring the Egyptian sun god worship, gained some adherents. More popular, particularly among Roman soldiers, was the religion of Mithra, which, among other things, demanded the sacrifice of bulls. To be sure, Christianity was not just "another" eastern religion. But it arose in a very favorable climate and it met, or was modified to meet, some of the elements that the other religions offered in a more limited, brutal fashion. The ritual of celebrating Christ's sacrifice with the symbolic consumption of his blood and flesh, through wine and bread, is an example. The ritualistic aspect of Christianity developed steadily. Also vital in these early centuries was the stress on the equality of all souls and the beauty of poverty. In an empire in which the rich lorded it over the poor and where the condition of the poor was soon to become ever more uncertain, a religion that strongly implied that the rich man would have a great deal more trouble getting to heaven than the poor man, who could more readily expect to find some compensation for a life of misery on earth, was obviously attractive. This was the social element of

Christianity. As rich people, too, were converted, and finally the Roman government itself, the social implications of egalitarianism were played down, but like other aspects of primitive Christianity they could surface again, for the common people remembered. Elements of the Reformation in the sixteenth century would invoke the evils of all wealth and the need for a total reordering of society to prepare for the kingdom of heaven.

Fervent missionary zeal, a favorable atmosphere, rituals and doctrines of obvious appeal—along with these, two other elements were needed and, by the second century, were increasingly provided. The first need was for some coherence in doctrine; by 100 A.D. the disciples of Christ and others, such as Paul, had produced a powerful literature concerning Christ as the son of God and dealing with Christian ethics. Many of their writings were eventually assembled into the New Testament. With a literature, some educated people who worried about the moral degeneration of the classical world were drawn into the new religion. The second element was a need for organization. Here Paul, not an original disciple but an early convert, was particularly important. It was he who encouraged the proselytizing of non-Jews, the vital first step in creating a Christian religion instead of a small, faithful body waiting for the Messiah to reappear. And, preaching in Greece and elsewhere, he realized that new converts needed some organization, that they all could not imitate the disciples by living in egalitarian communes—most had to work in the world to survive—and that some governing structures were needed. At first these were local; each local body selected elders, or presbyters, to govern them. But by 100 A.D. a single leader, a bishop, dominated each city. This reflected the need for greater specialization in government, for with a growing religion a part-time council would not suffice. It also obviously paralleled the centralizing trends of the Roman state. Just as Roman provincial governors supervised local activities to prevent dissent, so bishops worked to maintain unity of doctrine, governed the charitable activities of the provincial church, and presided over increasingly complicated religious services.

With their faith in God and their oft-stated disdain for things of this world, Christians could easily be annoying to other citizens of the empire and even seem a threat to the state itself. But persecution was sporadic, partly because the church, although steadily growing, was not overwhelmingly large and its organization was scattered and localized. Also Christians were by no means set against even a non-Christian state. Christ had said firmly: "Render unto Caesar the things that are Caesar's," and Paul was even more emphatic: "The powers that be are ordained of God." Here was a clear basis for downplaying some of the subversive political and social implications of Christianity and ultimately for converting it into an official religion. The church never wavered in its formal pronouncements on what was to come first, and that was religious duty. But people could work in the world, pay taxes, and fight wars without damning themselves, although there was always an element in religion that suggested that people who did not do these things were superior. Nevertheless, a large, organized church could not be based on the latter alone, so that Christianity was to build on a few phrases of Christ and involve itself very deeply in the world.

At first there were troubles. As the empire weakened, emperors turned savagely on Christians as scapegoats. Several times during the third century emperors ordered all their subjects to make sacrifices to the pagan gods and to the emperor, a belated effort to build on that imperial loyalty that now was declining. Christians refused to obey, and bitter persecution resulted. The final confrontation occurred early in the fourth century under one of the last strong emperors, Diocletian, who briefly restored the unity of the empire against foreign invasion and internal decay. A return to the classical virtue of loyalty first to the state was a part of his program. But the courage of the Christians, their ability to go underground—quite literally, by conducting services in elaborately constructed catacombs—and their sheer number doomed the persecutions to failure.

The next emperor, Constantine, entirely changed the official approach, only twenty years after Diocletian's efforts had failed. Like most of the late emperors, Constantine stressed the religious quality of his office and cast about for a god to serve as his patron. First he considered himself favored by the Sun, then by Apollo, but finally he shifted to the Christian God as the most powerful one available. He even claimed to have had a dream, in 312, in which he was ordered to have his soldiers mark their shields with the Christian cross; when they subsequently won a battle against superior forces, he was convinced. God had proved that he was useful. Christianity was now favored, and the emperor and his successors (all but one of whom were Christians) even deemed it their duty to run the church. They intervened in doctrinal disputes, for with their success Christian bishops and theologians could now afford to engage in more bitter arguments about the nature of God. Councils directed by the emperors helped produce the accepted doctrine of the Trinity, according to which a single God existed in three forms, Father, Son and Holy Ghost.

The Church in the Later Empire

The official embrace of Christianity was obviously a double-edged sword. It not only ended persecutions but allowed unprecedented conversion of people throughout the empire, people who were accustomed to having their religion promulgated by the state. How far Christianity might have penetrated geographically and socially without official backing is impossible to say. But with the state now not only tolerant but claiming active supervision over all church affairs, the danger of manipulation for worldly, political goals was obvious. Most bishops ignored the danger in their enthusiasm to end persecution. In the eastern Mediterranean this position was basically maintained, and in the eastern Byzantine empire that succeeded Rome, the state firmly ran the church; the same was true as the eastern, or Orthodox, religion spread to areas like Russia. Other bishops dissented, insisting that the church alone should determine its dogma and policies. This position, plus the growing weakness of the western section of the empire (Gaul, Spain, and Italy itself) left the bishops a freer hand. As the empire fell to Germanic invaders, the latter largely accepted the powerful position of the bishops in the administration of the church. Increasingly, the authority of the bishop of Rome was recognized to have some precedence in the West. Roman bishops claimed this by virtue of the fact that the Roman church was held to have been founded by the apostle Peter, and that Christ had told Peter "Thou art Peter and upon this rock [*petra,* in Greek] I will build my church." The traditional position of Rome, while now in disarray, gave its religious ruler an advantage. The bishop of Rome increasingly was called Pope (from *papa,* or father) and other western bishops saw the advantage in naming some central authority now that the state had collapsed. Papal leadership helped preserve orthodox doctrine against the many heresies that developed. Although this leadership was not yet formally organized, the church in the West was sketching a government not unlike that of the earlier empire: a central figure with local "governors," the bishops, and this was long to be the strongest institution in western Christendom.

The early church made one final contribution amid the growing weakness of secular Rome. Once adopted as the official religion, it provided the only vital intellectual element remaining in a shaky empire. Christian thinkers, building on an earlier doctrine, now tried to incorporate elements of classical philosophy, to build a true, convincing, intellectual base for the church and to aid in the sincere conversion of intellectuals who had long scorned the new religion as fit only for the rabble. Their efforts had a tremendously important side effect: by recognizing the value in classical learning, the church became the physical repository of innumerable ancient writings and even works of art that otherwise would have perished in the chaos of Rome's collapse. A few Christians questioned the virtue of any pagan learning or culture, and some of the basic features of classical civilization—its materialism, its man-centeredness, obviously its polytheism—had to be rejected. But much could be incorporated. Virgil, for example, had written a poem that could be construed as implying the coming of a new savior; so Virgil, although not on the recommended reading list, could be read and his works preserved. Also preserved were classical forms of construction, because Christian architects and sculptors followed them in building early churches.

Amid a long list of early Christian theologians the final synthesizer was Augustine. Thoroughly trained in classical learning, particularly Platonic philosophy, he was converted to Christianity in 386. His writings ranged from an eloquent statement of his conversion experience—his mystic, inexplicable flash of contact with God—to a long treatise explaining why the fall of Rome was not due to the abandonment of the old gods, which in turn led him to contrast the troubles of the earth, which God directed for man's ultimate benefit, with the perfections of the kingdom of heaven. Above all, Augustine, using many Platonic concepts, grappled with key problems in Christian theology. God was all-powerful; he directed all things for he knew all things. How, then, could man be free? Augustine sketched a complicated position which stated God's full power but yet left man with a free will. He similarly ventured to explain the philosophically complicated doctrine of the trinity: one God in three forms. In all of this Augustine implicitly admitted the power of human reason to advance an understanding of divine truth. But reason could never unravel the whole or even the bulk, for here on earth man needed faith. He should never try to reason without the guidance of faith, although a full understanding might come only with salvation. The role of faith and reason would later be vigorously debated, but Augustine's position remained central. It preserved an element of the classical belief in reason, against those who insisted that faith alone was enough. And it allowed the use of some classical philosophical concepts as part of the reasoning process, even if these were now to be firmly subordinated to the primacy of Christian truth.

With Augustine and the other early theologians the ancient world left its final intellectual legacy to the West. A body of patristic learning, so called because of its derivation from the early church fathers, was available for later theologians to work with and discuss. It was an immensely sophisticated body, capable of rivaling classical or other philosophical systems. Along with classical learning per se, it provided something that western intellectuals would need to master as part of an awesome legacy of the past.

But let us not leave the triumph of Christianity with the intellectuals and politicians alone. It had been a religion spread among common people and it was to spread still further. Theology played a role in popular religion; doctrines of the trinity were taught and perhaps vaguely understood. But we must remember above all that Christianity *potentially* could offer a new culture to the masses. It could help explain human misery and offer promise for the future. Karl Marx was later to call it an opiate in this sense, distracting people from their troubles; but we must see it as a comfort as well, when people could do little about their troubles. How much did the implications of brotherly love and the equality of souls under God affect ordinary behavior? Wars did not stop; domestic quarrels continued. But Christianity played a role in the virtual ending of slavery in the western world. There were many factors here, but certainly the church fathers frowned on such complete subjugation of man to man, and a more subtle system of servitude replaced it in Europe (though not in the eastern, Byzantine empire where political interests had greater dominance). The church may have improved the position of women, again along with other factors. Women were not given equal rights in the church, being unable to serve as priests for example, but they did have souls, could be saved, could be sources of religious truth. How this affected day-to-day relations we do not know. But it is true that women in Christian culture had more rights and a greater range of opportunities than those in almost any other religious zone, and certainly they had more recognition than they had been granted formally in the classical world. These are two illustrations of how Christianity could affect ordinary life, quite apart from its new rituals and ideas. And here was one of its real roles in the formation of a new, distinctively western civilization.

The Fall of Rome

Rome's collapse poses some fascinating questions about causes and about the extent to which great political structures inevitably effect their own demise. From its early decay to the present, Rome certainly offered lessons for moralists who gleefully or sadly pointed to corruption and greed as reasons for such demise and as a threat to any individual or society not rigorously pure. It left among Rome's heirs, even those invaders from outside the empire, a feeling of confusion that would long complicate rebuilding. The aura of Rome's greatness remained. How could it have failed? How could its puny successors hope to rebuild when some fatal flaws must have escaped even the great Romans? Classical greatness followed by collapse left the West with an enduring inferiority complex, a sense of past grandeur that could not be recovered and a fear that any new, risky ventures would be doomed to destruction. Contrast this with China, for example, where dynasties fell and periods of major disorder reigned but where a greater sense of cultural continuity existed and therefore a fuller confidence in the distinctive validity of Chinese civilization—a confidence that could survive even periods of western dominance later in history.

The beginnings of Rome's collapse go back to the second century when a wave of plagues decimated the population of the empire, increasing the problems of recruiting troops. The plague spread elsewhere without triggering such disastrous results. In Rome, however, population decline was accompanied by economic stagnation. Both farm and industrial production leveled off. Yet the budget of the state had to soar, for frontier defense became more and more difficult. Without eschewing arguments about a civilization locked in the selfish greed of an effete upper class, the first ingredients of Rome's decline seem clearly to have been economic-demographic weaknesses and new pressures on the frontiers. Particularly in Europe, waves of Germanic barbarians forced more costly recruitment and maintenance of troops; there also were attacks on the eastern frontier in Persia.

The end came with a new wave of invasions. A host of Germanic tribes pushed into the European section of the empire in the later fourth century, themselves chased, ironically, by invaders from central Asia, the dreaded Huns. Various Germanic tribes took over Spain, Italy, France, even parts of North Africa, and their rule had to be recognized by the emperors, now ensconced in Constantinople. The East remained safe, for imperial control, greater wealth, and greater civic spirit kept Greece, Asia Minor, and Egypt secure—where armies were not sufficient there was money enough to buy off the potential invaders. But during the period 400-450 A.D. the western empire essentially disappeared. Even the Huns, under Attila, had a go, as they took Rome in 452 and were induced to leave only by the appeal of the Pope and a large payment. But with Attila's death the next year the Huns dissolved in internal conflict; the bulk of Europe was now in the hands of the Germanic tribes and these in turn were split into a host of kingdoms, based initially on tribal affiliation and leadership. The empire had not fallen into new hands; it had disappeared and with it the unity and peace it had long represented.

Causes and Analogies

Was Rome's fall inevitable? Was it due to human failings or to elements beyond man's control? What does it portend for later civilizations such as that of the contemporary West?

Let's take the human argument. With early expansion three related things happened to Rome. The upper classes became more dissolute and pleasure-seeking, which benefited culture but threatened the virtues of the early republic. The lower classes were separated with new harshness, kept happy in the cities by doles and games and simply exploited in the countryside. So there was greed at the top, which could undermine sound statesmanship since the rulers came from this elite, and endemic social tension that also could erode a state. The third ingredient was a product of the first two; representative institutions could not survive and so an ever-stronger executive took over. This worked well at first but it weighed heavily on the ability of the ruler and it resolved the first two developments, greed and social cleavage, only by constant expansion. Yet overburdened peasants and effete aristocrats made poor soldiers, so that expansion proved impossible to maintain. With this, in turn, came collapse of the economic and tax base of the empire and thus, ultimately, its political demise.

We must remember, of course, that all of this took five centuries, which is hardly an illustration of immediate retribution for greed and ambition. And we have suggested elements of decay that involve less moralization. Rome's economy was active as its height but not innovative. The demographic blow to the empire due to plague was severe. Falling population always lessens creativity and weakens an economy. In this case resultant chaos reduced the incentive to compensate for the population loss and permanent damage was done. Not only did falling population reduce the possibility of economic and military revival but it also limited the kind of competition for survival that a rising population produces, the rivalry with others seeking recognition that produces friction but also innovation.

Obviously a host of factors are involved in Rome's decline, including the positive qualities of the tribes that Rome faced; for though called barbarians, they had not only numbers but elements of civilization and political-economic structure well adapted to fighting, and they had learned something from their contacts with the Romans themselves. It is tempting to combine human and less personal explanatory factors. Greed alone did not cause the empire's downfall, but it may help explain the lower birthrate after plague had struck; upper-class families were reluctant to limit their pleasure-seeking by the burden of raising too many children, while the lower classes, increasingly impoverished and underfed, also lacked incentive. Scholars continue to debate the causes, and students can profitably do so, too.

Suggested Readings

Rome's origins are covered by A. Alfoldi, *Early Rome and the Latins* (Ann Arbor, 1965); general treatment of Rome is provided by D. R. Dudley, *Civilization of Rome* (New York, 1960) and F. M. Heichelheim and C. A. Yeo, *A History of the Roman People* (London, 1962). Interpretive essays are R. H. Barrow, *The Romans* (New York, 1965) and M. I. Rostovtzeff, *Rome* (New York, 1964). See also M. I. Rostovtzeff, *The Social and Economic History of the Roman Empire* (New York, 1957). The best survey of Rome's fall is F. Lot, *The End of the Ancient World* (New York, 1951); see also J. B. Bury, *The Invasions of Europe by the Barbarians* (New York, 1928).

On Christianity, Henry Chadwick, *The Early Church* (Harmondsworth, 1967), C. N. Cochrane, *Christianity and Classical Culture* (New York, 1944), and R. K. Bultmann, *Primitive Christianity* (London, 1956). A stimulating essay is Bertril Albrektson, *History and the Gods* (Lund, 1967); for related background, S. W. Baron, *A Social and Religious History of the Jews* (New York, 1952ff). On less standard topics, Carlo Cipolla, *The Economic History of World Population* (London, 1962) and T. K. Derry and T. I. Williams, *A Short History of Technology* (London, 1960).

The Coming of
the Middle Ages

WE TEND TO THINK of the Middle Ages as centuries of stagnation dominated by political chaos, violence, poverty, superstition, and religion. This view was fostered by intellectual advocates of the Renaissance who thought that they were distinctly superior to their predecessors. On the contrary, the medieval period, from 500 to as late as 1600, produced a civilization as distinctive and notable in many respects as that of Greece and Rome; and borrowing liberally from the past, this civilization was definitely western. This was in fact the crucible of western civilization. The period was not one of ignorance and bestiality. In many areas the Middle Ages engendered institutions and values that are more relevant to contemporary life than are those of the classical period. Of course, medieval civilization was not modern; neither was the classical period. In order to assess medieval achievements in their own right, we will consider three factors: the Germanic tribes, the Dark Ages, and the Middle Ages.

First, there were the contributions of the Germanic tribes, wandering peoples whose political values and human relationships did more to establish a basis for parliamentary government in Europe than did all the assemblies of Greece and Rome. Their tradition of limitation on the power of the executive obviously set a precedent that broke with the later Roman Empire. Their superstitions and folkways proved to be extremely pervasive and merged with, rather than yielded to, Christian concepts.

Secondly, there was the so-called Dark Ages, a period when cities shrank to almost nothing, serving as little more than Christian religious centers, and trade dwindled in Europe (though not in the eastern Mediterranean). Large political structures were impossible to maintain, and the real power was in local units, in the hands of noble landlords. Cultural achievements were minimal, yet a tradition was set of trying to master the ancient wisdom, particularly Christian learning but also related secular knowledge. Religious vitality was shown in monasticism, for the monks were in a position, first of all, to devote themselves to intellectual activities, copying manuscripts at the outset but later involving themselves in the highest levels of Christian theology; and, second, to engage in agriculture and related economic activities, whereby they often served as examples to the farmers. From the Dark Ages came the basis for the civilization we can label as distinctively medieval.

So, thirdly, we come to the Middle Ages proper, with its great centuries beginning from before 900 and continuing through 1400. In this era, parliamentary institutions and the modern central state had their inception. Theology and Christian art were at their height. Major scientific advances occurred, along with the beginnings of a secular literature. Medieval people were not modern people, but they were definitely western. They were inferior in technology and culture to the Chinese and several other contemporaneous civilizations, and they themselves felt inferior in most ways to classical civilization—religion being the major exception. But they were beginning also to set the bases for technological advance and social change along lines which the ancient world had not known. The high point of the Middle Ages, everyone agrees, came in the thirteenth century, which saw the beginnings of the Renaissance, first in Italy and then spreading to the north of Europe by the fifteenth century. The sixteenth century brought the Reformation, which in many ways was a definite re-expression of medieval values. After the Reformation came a clearly new period, the beginning of modern times.

The Germanic Tribes

In the late nineteenth century, two great schools of historical study, the French and the German, were engaged in debate. The French claimed that all that was good in the Middle Ages—or all that was even typical—came from Roman sources (the French erroneously regarded themselves as Latins), whereas the German scholars were even more adamant in claiming that the bravery of medieval knights, the traditions of parliament, and virtually everything originated with the Germanic tribes. The Latin tradition should be given its due, since it provided the formal religion, a tradition of agricultural organization and technology (the manor, with its serfs and its tools), and a secular culture; but the Germanic tribes, which ruled and intermingled with native races all over southwestern Europe, including Italy, Spain, and France, and which obviously predominated in central and northern Europe, did offer something new beyond sheer muscle power and a willingness to fight.

The Germanic tribes brought with them a stem language, Indo-European, quite different from Latin. Modern-day European languages mix Latin and German elements roughly in proportion to their distance from Scandinavia, which is where the Germanic tribes had their origin. Along with language the Germans brought a folklore and set of ritual practices, and oral legends of great sophistication, including sung poetry, that were preserved and came to be written down in the Middle Ages.

Germanic customs, if rude, added elements to western civilization which the Romans did not. The position of women in Germanic tribes was more equal than that of women in classical civilization, at least in the upper classes. They could own property, even inherit rule if a king died without a male heir. Germanic tradition helped begin a gradual, often-interrupted reversal of the customary position of women in Mediterrean society. Limits on the authority of kings and military vitality might be added to a potentially considerable list of advantages the Germans had over the later imperial Romans.

Moreover, the Germanic peoples had a political system, though not a unique one. Their tie was not the geographically defined city-state or empire of the Mediterranean world. There were no cities, and although agriculture was practiced, these Germanic peoples were mobile, exploiting the soil and the hunting area simultaneously and then moving on. Clans of ten or twenty families, often interrelated, formed the basis of social organization, and beyond these were loose tribes, under a chief or king who was essentially a war leader. The king was elected by an assembly of elders and warriors, and around him he had a group of close followers, called in Latin a *comitatus,* or committee. This committee owed special loyalty to the king, fought and feasted with him, and in return received special favors. However, successful kings (success being defined mainly in terms of prowess in battle) would gain the allegiance of many clans. As primitive as all this was in comparison to Rome or the Greek city-states, it suggested the idea of election that was already present in Rome and to a degree in Greece; it also suggested an elite group like the early Roman senate, that would aid the executive and guide and direct him. Autocracy thus was difficult, but, on the other hand, the Germans had potentially stronger executive authority than the Greeks had ever formally developed. This ambiguous mixture was later inherited directly by the West, and the Middle Ages would later work out this duality more formally.

As they overran Roman frontiers, either as settlers or invaders, the Germans learned some of the Roman ways, although assimilation was difficult for them partly because the Roman culture itself had deteriorated to a point at which it was no longer creative. Hence a decline of civilization in a formal sense did occur, but a new mixture of popular culture was possible among the Germans, as the change in religion, modification of language, and admiration of Roman artistic works all suggest. What we are dealing with in these centuries when Rome was declining and the Dark Ages were beginning is a cultural fusion, immensely creative if not well articulated, and having great implications for the future. The mixture distinguishes the political tradition of western Europe from that of eastern Europe (where the state ruled the church and an independent nobility did not readily develop) and from that of most other advanced civilizations. Ironically, the combination came forth, implicitly, in a period when Europe was scarcely civilized at all, certainly far inferior to vibrant kingdoms and empires in Asia, Africa, and Latin America.

The Dark Ages

We have already implied that the Dark Ages did not constitute a total societal eclipse. Ingenious scholars have found signs of vitality, even renaissance, in virtually every century, although this was actually a rather grim time in which to live. Let us briefly consider several points in regard to the three centuries plus after Rome's fall. First, why were they dark; what were the signs of deterioration; what was the new grimness of life? Second, what were the signs of cultural revival? Third, let us outline the structure of the modern European state in its crude but durable form in terms of geographical boundaries. And fourth, let us look at the development of a new and even more durable popular culture, of which the spread of Christianity was an inextricable part.

The bleakness of the Dark Ages stems from poverty, the decline of cities and trade; most people not only lived off the land but produced all of what they needed to survive. There was scant specialization of labor, virtually no money economy. Even the lords lived badly in crude wooden structures and exacted food, labor, and occasional unskilled service from their subjects. Everyone was poor, although a few people—upper churchmen, landlords—were less poor than others.

Recurrent invasions in the Dark Ages made most people feel that life offered little if any security or predictability. The worst offenders were sea-raiders, the Vikings from Scandinavia, who could seize, burn, and kill in forays into Britain, Ireland, Germany, western France, and even southern Europe. Some settled down, the most famous being the Normans who appropriated a huge swath of western France. Establishing a stable government, they ultimately conquered Britain and, briefly, Sicily. The Magyars arrived from Asia, cutting through Germany before settling in what is now Hungary; and from the south came the Moslems, whose religion stemmed from Judaism and Christianity. The Moslems appeared on the world scene in Asia Minor in the sixth century, with a religion that exhorted them to conquest: Islam was to be spread by the sword, and unbelievers were given the option of converting or paying tribute. When Roman rule collapsed, Arab Moslems easily spread across North Africa and conquered Spain. They were blocked from further advance by a defeat at the hands of the Franks in central France in 732, and their principal conversions and military conquests turned eastward, reaching major portions of the Indian subcontinent, Maylasia, Indonesia, and to a lesser degree south into other parts of Africa. Their failure to subdue Europe, save for a long, prosperous rule in Spain, was fortuitous; initially they would have provided better government and a more advanced civilization, but they also would have prevented the development of distinctive western values.

Partly because of the invasions, no large political structures were formed during the Dark Ages. German and Roman inheritance merged to create vassalage and manorialism, both localized in their early forms as politico-economic systems.

Manorialism has been described as part of the politico-economic evolution of the late Roman Empire; we need only add that it now spread over most of Europe as the Germanic tribes settled down. Ordinary peasants needed protection; local rulers saw a chance for modest glory by offering defense for a price. A few free farmers remained, but most of agricultural Europe (even the lands held by the Church) were divided between a small elite of local landlord potentates and a mass of peasants. This was not a slaveholding system. Peasants were not free to leave their land, but the lords were not free to dispossess them either. Obviously there were exceptions: some peasants escaped; some lords arbitrarily seized land. But the system was based on mutuality and a concept of ownership far more complicated than the modern one. The lords offered the protection needed in the absence of a strong central state, law courts to rule on major crimes, and possibly some help to tide the peasant over if the crop failed. The peasant turned over part of his produce and also gave the lord labor service on that land which the lord directly controlled and whose produce went to him and his retainers as a major means of support. This proved to be a highly durable economic system, and it certainly made sense in the confused political context of the Dark Ages. But it was not designed to spur agricultural production. A lord, thinking mainly in terms of military and political activities, plus feasting and hunting, was not oriented toward the idea of improving productive methods. If a lord wished to expand his fortune, his logical recourse was to try to seize more land by force from another lord rather than to improve methods on what he already had. As to the peasant, his goal was subsistence; greater production would primarily mean more to be turned over to the lord, and in the Dark Ages there were virtually no markets for surplus produce anyway. The manorial system, with rare exceptions, was designed for a stable, low-level economy, and it helped perpetuate precisely that.

Feudalism

If the manorial system had its roots in structures set up in late Roman days, overlaying it was the feudal system of vassalage that owed more to Germanic than to Roman influences. The two systems were related—both involved mutuality, for example—but they must not be confused. Manorialism can exist without feudalism, as indeed it did in many areas from the end of the Middle Ages onward. Feudalism describes the relationship of lord with lord, and this began to take on some sophistication in the Dark

Ages. A successful lord, who had induced farmers to come under his protection and had gained land by local wars against other lords, could gather around him an increasing band of retainers. Initially these were simply paid henchmen, supported in the lord's household and preserved from the servile pursuit of agriculture. But gradually a clearer hierarchy developed. A lord might reward a follower with a bit of land and some serfs of his own. The follower then became the lord's vassal; and precisely because he now lived independently, elaborate rituals were developed, including Christian symbols as the tribes became converted, to assure mutual loyalty. The lord owed the vassal protection, providing courts of justice to rule on disputes, and sometimes extended special gifts, as when a daughter married or a son reached knighthood. The vassal owed the lord gifts and rents, but above all military service and advice. The system could become immensely complicated (vassals could have vassals of their own), but as it developed it did provide the possibility of some stable regional rule. A successful, powerful lord, with vassals spread out over, say, a large province such as Normandy in France, could control hundreds of square miles, prevent local squabbling, and even mount a military force capable of reducing the danger of invasion. The development of feudalism was gradual and uneven, but it was a characteristic medieval institution that managed to create some order out of chaos. Characteristic also were the regional quality of the system, which would only slowly be modified, and the mutuality theoretically involved. No one was completely in command, and although this was a hierarchical system, the lord could not act without consideration of his vassals' interests and periodically sought their advice. Mini-parliaments, with vassals gathering around their lord to consider local problems and deal with particularly difficult legal cases, were taking rudimentary shape under this system.

The Painful Rebuilding of Culture

The Dark Ages were most clearly "dark" because the level of cultural activity fell to near zero. The only people with the time and literacy to deal with intellectual activity were a few clergy. Like Bishop Gregory of Tours, they knew there was a body of learning to assimilate, arithmetic and rhetoric texts from the late Roman period, and of course the gigantic achievements of the Church Fathers, but they could not understand them. They copied them, literally, which helped to preserve them, and sometimes tried to do compendia of knowledge. A few centers, notably some monasteries in Ireland and northern England, went further and produced theological works of merit. But this was just the beginning of an overall relearning period.

Artistic achievements also were few. In the eastern part of Europe, where the Byzantine Empire held sway, churches were decorated with elaborate mosaics of great beauty. But in the West churches were small, copied from Roman style with simple arches and a squared-off appearance; not unattractive, but certainly on a humbler scale. There seems to have been little painting or sculpture, for even the stylized "primitive" Christian art, with awkward, unrealistic figures painted on wood against a gilt background comes mainly from the tenth century onward.

But more important were happenings at the lower levels of society. The Dark Ages saw a major geographical extension of Christianity in Europe and with it the creation of a durable popular culture. Christian missionaries fanned out to Britain, northern Germany, and elsewhere. Many of them were killed. The most successful were those who, like Augustine of Canterbury in England, persuaded local chieftains or the wives of chieftains to tolerate religion or to convert directly. With the leaders' backing, the subjects soon followed, and by 800 only Scandinavia in western Europe remained pagan. With conversion, even if initially forced by one's tribal ruler, came the possibility of new values—Christian ones, but also such things as reading and writing, for most missionaries had some education. The spread of their religion depended on training a local priesthood, which meant teaching some Latin. Also schools were set up that might delve into secular problems of rhetoric and logic. This influenced few people directly. Yet it is important to remember that Christianity brought some classical influence, even in the very language it used.

For the common people, Christianity made sense on one level and could be shown to make sense on another. Again, we do not know whether Christian precepts prompted better treatment of neighbors and wives, except by particularly pious people, but Christianity did help to reinforce a fatalism that already existed in peasant culture and would last well into modern times. The world was a place of pain, unpredictable and hostile. There was little point in trying to change anything. The social hierarchy was natural, and the new priests said that government was ordained by God. One should therefore worry about one's soul, not politics.

Work was obviously necessary, but striving for greater wealth was dangerous; one should maintain one's place in life and pin one's hopes on the afterlife. Peasants as a class, the mass of Europe's population, thus were confirmed in their sense that the world was beyond their control, that the best they could hope for was that things would not get worse; change was dangerous. Christianity softened this fatalism by extending the hope of comfort in the afterlife, which paganism had not offered.

Peasant culture was not entirely displaced by Christianity, however. Already peasants had learned that there were gods to be propitiated by appropriate ceremonies and that life could be lightened every so often, even if not permanently improved, by festivals that pleased the gods and provided occasion for drink, dance, and courtship in an otherwise work-filled life. The new priests could not get rid of this culture. Some practices they could not accept, but these might persist anyway. Others they tried to christianize, bending their doctrines flexibly. The end result was a peasant culture that accepted priests, accepted Christianity, but preserved alternatives as well. This gave a richness to the life of the common people which conventional pictures of the Middle Ages do not capture. The common people were not necessarily devout; some were, some were not—all we really know is that they did not reject the new religion. Many did not go to church regularly. Their basic life was a material one—raising crops, raising a family. Their culture surrounded this activity, which is why some Christian beliefs made sense but pagan ceremonies were retained as well. The specific content of the combination varied from one area to another, but the merger of cultures applied everywhere; and everywhere too this merger was durable, lasting through the Middle Ages and beyond.

Direct examples from the Dark Ages are impossible to come by, save through hints left by artifacts of the period and educated guesses, plus the comments of missionaries who bemoaned the continued paganism of their charges. Although we cannot claim that nothing changed in the intervening centuries, we can view the peasant religion in Ireland in the late Middle Ages as probably typical. There, says one observer, the average Christian did not take confession or communion more than once a year. They were far more assiduous in attendance at festival bonfires, funeral wakes, as well as celebrations for local patron saints. The traditional pagan harvest festival in one area had been christianized into a pilgrimage marking the beginning of bringing in the crops. In other cases, priests were given magic powers—which had nothing to do with religious dogma—to cure diseases, overcome rapacious landlords, and so on. But other rituals, such as those at planting time, remained fairly strictly pagan in form. St. Patrick's day was linked to the first sowing of crops not just because of traditionalism but because it seemed to work. May Day rituals, for example, were devoted to the health of milk cows, which provided the main source of food until the grain harvest. And personal rituals were retained to guard against the presence of witches at marriage, who might produce a barren wife, or to protect newborn babies against evil spirits. Many rituals would survive the Middle Ages into the nineteenth century, not only in Ireland but throughout much of Europe.

We should consider one final point: Did the spread of Christianity to the common people, even though incomplete, have subtle influences that helped to create a distinctive western culture at the lower levels of society? Although focusing on God, Christianity nevertheless placed man in a special position. He alone of all the earth's creatures had been fashioned in God's image, and it was clear that the plants and animals were inferior to man; they did not have souls, and they were meant to serve man. This may have gradually encouraged a distinctively western attitude that nature was man's to exploit. Obviously, this did not produce new economic activity in the Dark Ages, but for a converted people, it reduced the awe in which nature previously had been held, and may help to explain the greater economic bustle of the Middle Ages. On a larger comparative basis, it differentiated western from Hindu civilization, in which nature's creatures were treated with respect or, in some cases, as sacred in their own right. The western person saw a cow as provider of milk and meat; the Hindu saw the cow, despite its potential as a source of food, as an object meant to roam free. Here may be the remote origins of a western attitude that would lead to economic expansion by exploitation of the earth's resources, although we must reemphasize that no economic revolution occurred until long after the Dark Ages and the Middle Ages were past.

The Carolingian Empire

It was not surprising that the Dark Ages drew to a close with a more ambitious political undertaking that had intellectual implications as well. Beyond feudalism Europeans showed signs of being able to create larger, effective political units, even if these did not always endure. With Rome's collapse the Germanic tribes had divided into relatively settled kingdoms, although few kings had significant influence beyond their local area. Indeed two kingdoms, called East Land and New Land (Austrasia and Neustria) sketched out territorial divisions that later would jell into the modern states of France and Germany. Austrasia was Germanic in race and culture; Neustria combined Germanic and Roman peoples and was strongly Latin in culture. In the late seventh century a strong group of rulers, the Carolingians, arose and unified both areas by successful battle. It was one of these rulers, Charles Martel, who defeated the Arabs in 732, sending the Moslems back to Spain. His son Peppin III thus inherited a strong empire and was able to push further, notably into Italy. The Pope was in trouble, for another kingdom, the Lombards in northern Italy, was pressing south against Rome. The Pope invited Peppin to save Rome and papal freedom; Peppin marched to Rome and was annointed king by the Pope, in return for which he defeated the Lombards.

His son, known as Charlemagne or Charles the Great, thus held much of modern Germany, France, and northern Italy; the territories of central Italy were given to the Pope and were known as the papal states. Charlemagne proved to be a giant of a ruler, equal to any of the Caesars. He extended the boundaries of the Carolingian empire further east and north in Germany; he defeated the barbarian Avars in the southeast, thus gaining Bavaria and pushing to the Adriatic Sea. He even tried unsuccessfully to conquer Spain. A famous defeat against the Moslems produced the legend of the heroic Roland, one of the earliest medieval epics. But Charlemagne must not be judged by conquest alone: he made three other, more durable contributions.

First, again finding the Pope in trouble, this time by a faction of Roman nobles, Charlemagne marched in to restore him and in turn was crowned emperor in the following terms: "To Charles Augustus, crowned of God, great and pacific emperor of the Romans, life and victory." This suggested the revival of the Roman Empire; it certainly indicated that Byzantium, Rome's more direct heir in everything but geography, had lost out in Europe. It began a fiction of a continuance of empire that had symbolic importance for a full thousand years. From this time there was always someone claiming to be Roman emperor. More concretely, the new empire tied Italy into the Germanic kingdoms, and while Italy was not consistently ruled from the North, German kings for several centuries periodically descended to make their claim. Finally, the gesture signalled a new relationship of church and state. Charlemagne was no Constantine, but he did believe that, annointed by the Pope, he had divine backing for his rule and therefore special religious duties. State aid might help the church, as in converting some of the newly-conquered peoples, but there was also the potential here for state-church clash, for lines of authority were not clearly drawn.

Second, Charlemagne had to administer the empire. He did this mainly by giving his bureaucrats permanent grants of land, which they could pass on to their sons in return for military and administrative service and a firm oath of loyalty. Essentially he turned bureaucracy into a system of large-scale vassalage. There were immense dangers in this, for a powerful hereditary duke could well renounce his loyalty and turn against the central ruler. Briefly, however, the system worked, and Charlemagne's empire was well run.

Third, Charlemagne played a direct role in the revival of learning in the West. He set up new schools associated with major cathedrals and brought in the best scholars of the day. The quality of the teaching of Latin, rhetoric, and even the understanding of theology improved.

In other respects, however, Charlemagne's empire proved only a temporary interruption in the more basic patterns of the Dark Ages. It spurred no economic revival, which might have been fundamental to real change, and it was divided within a short time into three parts: one, basically France; two, basically Germany; and three, a central stretch of land running from the Low Countries through Alsace-Lorraine and Switzerland to northern Italy. This division has in many ways lasted to the present day, and the central kingdom, intended to be the most important, proved to be the recurrent battleground between the states on either side. By the ninth century the central kingdom had already fallen into fragments while France and Germany retained some superficial unity.

But it was only superficial. These states were too big to be ruled with the weak economy and primitive transportation of the day. A strong king might win some allegiance from putative vassals, but now that monarchy was hereditary (another change from German custom introduced by the Carolingians) there was no guarantee that a king would be strong. This was also the period of the most intense Viking invasions, which both confirmed and heightened the weakness of the central state. Charlemagne had sketched many potential developments, but he had not ended the Dark Ages. In France a strong king turned back the Vikings at the end of the ninth century and began to build strength around Paris, deriving only the vaguest allegiance from powerful nobles elsewhere in France. Germany was also divided, though the German king claimed the title of Roman Emperor. Effective political rule was local. Laws, too, were local, so that a crime in one small region might be meaningless, or at least subject to different kinds of punishment, in another.

The only clear, relatively binding institution in the West was the church. At least on the regional level the church had much clearer institutional ties than those provided by vassalage. Church doctrine now had clarified to hold that only certain men could administer the sacraments. Through baptism original sin was washed away; confirmation, penance, and Eucharist, if regularly performed, would compensate for the sins that inherently evil man was bound to commit. But the mystical powers capable of administering these rites were reserved for the clergy, who also received the sacrament of ordination which conferred upon them direct authority from the deity. For Christ had laid his hands on his apostles, giving them divine authority to continue his work of salvation; they had commissioned others, and the succession (called Apostolic Succession) continues still. The bishop received the full apostolic power, part of which he then conferred on priests, the local representatives of the church. This potentially provided a taut organizational structure, although it was not yet capped by international leadership. Ruling his own territory, the pope was, after the Carolingian period, freer to direct his attentions to claims of special authority, but he was not in direct contact with most bishops, indeed did not appoint most of them. The eastern church in fact was now largely split off, recognizing neither papal authority nor some of the theological doctrines maintained by the western church. What became the Orthodox religion of the East with state control, tolerance of marriage for priests, and so on, profoundly differed from what would become known as Roman Catholicism in the West. But in the West the stronger popes did maintain some ties with bishops from North Africa to Britain and Germany, also sponsoring missionary activities further into northern Europe. But the quality of popes declined after the Carolingian era. Poor, disunited, open to raids and attack, Europe was still a puny place in the tenth century.

Popular Culture and Popular Toil

Let us return to the common people. Agricultural techniques were unchanged from Roman and German customs. The Roman plow was used in the light soil of southern Europe, a wheeled plow was pulled by oxen on the heavier soils of the North. Craft techniques, almost gone given the withering of the cities, actually deteriorated from late Roman levels. Lacking many animals, peasants had scant fertilizer. To restore their soil's fertility they left half, or more commonly a third, of their land fallow each year. Productivity was low, for grain was of poor quality and a fourth of the seed produced had to be saved for the next year's planting. Since transport was too primitive and the money economy too illdeveloped to bring in food from the outside, famines occurred about once every four years. Too little food was produced for most animals except those needed for breeding, so the surplus was slaughtered in the fall—most of the meat going to the lord. The peasant lived on bread, produced his own simple clothing, and built his own shack. Even this stark system was maintained only by village cooperation. Village cooperation and approximate equality were again vital and durable traditions, for even if they did little but keep village members alive, they provided a subculture and subgovernment (ruling, for example, on property disputes) beneath the manorial system. The economic principles of the village were expressed in two distinctive features: First was a considerable amount of common land owned by no one, on which peasants could graze animals, seek wood, and so on. Second was the division of individual holdings into strips, rather than single plots, so that if something went wrong with one section of land or if one section was more fertile than another, no one family would be the exclusive sufferer or gainer. Again, approximate equality and mutual protection were vital when no one had much to spare, and village principles of organization would outlast almost every other feature of the Dark Ages.

The Coming of Middle Ages

The Dark Ages began to end by the tenth century—the pressure of invasions and raids decreased, stronger regional political structures, sometimes even national structures, developed; and, because of greater stability, the population began to increase, forcing further economic and political change. The ending of the Dark Ages and the advent of the Middle Ages were due to various interrelated factors and covered a rather long period of time. Cessation of the invasions was vital, because the peasants could plant without fear of being wiped out by attacks; merchants could plan trade without fear of seizure of their goods by pirates; and, governments could develop on a regional, or even a national basis. These factors all contributed to Europe's revival.

There had been three sources of invasion. The first was from Asia, by tribes who were drawn into the weakly ruled lands of what is now Poland, Austria, Hungary, and the Balkans. Central Asia had produced a host of peoples whom it could not support; these peoples had a military tradition, based on fleet cavalry, that was hard to withstand. The Byzantine Empire, with its capital in Constantinople, was no great barrier to the advance of these eastern invaders, so that during the post-Roman centuries, Byzantium steadily lost to the conquering Arabs its rich territories of Egypt and the lands bordering the eastern Mediterranean. In Europe itself, the invasions ceased as the invaders, traditionally nomadic peoples, settled down in territories they had conquered, turned to agriculture, became converted to Christianity, and established stable political institutions. Besides, there was increasing and recurrent chaos within central Asia itself which drew the invaders away from Europe. Yet, in the thirteenth century the Mongol hordes, led by the military genius Genghis Khan, poured into Europe, reaching well into Germany. They produced nothing but decades of disruption, however, and eventually withdrew because of troubles at home. More durable was the incursion of the Ottoman Turks, another central Asian tribe, of Islamic persuasion, which began to move west against both the Arabs and the Byzantines in the tenth century. These people were settlers, and gradually they built a dominant empire in the Middle East, extending through North Africa. The Byzantine Empire fell to them in stages, with Constantinople being conquered in 1453. This gave the Ottomans not only Asia Minor, but also the Balkans, and they continued to press Europe until the seventeenth century, when an effort to capture the city of Vienna failed and they gradually retreated. Thus, we see that the eastern invasions were complicated and extremely prolonged. This prolongation explains why what we

now know as eastern Europe, although christianized (the Ottomans, a tolerant people, did not normally mistreat the Christians), entered the story of *western* civilization only after the
Middle Ages, and why even then their diverse cultural background
made their westernization tentative and distinctive.

The cessation of Viking incursions is more simply told.
Christianization of the Norse kingdoms and the development of
agriculture reduced their marauding spirit. In several cases, major
groups of raiders decided that it was more profitable to settle down
as rulers in an area than to continue periodic, arduous sea trips.
The classic case is Normandy, an area of present-day France, rich
in soil, and long a scene of brutal coastal raids. But in the tenth
century the Vikings conquered that rich province and set up a well-
administered state. Led by a duke, they adopted feudal institutions, so that the old Viking warriors were given land in the
province and became vassals who swore allegiance to the duke. A
century later, in 1056, William the Conqueror, a Norman duke,
successfully conquered England and imposed the same system
there, with a largely Norman nobility headed by the king (who
remained duke of Normandy) ruling the Anglo-Saxon people. We
have noted already that around Paris the king of France was
operating in much the same fashion, building a regional government where the vassals owed him direct allegiance, including aid in
war where they served as cavalry. The king controlled stretches of
land that could provide direct income (a system also used by the
Normans in England, where royal lands were scattered throughout
the whole kingdom).

Finally, the cessation of southern invasions was due in part to
the temporary grandeur of the Carolingian empire but more to the
disarray of the Arab Moslem world. Moslem rule in Spain,
although eliminated completely only in the fifteenth century, had
degenerated increasingly into bickering local dynasties. The entire
Arab world was under pressure, politically divided, and then
assailed with growing success by the Turks; small wonder that they
were on the defensive in their small European holdings. As European states became better organized, and as the papacy gained
greater influence over the western church, a holy war was
proclaimed against the Moslem world in order to regain for
Christianity the lands in which it had first developed. Even before
the crusades, feudal adventurers attacked Moslems not only in
Spain but also in Sicily and southern Italy; a group of Norman

adventurers, for example, set up a kingdom in Sicily. Merchants as well as knights, particularly in the Italian ports, saw that there were personal and religious gains to be had in further conquests. As Byzantium lost the Near East to the Turks, it seemed vital to protect the Christian holy places from control by the infidels. So in 1095 the first crusade was launched with great religious enthusiasm fomented initially by Pope Urban II. Many joined the cause: knights who could not fight at home now that governmental controls had improved; holy men; important kings such as Richard the Lion-Hearted; even in one case some misguided children—all periodically attacked the Middle East. Thanks to the heavily armed and armored cavalry that was the hallmark of the feudal lords, initial conquests succeeded in establishing western kingdoms in Jerusalem and elsewhere in the eastern Mediterranean. These soon were lost, however, as the Turks united, and a series of subsequent crusades, lasting into the thirteenth century, became more and more insane. Crusading zeal had waned, kings were busy expanding their home territories, and the Turks were unbeatable on their own ground. The small western holdings were quickly wiped out and the later crusades were chiefly commercial affairs fostered by Italian merchants to gain territory, not in the holy land but along the Adriatic (one crusade even captured Constantinople, then still a Christian city) for the purpose of facilitating trade.

The crusades proved, certainly, that the threat from the South was gone, but more importantly they acquainted Europe with aspects of other civilizations more advanced than the West. The fact was that both the Byzantines and the Arabs had preserved vital elements of classical learning in literature and art but particularly in the realms of science, philosophy, and mathematics. From Constantinople, Italian merchants had brought back books as well as eastern spices and jewelry, and scholars had labored there to collect and translate Greek works. Even more important were the efforts of translators in Spain, who found in Arab learning not only preservation of classical wisdom but also independent advances in science and philosophy.

Signs of Revival

Western Europe could now assume a more durable political shape than had been possible under the talented Carolingians. Germany was ill-defined, although an important ingredient in medieval civilization. Political units in France, the Low Countries,

Britain, and increasingly Spain, grew capable of preserving internal as well as external order. This was both cause and result of the
reduction of pressure from the outside, and we must deal shortly
with the unique political structure that characterized the Middle
Ages. Thus, the invasion-political advance equation is one vital element in the transition from Dark Ages to Middle Ages.

The second major element was economic-demographic revival
which coincided with the political advance. It would be tempting to
view political stability as leading to economic gains in a neat
pattern, but, in fact, economic revival was somewhat
autonomous—witness the fact that it occurred in some badly
organized areas such as Italy and could serve as the base for
political revival by providing new money for governments, new
skills, even a new mentality.

Commercial revival began as early as the eighth century.
Venice, an independent city-state endowed with shrewd merchants
and an unfailing thirst for profit, was the leader. Venetian ships
supplied the Byzantine Empire with the primitive goods of the
European economy: salt, fish, wheat, wine, and timber. In return,
they carried back fine fabrics and spices from the Far East. The
Venetians cleared the Adriatic Sea of pirates, and by the end of the
Middle Ages their great fleet dominated the Mediterranean. Venetian success served to spur the inland Italian economy as cities
began to manufacture cloth and metal goods as well as engage in
commerce themselves. Gradually, this new commercial spirit
spread north of Italy, as Italian merchants extended their trade to
southern Germany and France; by the late eleventh century they
had even reached England.

At the other end of Europe things were quieter, but here, too,
commerce took a new hold once the Vikings settled down. Indeed
the Vikings themselves helped the transition to commerce by learning that trading was safer than raiding. It was the Vikings who
sponsored trade in Russia, bringing raw materials from the North
and meeting merchants from Constantinople whose goods they
carried to England, Germany, France, and the Netherlands. This
latter region, with ports on the Atlantic, proved to be central to the
northern economic revival; located between the commerce of the
North (north Germany and Scandinavia) and that of Italy, it was
the meeting ground for the two currents of European trade. This in
turn encouraged manufacturing.

With trade revival came new functions for cities, for although most manufacturing was done by part-time workers who lived in the countryside, the highest quality production demanded specialized urban labor. Merchants needed cities as centers where they could meet, exchange goods, and promote new commercial institutions such as banks which might further spur the economy. With cities came new opportunities for human contacts, and urbanization was just as important as political stability and contacts with other civilizations in promoting a steadily rising standard of intellectual life.

This is not to say that, although medieval economics were highly sophisticated, they were modern in the sense of a uniform commitment to international trade and capitalism as the basis of economics. The ordinary individual in this era was still rural. In Flanders and northern Italy, the most vital trade centers, perhaps twenty percent of the population lived in cities, and some rural inhabitants did at least some manufacturing work, but most people were farmers. Peasant life and values characterized the vast majority of European people elsewhere; they did not alter much as medieval civilization unfolded, although two forces for change were present: the peasants had large families, and they adopted a more productive technology.

An agricultural revival had to be the basis for a new civilization. Only greater crop production could allow towns to grow, trading to expand, population to increase. Exactly why food production increased is not clear, but better government and cessation of invasion played a key role. Peasants had more children; increased family size required new methods to produce food; and fewer people died so that there were more hands available to help with farming. Increased production in turn encouraged still larger families and population growth stimulated agricultural change. It allowed Europeans to spread out into previously uncultivated lands, leading to the formation of new villages and cities and the consequent adjusting of old political structures to meet new situations.

More important, by the tenth or eleventh centuries new agricultural devices were either invented or spread from areas where they had been used before but only on a local basis. Northern European farmers adopted a heavy, wheeled plow now equipped with a mold-board, which not only dug a furrow but turned the dirt over, thus greatly increasing crop yields. The plow required extensive animal power. Oxen had been used for more primitive versions of the plow, but horses were quicker. During the Carolingian era peasants learned, perhaps from Eastern invaders, the use of the horse collar. For the first time, for even the Romans had not known the method, horses could pull a heavy load without choking themselves to death. The horse became thereby more efficient than the ox, though oxen, easier to feed, remained important. Finally, more and more peasants learned to leave only a third instead of a half of their land fallow each year, again producing a potential increase in output. Except for the horse collar none of these developments was entirely new; even added up they hardly sound revolutionary. But prosaic as they are, they were the foundations of medieval civilization, as they had to be in a society still overwhelmingly agricultural.

And again, without pretending to know which came first, the chicken or the egg, we must stress that more eggs resulted. Population growth stimulated agricultural change. It allowed Europeans to fan out into previously uncultivated lands. It stimulated the formation of new villages, even the spread of peoples, as in the movements of Germans further and further east. Population growth is inherently creative. It forces people to make new decisions in order to survive, even in order to preserve some semblance of traditions. Fathers have to innovate to take care of their children in the traditional manner—to provide land, dowries, and so on. Children must innovate, when they turn out to be unprovided for. Hence the movement to new villages, to cities. Political structures must adjust. Local manorial regimes had to deal with new people and new economic opportunities; on the whole the result was a loosening, though not the destruction, of the manorial system in the West. Regional and national governments had to deal with cities and totally new social types, such as the craftsman and, above all, the merchant. Adaptation was creative, so that the population spurt could continue well into the thirteenth century; when it ended, as we will see, medieval civilization itself began to decay.

Developments outside Europe; new politics; new intellectual contacts; a new urban base; a rising economy—all fed medieval civilization. Beneath them all was the silent upheaval among the European masses, who began to turn out more food and more people.

Medieval Civilization

A NUMBER OF PROBLEMS ARISE when one tries to capture the essential aspects of medieval civilization. One pervasive notion is that the Middle Ages were filled with ignorance and chaos, or, at best, were merely a learning period which bridged the gap between the great classical ages and the Renaissance. This is simply not so. The Middle Ages produced a culture which was neither classical nor modern but which rivals both in sophistication. By the conventional standards of judging how civilized a people is, the Europeans in the Middle Ages had gained the right to serious attention. In technology as well as politics, Europe was as advanced as most of the other civilized areas of the world, even if it still lagged behind a bit. In art and philosophy it could certainly claim competitive stature. And in trade it was more active even than China. The Chinese, although rightly convinced of their superiority, found that they could learn some things from early European visitors (beginning with Marco Polo in the thirteenth century); but the Europeans learned even more from the Chinese, which shows that they were able and willing to adapt.

None of this is meant as a proclamation of "hurray for the West." It simply states that by the conventional measures of how civilized a people are, the Europeans in the Middle Ages themselves were advancing in most areas. And if it was true that Europeans learned more from the Chinese, from how to make paper to how to make gunpowder—the latter a celebratory device in China, for making firecrackers, that should never have been given to the more aggressive West—this showed two things: first, that the Europeans were able and willing to learn and to advance on this basis, and second, that, even if still backward in many respects, they had some peculiar venturesomeness that pushed the Marco Polos and the Christian missionaries all over the world by the end of the Middle Ages. Even the Chinese, whose traders stopped at the eastern part of the Arab peninsula, never ventured around it to Europe and never pushed into the western unknown where they would have found America. The Middle Ages must be seen as a vital, creative period, even at the level of popular culture. Most people were ignorant; so they had been in classical times and so they were all over the world. They had little, if any, ability to read or any contact with formal learning. But they had an evolving culture, mixing superstition with a willingness to try some new technology, such as the horse collar; by no means should they be dismissed as the benighted church-going, landlord-ridden poor.

The Middle Ages must be seen as a vital, creative period, even at the level of popular culture, so that it deserves attention as a major period of civilization and, thus, a major contributor to the ongoing development of western civilization. But medieval civilization did not produce political unity as Rome had done and as Hellenism had done to some extent. There were separate kingdoms and city-states, and even though the Holy Roman Empire pretended to provide a basic unity, it never dominated a major part of Europe. As Voltaire later said, the Holy Roman Empire was not holy, Roman, or an empire. In fact, Europe's political gains continued even as medieval civilization declined. There was a medieval political style, but it never extended uniformly from one area to another; it never united Europe or even intended to unite Europe. It is even difficult to determine exactly where western civilization ended during the Middle Ages. All one can say is that the eastern boundary of western civilization was flexible and that some eastern peoples, Slavs as well as Magyars, although outside the real orbit of western civilization, acquired through their trade and cultural contacts some bases for later inclusion therein.

The dynamic center of medieval civilization was France and the Low Countries, with England and western Germany actively participating. Italy, a leader in trade, never developed typical medieval political forms, but relied rather on the traditional city-states, which were overrun occasionally by invaders under the German emperors. Italy was highly civilized but did not extensively copy such typical medieval styles as Gothic art, preferring rather to follow more closely the classical tradition. Spain, as it threw off Moslem rule, did acquire some medieval elements (the Gothic style of building and a medieval monarchy), but it too was always a bit different because the conquest had produced a militant, intolerant attitude and Moslem influence remained in art and intellectual life. Farther north, medieval styles spread belatedly. The first Gothic cathedrals were being built in Scandinavia as the Middle Ages seemed to be in full decline in its seat of origin farther to the south. Again, this reminds us of the lack of unity in western Europe, even as a common civilization spread gradually throughout most of the region.

We have said that the high point of the Middle Ages occurred in the thirteenth century; this was true of France and the Low Countries, but for Britain it was the fourteenth century. For two centuries thereafter we can discuss symptoms of decline. First of all, decline was primarily cultural. Political structures changed along lines already marked out by medieval developments; one can say that at some point they changed so much that they were no longer medieval. But there was no collapse as in Greece or Rome. The same holds true for economics. Again in contrast to Greece and Rome, there was no long period of deterioration in economic levels and no easily identifiable change of direction, although there was an important period of difficulty in the fourteenth century, caused by plague and economic decline. Medieval civilization did not fall or die but rather merged into later versions of western civilization.

This brings us to the question of whether the Middle Ages were over by the time of the Renaissance and Reformation. Most historians make sharp divisions by period at this point, and we will bow to this convention by having a separate, brief section on the Renaissance and Reformation. But it is well to point out now that these periods were essentially medieval, part of the ongoing evolution of medieval civilization, and despite there being a new period in western history, the bases of the medieval world were not changed. We deal, then, with a civilization that began to take clear form after the chaos of the Dark Ages, by the tenth century. It found its most typical expression three centuries later and underwent further stress and change, but yielded to a fundamentally new set of intellectual premises, political and economic structures, and popular attitudes only by the seventeenth century. This was a civilization which had a long and varied life and which never definitively collapsed—in other words, a civilization of which we are direct heirs.

There is no single term that adequately describes the Middle Ages. Historians can pretend to unite Greek civilization, from politics through drama to philosophy, with the word moderation. Rome's central heritage seems to be dominated by order and power, and the Romans simply were not very talented in certain areas of human endeavor. But medieval civilization was active in high intellectual life, art, politics, economics. Participants were not only upper class individuals but also common people, such as the hosts of nameless craftsmen who labored through the centuries on the details of Gothic cathedrals, or even the peasants who steadily continued to blend Christianity with tradition into a comprehensible popular culture.

If there is a common theme to this it would seem to be tolerance of ambiguity. We illustrated this in discussing the manorial system: medieval people, unlike both classics and moderns, readily tolerated a situation in which both peasants and landlords had defined rights to a given piece of land with neither owning it in the sense of being able to dispose of it at will. This ambiguity extended to political relationships at higher levels, where central rulers similarly shared power and property with the landed aristocracy and sometimes even with rich merchants; rights and duties were mutual.

Taken overall, medieval philosophy constituted an effort to blend the dictates of Christian faith, taught by the Bible and the classical Church fathers, and a belief that man could know a good bit on his own in an expanding area of secular learning, most notably in science and mathematics. The Middle Ages thus involved the reconciliation of very diverse kinds of knowledge, such as Thomas Aquinas attempted to do in his great *Summas.* Through the Renaissance and into the seventeenth century, philosophers thought they could know everything knowable, and answer every basic question except those that had to be referred to faith. Modern man not only has abandoned this confidence, with the specialization of knowledge, but has dropped some basic questions as not necessary to human life or worthwhile; and this, as we will see, was a seventeenth-century development, based on a new kind of confidence in advances in a narrower range of learning than Aquinas would ever have tolerated.

Ambiguity also extended to economics, where we see the rise of a new, vigorous capitalism but institutions that typically were not capitalistic, but rather designed to protect stability even at the expense of individual advance. We see economic ambiguity in the individual merchant who had made his fortune, but worried lest his concentration on material things reduce his chances of salvation. He was then prey to sudden bouts of conscience (usually but not always on the deathbed when there was no chance to spend any more money anyway) in which everything would be given to the church or the poor.

So there may be a medieval theme, the attempt to reconcile, which was compatible with vigorous, proud achievement in many fields. The major fields of endeavor were, of course, interdependent. Intellectual advance depended on better farming and the rise of cities, which could support a population of philosophers and students. And all of the fields yielded direct legacies to modern western civilization. Even if few of us read Aquinas now, we depend heavily, in our intellectual makeup, on his contribution to rationalism and science. We certainly depend on the medieval contribution to the institutionalization of learning, the creation of formal universities, replacing the classical reliance on groups of students informally gathered around a great mentor. But our ordering of fields is meant to suggest the extent to which each contributed to the future. Medieval art and philosophy can correctly be taken as the highest achievements of the civilization, but they left the least complete heritage to later ages. Political developments were carried on much more directly. We no longer have medieval political structures but we are working with their direct successors and grappling with problems that a medieval politician could to an extent identify. In intellectual life, in contrast, modern western civilization has pulled vital elements from the medieval achievement, but has rejected its basic thrust. We inherit as much if not more from medieval economics as from politics, and it was certainly in this area, which touches on the common man as on the merchant prince, that medieval civilization proved to alter the classical balance, in which economic innovation took a back seat to formal culture or political activity. This rank order of fields is not conventional, from the standpoint of the medieval historian, who likes to work up from economic change and political stabilization to the Gothic cathedral and the philosophical *Summa*. But it fits our purpose, which is to find out what is durably western, what makes us what we are. And it captures a useful van-tagepoint on medieval civilization itself.

Medieval Thought and Art

Architecture most clearly demonstrates the distinctive tone of medieval culture. The soaring spires of Gothic cathedrals are living testimonies to the worship of the Christian God, but are also major artistic and engineering achievements (for the Middle Ages produced one of the three major architectural styles in Western history). Music flourished as well, also mainly in a church context. So did painting, but early medieval art yielded by the thirteenth century to more realistic portrayals of man and nature, indicating a more positive conception of life.

Medieval philosophy left a clearer legacy. In the twelfth century philosophers stepped up the work of assimilating classical learn-ing and the Christian faith. One monk, Peter Abelard, one of the founders of the University of Paris, ventured to set out major premises of faith in a question-and-answer framework, challenging logicians to apply their reason. His effort was condemned, but Abelard's questioning spirit survived. Later in the century the translation of Greek and Arab philosophy greatly broadened the scope of knowledge seemingly accessible to reason alone. Aristotle's comprehensive learning was particularly challenging, for few dared to question the classical past, yet Aristotle could not have been in-formed by true faith.

It remained for Thomas Aquinas to attempt the key medieval synthesis. Thomas expanded the area of knowledge open to reason, but he asserted that faith still should procede understanding; vital areas of religious truth could be penetrated by faith alone. Yet he tried to deal with rationalism, particularly as represented by Aristotle, on its own ground, for there could be only one truth, and faith and reason had to coincide. His *Summas* set forth all possible objections to truth as taught by reason and faith alike, disposed of them logically, and set forth the correct premise. Later in the thirteenth century, philosophers such as Roger Bacon became still more interested in classical science, applying not only logic but also empirical investigation, beginning a thread of scientific inquiry that continues to our own time.

The rich diversity of medieval thought must be stressed: there was reason, anti-reason, experiment. At the end of the thirteenth century some scholars fell into petty applications of reason to religious truth, such as: how many angels can dance on the head of a pin. Thus, medieval scholasticism, the wedding of faith and reason through logic, was brought into disrepute. But its legacy was that medieval philosophy developed logical reasoning to its highest point and suggested a host of new directions for knowledge.

Political Culture

Let us begin with the major features of the medieval political synthesis. The key medieval political institution was the feudal monarchy. It was not a permanent political form, for once the Middle Ages were over, it tended to become more nearly a pure monarchy or, in a few instances, a parliamentary state.

Feudal monarchy was composed of three elements. In the monarchical element, kings steadily extended their powers. Centralization of the state began in the Middle Ages, and in a sense this trend has never stopped. Medieval kings used the lands under their direct control to afford armies, and diplomatic leverage to expand—by force, by marriage alliances, and by negotiation. In the classic case, the king of France, enthroned at Paris, continued to acquire territory and made more and more local rulers his vassals (although at the end of the Middle Ages he was still far from controlling all of the territory of modern France). In addition to the geographic expansion, a rudimentary bureaucracy began to develop around the monarchs. Specialists in matters of finance, the administration of justice, and military affairs appeared on the scene, so that the king did not have to rely solely on occasional councils of his vassals. Moreover, by the eleventh century, emissaries were, in some cases, sent out from the central government to see how things were going in the provinces. These emissaries might oversee the collection of taxes, hold courts of law, or report back on the loyalty of local nobles. Thus, medieval bureaucracy evidenced the two key principles of centralized rule: specialization and contact of the center with the rest of the country. Direct contact with subjects, except those who lived on land that the king owned as manorial lord, was slower in coming. Only at the end of the Middle Ages were kings beginning to tax directly the populace and recruit soldiers. During most of the period, fighting was still conducted primarily by cavalry (the common people were not of much use in this regard) so that the kings had to recruit their soldiers from among their own vassals. Money was obtained from the vassals, too (although this source was an unpredictable one) and from what was produced on the kings' own estates. But at the end of the Middle Ages, by the fourteenth century, kings were beginning to impose light taxes directly on their subjects and to recruit soldiers for the army; this latter development was aided by the new effectiveness of archery, which reduced the importance of cavalry by allowing the use of foot soldiers. Finally, the kings or their representatives had held courts of law for the dispensing of justice; the court system was particularly well developed in England, where court officials were the king's men, aided periodically by visits from judges of higher courts who took care of major disputes and crimes.

The centralized monarchies grew because they could provide more internal stability and a greater measure of justice than was possible under the feudal system. Centralized monarchy was aided by the revival of Roman law, which stressed that the line of authority was from the top down. Not surprisingly, monarchs sponsored research in Roman law and used that law against customary feudal law. By the thirteenth century, political theorists emerged who hailed the king as absolute ruler, in the tradition of the Roman emperors.

Centralized monarchies grew because they had a new social class that could be played off against the military aristocracy. The increase in wealth and the rise of cities created new resources to be tapped for armies and expanding bureaucracies. It also created a merchant group which would welcome central regulation of a territory in the interests of trade, as against piracy, local tolls, and so on, and one which naturally resented the pretensions of the aristocracy. The merchants tended to be natural supporters of the monarchs well into the seventeenth century. In return, kings often extended special privileges to the cities and selected bureaucrats from the ranks of merchants who might at once be more dependent on royal favor and more skillful at, say, royal financial administration than were the noble vassals.

Restraints on the New Monarchs

But the growth of the central monarchy was balanced by two factors: the church and the tradition of the vassalage. First, the church served as a counterpoise. Like the kings, indeed even before them, the popes were strengthening their administrative position as head of the western church. They first introduced direct taxation, taking a portion (an increasing portion, indeed) of local tithes and fees imposed on ordinary churchgoers to be sent to Rome. Papal bureacracy steadily expanded. Emissaries checked up on local bishops and abbots to keep them in line. A system of courts was developed to deal with any crimes committed by clergy and religious offenses of any sort, no matter who the perpetrator. Here, then, was a powerful government, lacking an army but claiming direct, divine authority, in immediate contact with the common people through the local priest. Each person owed loyalty to the church as well as to the state; the king himself owed loyalty to the church in key matters. Thus, royal authority could not be absolute. Kings and popes inevitably clashed. How far did the jurisdiction of church courts extend, compared to that of royal courts? How much tax money could the Roman papacy take out of the country? What about the traditions, which Charlemagne had revived, that held that kings had religious functions?

In the early Middle Ages, the pope usually won when a clash developed, for the king was not all-powerful and besides, his own religious loyalties were still great enough that he often backed down. The most famous instance was the Investiture Controversy that pitted Pope Gregory VII against Henry IV, emperor of Germany. Kings, and even local nobles, had often appointed bishops and priests; this expressed their religious function and gave them obvious advantages, for they could give these offices to loyal supporters. Gregory, who greatly strengthened the papacy, insisted that only popes could appoint bishops. Henry refused to concur in this view and was excommunicated from the church, which meant that he could not receive mass and was denied salvation. It also meant that Henry's subjects owed him no loyalty, for the divine sanction of his secular rule had been withdrawn. This naturally encouraged rebellious nobles to revolt, and Henry had to yield. For three wintry days in 1077, Henry stood barefoot and pleaded for forgiveness at the papal castle of Canossa. He finally got it, which made the church seem clearly supreme over the secular state. Papal authority was heightened by direction of the early crusades and by attacks on new heresies. By 1200, courts of Inquisition were established under direct papal control, to prosecute anyone suspected of heresy. Trials were secret and torture was freely used to gain confessions. Those who confessed were imprisoned for life;

those who refused to confess but were deemed heretical were turned over to the civil authority to be burned at the stake—the pope would not shoulder this responsibility directly.

But papal power was not to continue to triumph over the central state. Popes became increasingly concerned with their temporal authority—their courts, the amount of taxes they received, and so on; the spiritual force behind the successful papacy of Gregory VII was lacking. And the kings were gaining more power. Early in the fourteenth century, just three and a half centuries after Canossa, the French king imprisoned a pope with whom he was in dispute and set up an appointee of his own—and not even in Rome, but in Avignon where the French could keep a closer eye on him. This situation did not last, however, and after almost a century of confusion the papacy returned to Rome. But the balance of power had definitely shifted.

If the institutional control of pope over king was of brief duration, the church nevertheless retained great organizational cohesion. It wielded international influence in contrast to the limited territorial sway of individual monarchs. Above all, it retained loyalties that kings could not readily tamper with, a factor which has remained an enduring ambiguity in the western political heritage: church and religion in competition with the state and secular government for the loyalty of the people. Certainly this quality existed in the Middle Ages and is still with us in a more secular age.

Secondly, the medieval kings were restrained by the traditions of vassalage. The example of Henry IV shows how easy it was for vassals who were resentful of claims of power by a king to rise in rebellion. After all, a landlord of any substance had vassals of his own who were a potential military force; sometimes he was stronger than the king, at least in alliance with some of his fellows. But vassalage meant mutuality, however imperfect an arrangement, and the king as feudal lord owed his vassals protection, justice, and the right to serve as his advisers in important matters.

Like the church, however, vassals gradually lost part of their power to the king, as the latter assumed some of the administration of justice and began to obtain military recruits from the general populace. The reaction of the vassals to a loss of power gave rise to a new institution—parliament. Here, the aristocracy might at times join forces with such other powerful groups as churchmen and merchants, for once a king launched direct taxation or engaged in wars that disrupted trade, these diverse groups could through parliament mount a powerful opposition. This occurred in 1215 in England. King John was unpopular; he quarreled not only with nobles but with the church. He inherited from his popular brother, Richard the Lion-Hearted, a bankrupt treasury, which meant that he had to raise taxes. Moreover, he lost an important battle against the king of France. Nobles and clergy easily forced him to accept a list of proposals known as the Magna Carta. This has been considered a statement of great modern significance, England's equivalent of the Declaration of Independence. Such was not the case: It was a very feudal document in which John promised not to encroach on the rights of the feudal aristocracy. A few concessions were made to the rights of the city of London and of the Church, but the ordinary Englishman was not mentioned. Yet it did state that the king was not above the law, which was essentially a restatement of the feudal principle that no king could act in an unrestrained fashion; and it did serve as a basis for modern constitutionalism in England in the seventeenth century.

After John's death, royal power increased again in England. The kings developed more and more comprehensive legal systems, working to assure fair, even justice, partly in a competitive effort to win cases away from the courts of the nobles and the church. If the king admittedly was under the law, he could also claim he could most effectively administer it. Local appointees and the traveling circuit judges were multiplied, and by the mid-thirteenth century the royal state controlled all major courts. But with this came the formalization of a checking institution, the parliament. It had always been customary for English kings to convene a council of major vassals whenever extra taxes were needed or other major problems arose. In the thirteenth century the great barons were more regularly called to national assemblies, and the word *parliament* began to be used. Here was the origin of the House of Lords (a real political force in England into the twentieth century), in which great nobles inherited the right to sit in a separate body to advise the king. At the same time the growing need to tax rich merchants and lesser nobles made it desirable to create another body, the House of Commons, where consultations on various measures took place between the kings' representatives and the representatives of the merchants and smaller landlords. The first such full parliament was convened in 1295 (the lower clergy met separately) and the principle was gradually established that representatives to this body could be elected by a propertied element of each district. English kings sometimes passed laws without consulting parliament, merely getting the advice of the House of Lords, but generally they made laws and levied taxes only with parliamentary consent. Quite soon the idea that taxes could not be levied without this consent was widely accepted, and because it had this basic power, parliament could often force kings to rescind unpopular measures or, more rarely, undertake new functions to aid the kingdom. In other words, parliament transformed the feudal tradition into an institutional check on the central government.

The English parliamentary tradition proved to be particularly strong, but the institution was a natural medieval creation. Parliaments were called in France by the early fourteenth century, again with a major voice in matters of taxation. The French parliament, however, and most of those that developed on the continent, more fully expressed the variety of medieval checks on feudal monarchy. They met as estates: the first estate was composed of church representatives, the second of aristocratic representatives. Here were embodied the religious and the feudal traditions. The third estate represented the "common people," primarily the merchants. In addition to periodic national parliaments, called Estates-General in France, various regions such as Normandy, had Estates, for France was not so united as England and regional interests ran strong.

As the Spanish monarchy developed with the conquest of the Moors, it reproduced the creation of a parliament. The regional states of Germany and Austria established parliaments, called Diets, also based on representation of social orders (clergy, nobles, commoners), each body with one vote. Much later, the reestablishment of a Polish state (that for a time, during the Middle Ages, virtually dissolved into fiefdoms of individual local princes) and the creation of effective Scandinavian governments also saw the creation of parliaments as checks on monarchical power.

Thus, by the end of the Middle Ages we can see many of the elements of the modern state, although in embryo form. Feudal monarchy was an evolving but distinctive kind of government, but in no sense modern because of its lack of any notion of democratic participation. People were *subjects,* not *citizens,* and their rights depended on the class to which they belonged. However, unique to the western political heritage established essentially in the Middle Ages was a duality, a recognition of the rights and possible usefulness of centralization of power but with a belief that the state should be controlled, that it was subject to higher principles and laws. Various countries had different combinations of these dual forces even in the Middle Ages, and their political histories would diverge even more as the Middle Ages ended, but the dual tradition was everywhere present: centralizing tendencies vs. efforts at control of the central power. No other major civilization produced this type of political tradition; most of them had tended more toward unqualified central rule, whether by a priestly caste or secular rulers. Because of the unique juxtaposition of political forces in the West, European political history from the late Middle Ages onward has been dotted with rebellions and resistance, at first mainly by nobles but then increasingly by common people against the central government.

Europe and Unity

Europe's pattern of political development created one definite problem: from the Middle Ages onward the continent had a common civilization but no political unity. Although this situation was not unique in world history (for example, India was often divided while maintaining common cultural values), most civilizations have had a central political base. But Europe's method of political development guaranteed disunity, indeed endemic internal conflict, despite shared religious and political principles and a considerable economic interchange. The new kingdoms had expanded like grandiose feudal units, with no single secular overlord. Hence territorial units came to exist without any institutional links to one another and, indeed, they had every reason to oppose one another. The classic example involved England and France. The English kings by 1200 possessed Normandy and large portions of southern France around Bordeaux. The French kings, in expanding outward from Paris, could not help but collide with the English. So there was a steady series of wars, with the French nibbling away at Normandy. Both England and France had sufficiently centralized governments to risk fighting. And fight they did, off and on for over two hundred years. The long-term result was an abiding enmity between France and England that played a vital role in European diplomacy through the nineteenth century and retains in our own time an influence even after seventy years of putative alliance.

Wars were not only an expression of royal ambition, but also helped to keep a rein on the nobles by giving them an external outlet for their combative tendencies, and provided an excuse for strengthening the royal powers of taxation and military recruitment. But by and large, standard feudal bellicosity was now transformed into international conflict. Part of the European heritage has included belligerency and expansionism.

Spain, the other principal medieval monarchy, did not play a direct role in European diplomacy until the end of the Middle Ages. It developed as a series of feudal regions, most notably in the Castilian region which earlier had thrown off Moslem domination, and Aragon which extended over the central part of Spain. These regions not only had local lords but their own separate kings, and in typical feudal fashion they proved as willing to fight each other as to drive the Moslems from southern Spain. Gradually, however, greater cooperation was achieved, along with the typical creation of parliaments, the *cortes,* to provide representation that would approve higher taxes. In the fifteenth century the two main kingdoms, Castile and Aragon, were united, and the few remaining pockets of Moslem territory were eliminated, with the Moslems being required to either convert or leave the country, the same option given the Jews. Once Spain was united under the kings of Aragon, it was fully prepared to enter the European diplomatic scene, adding further to nation-state belligerency. Spain had a tradition of militarism (Spanish Christians had fought Moslems for centuries.), and in the sixteenth century it had the largest, best-disciplined land army in Europe. Religious fervor was added to the Spanish militaristic bent, and whether fighting heathen Indians in Latin America or Protestants in Germany or brother Catholics in neighboring France, the Spaniards brought a special, traditional zeal to their work. In summary, at the end of the medieval period Spain was ready to assume a European role, having fought the French and German dukes, and having directly conquered the Low Countries.

Thus, England, France, and Spain all had the outlines of the nation-state structure by the end of the Middle Ages, and all were prepared, because of the values that were transferred to the nation-state, to do battle with each other. Spain briefly had exceptional military power, reinforced by religious zeal and gold from the colonies of the New World, but by the end of the sixteenth century her power had waned. Unable to convert her New World holdings into a viable economy, Spain lost her influence in Northern Europe because of this and through the combined factors of vigorous Protestant Dutch armies and the English fleet, which sank Spain's

great armada in 1588. France, with a larger population, was militarily more durable. But our main point is not to stress what particular nation was supreme at any given moment, for this would fluctuate, but to emphasize that the nation-state system was imbued with a desire to fight. Feudal monarchy had essentially three purposes: to preserve internal order, to administer justice, and to make war. Wars usually were assigned some plausible excuse: a defense against foreign attack; the legitimate exercise of a king's right against his vassals; a means of defending true religion against heretics (the justification for undertaking the Crusades and, later, fighting the Protestant Reformation). Although these justifications were often tenuous, expansion through the conduct of war was one of the purposes of the nation-state under the feudal monarch and continued long after the specific forms of feudal monarchy were gone.

The Alternatives to Feudal Monarchy

France, England, and Spain were clearly powerful feudal monarchies, but the rest of western Europe, as geographically and culturally defined, presented a picture of chaos. In Scandinavia, stable kingdoms were just being formed, and western values were just beginning to be assimilated; actually the whole region was too distant for the concern of any potential conqueror. But the Low Countries—part of that stretch of territory which the heirs of Charlemagne had failed to organize on a strong basis—were open to the interest of well-organized powers to the south and east. The Low Countries were prosperous; no centralized kingdom had arisen, so that the area was divided and politically weak, an open invitation to attack.

Italy was another anomaly, with the basic political unit being the city-state. As in ancient Greece, these small units were intensely productive culturally and economically, but continued to fight among themselves rather than unite so as to present a common front to foreign foes. Hence, Italy constituted what modern diplomats would call a vacuum of power, which, given the aggressive bent of the western states, encourged better organized political entities to move in. During most of the Middle Ages the invaders were Germans whose emperors, in the tradition of Charlemagne, believed that they had a mandate to rule Italy as part of the heritage of the Roman Empire. But by the late fifteenth century, at the height of the Italian Renaissance, both the French and the Spaniards overran the peninsula and all but destroyed the city-state tradition. Italy became a political backwater, a prey to the larger, better-organized powers which had copied some of the methods of rule initially applied in the small Italian city-state. Most Italian city-states had been ruled by individuals or oligarchies of the wealthy who had employed such modern measures as census-taking; exchange of formal ambassadors with foreign powers (to prevent needless antagonisms and facilitate trade); provision of grain to the urban population in times of famine; and various means of economic encouragement. But these measures could all be applied equally well in the centralized monarchies, which had a far larger economic and military base, so that Italy's inability to create large political units doomed the peninsula to political chaos and vulnerability to outside control. Ironically, even in the nineteenth century, only outside intervention permitted the establishment of a united Italy.

Germany provides the oddest case of medieval political failure. Despite the fact that in the division of the Carolingian Empire the German kings had inherited the mantle of Holy Roman Emperor, this proved to be a misfortune for two reasons: no national parliament emerged in the feudal monarchical system of Germany, and the German tradition of politics prevented the establishment of a clearly national kingdom such as already existed in England and was under development in France and Spain at the end of the Middle Ages. Not until the nineteenth century was a central government established in Germany.

We must conclude that medieval Europe, by organizing on regional or national rather than cultural lines, was politically creative but also in an ultimate sense a tragic failure. Every century from the beginning of the Hundred Years War (in 1338), onward was to experience major national battles, some of them, such as the Thirty Years War in Germany early in the seventeenth century, devastating even before the invention of modern weapons. At least until the second half of the twentieth century, no area as small as the European continent was so constantly wracked by major conflict.

Perhaps this particular aptitude for belligerence may explain Europe's vitality in other areas of endeavor. Technology, for example, owes something to the desire to make war more brutally and effectively. In no sense are we claiming that frequent war is unique to western civilization, but few cultures were so permanently aggressive, few so unsuccessful in organizing large political units as Europe, while attaining in other fields comparable levels of civilized achievement. Reluctantly, one must conclude that a medieval political legacy was an unusual propensity to go to war. Indeed, the calmer, more familiar medieval political achievements partly related to this: central bureaucracies grew so that the state might make war better, and parliaments were called, usually to approve taxes that would also facilitate preparation for battle.

A final point: the relatively small but coherent political unit—England, say, as a national monarchy—was a European invention. As we have seen in classical civilization and in reference to kingdoms from Africa to Latin America, the typical civilized political unit was larger. But as Europe spread out it carried along the nation-state idea. China, of course, did not ever use such a political division, but in Africa, Latin America, and to an extent the Near East, European rivalries and the basic nation-state concept created almost an entire world of nation-states, some of them brand new, the result of arbitrary boundary-making by European powers abetted by new native elites. For medieval Europe had created a distinctive political form, very promising in terms of internal checks and balances, less impressive in its self-control.

Economic Development

Medieval economic development, while just as vital as political development, is harder to capture than politics, although it did produce a few key institutions. This was an economically active period that produced entrepreneurs who would not be totally uncomfortable in contemporary corporations, because they loved to make money and had a sense of organization beyond sheer individual enterprise that facilitated this goal. The Middle Ages saw the western birth of capitalism, a money economy, the profit motive, and the corporation.

The Middle Ages was obviously more than a poorer version of our own consumer society. There were many critics of the new economy. Aristocrats were nervous, for money power was different from land power, and successful merchants might rival their style of life and political influence without sharing their values. Thus, aristocrats did two things, particularly along the Atlantic coast and in Italy where the merchant spirit was strongest. First, they tried making money themselves. This was most easily done by modifying manorialism and converting traditional obligations to money rents. Such a procedure made sense in the short run by providing cash. However, in giving serfs greater latitude—paying money was a more flexible obligation than working two days a week on the lord's estate—the aristocrats undermined part of their basic social power. Second, aristocrats tried scorning the new merchants, and in this they had support. Peasants could easily resent strange peddlers who tried to convince them to buy a city-made hoe instead of one that was locally forged. Money was still associated with filth and corruption, and medieval peasants never made a full conversion to a money economy. And certainly the church agreed. According to Thomas Aquinas, the profession of merchant was economically necessary but exceedingly dangerous to the salvation of the soul, for it easily encouraged greed. Prices should be set at the true value of the good—the labor put into its production and sale—not what the market would bear. In other words it was wrong to jack up prices in periods of shortage. If someone needed a loan the lender could legitimately charge what he lost by not having the money at his disposal; but he could not charge interest beyond this. Yet the capitalist ethic made progress. By the fifteenth century theologians admitted that it was all right to take interest on loans—they had to, since the papacy was a major borrower and lender of money in what was now a complex economy. But we should remember that there was resistance to the new economic system both from the church and from important social groups.

This leads to our main point. There *were* outright capitalists in the Middle Ages turning over huge fortunes through trade, money-lending and the like, but capitalism of the modern sort—striving for maximum profit through openness to technological development—was not characteristic. More typical were new organizations designed to serve a market or money economy but to preserve older economic values, including setting limits to economic inequality, preserving standards of the quality of the product, and in general, avoiding disorderly competition from which a few might benefit but many would suffer. Merchant and artisan guilds in the cities most clearly expressed these values, indeed institutionalized them, but the village economy of the peasants, drawn slightly into the market orbit, preserved them as well. It was peasant values, in fact, that probably served as the basis for the typical medieval economic institutions; for as we have seen, peasants wanted self-protection, an element of equality, and, above all, stability. Village agriculture preserved these values on the whole.

This gives us a mixed, ambiguous heritage when we assess the Middle Ages as an economic period. Wealth and population increased, as we have noted. The ordinary peasant or artisan in 1300 was desperately poor by our standards, but he or she often had a slight margin above subsistence, to buy slightly nicer clothes, furnishings, or periodically to enjoy village festivals. Europe thus reached above the poverty line as defined by the ability to produce more than enough to survive on. It was on this base that kings, churchmen, scholars, warriors, and merchants survived in some genuine luxury.

Signs and Sources of Capitalism

Many individual examples of the modern capitalist in medieval Europe must be stressed, because of their wealth, against the common notion that the Middle Ages was locked in poverty, and because they launched motives and business forms that have long survived the period. Religion might make capitalists feel a bit guilty, but on they went, amassing huge fortunes. We have seen that this was one of the bases by which central monarchs could build up independent strength. Trade ranging from the grain, fish, and timber of the Baltic regions to the cloth of Flanders to the eastern spices and jewels imported by the Italians showed the venturesomeness of leading merchants. Bankers sent representatives to trade fairs in northern France, and could discount notes from an English merchant so that he could buy Italian goods without exchanging cash. This was capitalism. It antedated the Renaissance or the Protestant ethic. It surpassed the trading interests of the Romans or even the Greeks. *Why* it thus developed is not clear, particularly given the widespread opposition to merchant and banking activities. But the best guess is as follows: Italian seafarers, not controlled by a strong central government, early discovered that there was a richer civilization to the east. Scandinavian seafarers-turned-merchants made similar discoveries in the markets of western Russia. Byzantine goods and especially those from Asia, did more than revive a Mediterranean trading spirit; they created a new sense of profit making in areas remote from this new tradition.

This in turn had immense social impact, for medieval society had an ambiguous structure. It was not as rigidly hierarchical as Greece, Rome, or even the Germanic tribes. Slavery, common to all three previous cultures, was virtually unknown. The serf, as we have seen, had some rights, although he was clearly lowest on the medieval totem pole and definitely not free in the modern sense. But the serf was equal in God's eyes; the church told him this. If bright, he might escape his condition by becoming a priest or monk. This was not, then, a totally static social hierarchy. With growing economic opportunities the rare serf might strike out for the cities, especially since medieval law provided that a serf living in a town for a year and a day was no longer the property of his lord. Some of these venturesome escapees might in turn become merchants or instill merchant values in their sons. Thus we can cite trading contact with more advanced civilizations, particularly via Italy, and the ambiguities of the medieval social hierarchy as possible explanations for the development of capitalistic economic forms.

But as we have noted, capitalism was not the typical medieval economic expression. Capitalists, in the sense of profit-hungry innovators, were a rarity. International trade was vital for bringing luxuries to the rich nobles and essential raw materials to the more urbanized areas such as Flanders and Italy, but none of this was characteristic. As urban economy developed, institutions arose which were meant to avoid innovation, avoid undue wealth, and protect both consumer and producer within an economy that was assumed to be relatively inflexible. Long after the Middle Ages were over, people bred in the tradition of merchant or artisan guilds, the genuinely characteristic products of the medieval economy, attempted to preserve their values and indeed, well into the twentieth century, attacked the capitalistic innovators in the name of traditional values. In other words, the more characteristic medieval economy also had a fantastic survival rate. In a sense, though, both artisans and merchants were capitalists. The merchant needed capital to buy timber or food but had to wait until it was sold to realize his return, hopefully with a profit. The artisan master owned his shop, tools, raw materials, and so on. But neither of these groups had the modern capitalist ethic. We can best approach their distinctive and attractive set of values by describing two related institutions, the merchant guild and the craft guild.

With economic and population growth, new people poured into the cities to flee manorialism, escape a harsh parent, or to take advantage of new opportunities. Most cities were not ready to receive these newcomers, and sanitary conditions and other urban facilities remained poor. Running sewers, carrying effluent along the edges of walkways and streets, were only the more dramatic signs of the unpreparedness for urbanization. Houses were typically built with each floor jutting out slightly more than the one below, which let a housewife throw out the slops without hitting her downstairs neighbor. But woe to the passerby on the street below! Here was the origin of the custom that a man escorting a woman walked on the outside, so that if slops were to be received, he would get them.

With the economic functions of cities proving increasingly vital, a political role soon followed. Some cities were directly run by feudal lords or bishops; most, however, were able to persuade kings or dukes to give them independent government, and of course in Italy the city-state became an entity controlling even surrounding rural territory. Generally, the key to position in the city was being *bourgeois*. This is a word we still use, often derisively, but originally it simply designated a recognized citizen of the city. Like other medieval social positions it was inheritable. To this extent the town function, primarily the merchant function, was integrated into medieval social structure. This did not mean that every town resident could become a bourgeois, for because this was a medieval right, that is a right belonging to a society in which you were born to your position or, rarely, advanced by merit and judicious expenditure of money, becoming a bourgeois was no easy matter. Yet the fact that the status existed and never entirely disappeared was crucial. First, it provided some social and political mobility. Dukes and kings found it profitable to grant cities a large degree of self-government, because they realized that these same towns generated money and taxes. So more often than not towns received charters allowing them to govern themselves. The leading citizens, usually merchants, set up commercial laws, assessed taxes, ran judicial courts, and so on. They served as sort of a collective vassal with special privileges in law just as vassals had.

Leaving the Italian city-states aside, note how unusual this development was in the pattern of agricultural society. Merchants were free to run their own internal affairs, and they were given a recognized place in society. Western society proved unusually tolerant of commercial activity, even giving it political recognition. Again the reason seems to be the felt need for money and goods that only merchants could provide, plus the competition among nobles and kings that could make either group decide to "sponsor" a town's freedom as an extra source of support outside the normal feudal monarchy relationships. Towns increasingly meant economic activity, and economic activity meant merchants and artisans who would ultimately gain powers foreign to their counterparts in the cities of eastern civilizations.

The Mainstream Economic Mentality

And so we return to the guild. Merchant guilds ran great cities like London as well as the more typical medieval town of 5,000 to 10,000 people. They provided their own law as well, particularly in commercial matters, since no clear precedent for this existed. This facilitated international trade by establishing standards to inform foreign traders how they would be treated in a distant port or commercial fair. But the typical merchant guild served to develop an urban upper class, which was not necessarily venturesome in commerce although certainly willing to engage in trade. A merchant guild, particularly when it participated in the running of a city, might simply exclude new entrants from citizenship, and if one were not a citizen, one could not legally trade. London merchant guilds gave their members first pick on the produce from any ship that came into the harbor; nonmembers might trade but only if times were so prosperous that a surplus could be sold. Social events, political events, and trading activities were dominated by these groups.

This was hardly stereotypic capitalism, with every man fighting for his own interest at the expense of others. This was corporate protection. And while it did not prevent some men from becoming rich, it did discourage innovation; with sources of supply protected, why worry about doing something new, particularly on the technological or production side? Medieval merchants in the richest regions, such as Flanders and Northern Italy, spread production into the countryside, but the peasants used traditional, manually-operated textile machines to produce common goods that the merchants could direct to the appropriate market.

Urban artisans were even further from capitalism, although some, such as fine weavers, produced for an international market. Their guilds were less likely to serve political roles in urban government, although these in some cases were represented. The social and ritualistic emphasis was extremely strong, for dances, festivals, and processions, in which guild members displayed their distinctive uniforms and symbols, constituted a vital part of medieval urban life. However, the guild was first and foremost an economic institution. It carefully limited the number of entrants to each occupation by stipulating that a master craftsman could maintain no more than a certain number of apprentices at any given time. Since one had to be properly apprenticed and graduated to enter a given occupation—and these rules were enforced not just by guilds but by city governments—this was a fairly effective control over the labor supply. Assuming proper calculations, this meant that there were no more artisans than the city's economy needed, which meant in turn that wages and profits would be predictable and stable. Guilds attempted to regulate not only the number of apprentices taken but also the conditions of their training—usually a teenager was signed up after a fee was paid by his family for a five- to seven-year live-in period. Guild officials tried to make sure that apprentices were treated properly and received the guidance they needed, although there is no doubt that much of their work consisted of servant labor, cleaning the shop, even helping in the kitchen. But ideally the artisan system worked to protect all its elements, and even when the ideal was not fully realized artisans retained it as a goal: first, a period of training, which separated you from the urban unskilled masses. One emerged from apprenticeship with a definite skill, proved by a master creation, whether in butchery or jewelry, that showed you were a real artisan. Then came a second stage of the career, in which one was a journeyman. Journeymen had skills, often owned tools, but they fit no neat definition of worker or employer in modern terms. No master was allowed too many journeymen, lest he advance his wealth to the detriment of other guild members. Masters were employers, but not in the modern sense. They worked alongside their journeymen, guiding but not superior except in their greater experience and their ownership of the shop. They housed and fed the journeymen. And, according to artisan tradition, the journeyman would become a master in his turn. By saving money from his wages he could buy a shop. By careful courting he could marry the master's daughter and be given the shop. Or, perhaps most commonly, he was the master's son in the first place, and had only to wait for papa to die or retire to take over.

Finally, guilds imposed strict standards of quality on their members; they were not just producer/seller organizations, but held to charging a fair price and delivering a high quality good. This was not, we repeat, a modern economy, though we continue to recall these older economic principles in asking for fair prices—not what the market will bear but what the worker needs to recompense his labor, or the merchant his enterprise. The guild system embodied a public spiritedness that now is more rarely achieved.

Yet the guild system was weakening as early as the end of the thirteenth century. Apart from Italy, where the merchant spirit already was keenly developed, more and more traders operated as individuals. Some set up their own manufacturing systems, as in Flanders, where merchants bought raw materials, particularly textiles sent them via foremen to rural producers, then had the finished cloth picked up to be sold on a massive market. The workers in this system had modest skills, but they were workers, dependent on capitalist controls. Even urban artisans saw a partial breakdown of their carefully contructed system as some masters took over the guilds and began treating journeymen as mere employes, never as equals.

Thus we can identify more and more modern business methods arising by the end of the Middle Ages. In the great merchant establishments accounting procedures developed; partnerships and even groupings of dozens of capitalists investing money according to strict legal regulations—the forerunner of the big business combine—developed. Commercial law, created by businessmen themselves, and common units of coinage exchange were vital for international commerce.

For the artisans it was always tempting to defy guild restrictions and build a larger manufacturing empire. But most medieval merchants and certainly most artisans lived within a recognizable and distinctive economic framework. They did not seek to build vast economic empires. The basic medieval economic ethic, even in the urban economy, was stability.

Thus medieval civilization was vastly richer in 1350 than it had been in 1000. The wealth was unevenly distributed, shared by new merchants and to a lesser extent by new artisans, along with the traditional classes. But despite innovation and relative wealth, basic medieval values, embodied in institutions such as guilds, held to the ideal of stable economics, a fair price for a high quality good. We can see the origins of further change in this new urban, economic thrust. We also can recognize that the economic goals preached and to some extent realized were attractive and possibly superior to what richer western civilization would later produce.

Popular Culture

Most people during this period of western civilization were rural; most were illiterate; most therefore leave us no direct records of their thoughts. What we do know suggests that the culture that developed in the merging of Germanic and Christian strains continued. Peasants remained fatalistic but were amazingly calm, in contrast to the periodic rebellions of the classical age and the new current of rebellion that began in the last phase of Middle Ages. It is probable that more stable political structures and an advancing agricultural economy kept protest down. A better judicial system, a sense that God ordained the existing order, a belief in just kings—all could account for a relatively calm popular mood.

The peasant had no cause to feel concerned about the economic system. Although "international capitalism" had emerged, its impact on the ordinary person was slight. Few people were controlled by capitalists. Most worked for themselves and their lord, producing almost everything they needed in the traditional manner. The tightness of the manorial system loosened.

New goods and a decline in local wars softened the manorial landlords and made them eager for a more civilized life. Moreover, the population was growing, which meant that the peasant family could not assure land to all its members and the landlord risked losing serfs who were landless. Some indeed were lost and poured into the cities. But landlords and peasants alike took an interest in founding new villages—*villeneuves,* or new towns, in France.

From all this came an easing of burdens on the peasant himself in western Europe. Landlords increasingly converted crop payments and labor services to cash dues, so they might have ready money to keep up with the style. In the new settlements money rents were even more common. This presented a problem in that the peasant now had to consider marketing some of his crop for funds. But the transfer freed the peasant from some of the most direct servility to the landlord. When prices rose in the late Middle Ages, making money less valuable, it meant that the landlords were the losers, as peasants could devote less of their produce to paying off their obligations. The manorial system was not dead, but particularly in England, and to a lesser extent in the western part of the continent, cash relationships made considerable inroads.

All of this gave freer play to the village economy. Peasants did not introduce new agricultural techniques for there was no need. They might develop a new awareness of the king and a loyalty to the office, but national politics did not preoccupy them. Religious changes were important but not the great scholastic products of the scholars. Rather, in the later Middle Ages peasant Christianity seemed to become more emotional. The clearest sign of this was the new interest in worshipping the Virgin Mary. Formal theologians had long debated Mary's position as Christ's mother. For Christ to be born without original sin, she had to be a virgin, but once this was said the theologians played down the personal factor. Not so the common people. Mariology, as encouraged by the papacy, gained increasing favor, and Mary was seen as a spirit who could intercede with a remote God and grant special favors. Statues of the Virgin appeared in almost every church. Religious symbolism extended to saints. Holy places where they were buried, bones and drops of blood that could be enshrined in the local church—all gained increasing favor and formed a bond between the common people and the devout upper classes, who were eager to acquire such holy relics on their own. Credulity was strained as the Church, while seeking piety, often made money from the sale of relics (some popular saints had enough bones attributed to them to form over a hundred complete skeletons). Here was a rich support for the church but also a double danger. First, the scholars of the church were moving away from this kind of simple faith to elaborately rational constructs. This did not bother the common people who did not know what, say, Aquinas was all about, but neither did it support popular religion, and a gap between popular practices and intellectual activity led some thinkers to question where the church was going. Still more significant, the elaborate institutional structure of the church, the political concerns of the popes and bishops, removed the leaders of religion increasingly from the devotions of ordinary folk.

But popular culture was by no means purely religious. An increasing secular pattern of festivity developed, particularly among the merchants and common people in the cities. Jugglers, circus acts, and plays that could be downright vulgar completed medieval culture and set the stage for further developments.

The Later Middle Ages: Change or Decline?

By the fourteenth century, we begin to note a decline in medieval civilization, not because key political units were destroyed, not because of new barbarian invasions, but because people began to modify or to corrupt typical medieval forms of thought and behavior.

By the latter Middle Ages the aristocracy was in trouble. The decline in the importance of cavalry was a problem, for aristocrats had depended on their monopoly of the principal medieval military tool. The growing importance of monarchy also hurt the aristocrats—such as in the administration of justice. Aristocrats had derived not only power but fees from this service, and now monarchs were doing more and more of the work. Some nobles, pinched for funds, turned to crime in a mild revival of the early medieval pattern. Others pressed weak vassals or ordinary peasants with brute force. But generally the central monarchs were powerful enough to prevent any large-scale violence or extortion.

By the fourteenth and fifteenth centuries, two other ominous developments occurred. First was inflation. Manorial lords in France or England, who had converted manorial obligations to money rents in order to buy the new goods the merchants were bringing in, were hard hit, as their rents were not worth as much as before. Second, the introduction of cannons with gunpowder weakened another military bastion of the class—a literal one this time—for even with primitive cannons huge holes could be shot in castle walls, and a monarch would have little trouble disciplining a rebellious lord.

Thus, a lot was happening to the ruling class. Although they still had parliaments and normally provided the chief advisers to the kings, they now had to share some of these functions with clever merchants. Here was just a hint of class rivalry that would become a dominant theme in later European society. Above all there was a crisis of function. Aristocrats still ran most of the armies; vassalage was not entirely meaningless. But their role as local protectors of the populace and indispensable servants to the king was greatly reduced.

Nevertheless the class survived in three basic ways. First, it managed to keep most outsiders out of the top military slots. This sometimes meant bad generals, for being aristocratic was no assurance of military skill; but there were also leaders of real quality. More generally the class developed administrative functions, with members serving as major bureaucrats in the central state and retaining important local political powers. They could use the new parliaments; they still had manorial courts, even if the range of crimes tried was less than before. The administrative function, with its base in the landed wealth that the class still possessed, became the real sustainer of the aristocracy. Finally, the class was open to new blood, particularly that of successful administrators of merchant origin. The average aristocrat of 1800 was not descended from a feudal warrior but from a sixteenth or seventeenth century bureaucrat. He might have traditional class values, including the desire to pretend that his family went back to William the Conqueror, but his origins were recent, and this strengthened the class.

All this occurred most clearly after the Middle Ages, even if maintenance of new military roles and expansion of administrative functions reflected a tradition aristocrats had developed in feudal society. During the last two centuries of the Middle Ages, because of the problems of defining new roles and because they retained great resources, the aristocracy went through a foolish period. Rituals became idle gestures. Tournaments, for example, originally training operations for war, now were carefully arranged so no one would get hurt. The clash of armor was replaced by prancing charges in which no one was touched with sword or lance. Increasing attention was given to decorating the castle, to polite entertainment, and to courting the ladies. Minstrels wandered about singing ballads about the nobleman's duty to his love. There was a good side to this development, for this was the final age of noble chivalry. Men became more polite. Real romance blossomed. Many fine poems and ballads were written by both men and women. But this was not the stuff of the medieval warrior and it often could become a travesty. By mocking its former functions, the aristocratic class was in danger of becoming effete, more concerned with the latest style of hose or costume than with anything useful.

Long-standing medieval traditions thus were changing. The state continued to function, for a frivolous aristocracy made it easier for monarchs to increase their powers while continuing to use individual aristocrats as generals and advisers. We cannot speak of a general political decline in this "waning" of the Middle Ages, but when part of the ruling class became effete this was a clear sign that something basic was changing.

Cultural Evolution: A Case of Decline?

The second area of change, being to some extent subjective, is harder to define than the aristocratic lapse. Medieval artistic styles became cluttered, losing their original freshness and purity. Late medieval painters such as Jan Van Eyck filled their work with every imaginable detail. No space could be left empty, and art historians often regard this as a sign of decadence. But even if they filled their canvasses unduly, painters were becoming more naturalistic in their ability to portray people and things realistically; this portrayal of real people in contemporary settings was a technical gain of significance, indicating that the medieval fear of nature as innately evil had waned.

In religion, decline seems obvious if one judges by the institutional church. There is no question that the papacy was in serious trouble. The successful defiance by French king Philip the Fair in the early fourteenth century had led to a period in which various rulers attempted to control papal elections. There were rival popes—one in France under control of the French king, another in Rome influenced by the German emperor; and briefly, even a third. Clearly, the institution had lost not only power but respect. There was a brief effort to revive it by means of councils of bishops not unlike the parliaments of the secular monarchies, and a council did manage, early in the fifteenth century, to reestablish a single papacy in Rome. But conciliar rule was too difficult over such a vast territory of western Christendom. In Rome, the popes became mired in the politics of the Italian Renaissance and even in Italian secular culture, defending their territories like any secular prince, and, in general, giving neither leadership to the international church nor religious inspiration to ordinary Christians. The papacy recovered great international power only after it was directly attacked during the Reformation. But as the papacy faltered, popular religious belief increased, as for example in the Low Countries, where laymen began to form a new monastic movement, the Bretheran of the Common Life, based on pious devotion to God. This popular piety became one of the bases for the Reformation, although it proved capable of being channeled back into a revivified Catholic Church.

Demographic and Economic Crisis

In the fourteenth century Europe was devastated by plagues, particularly bubonic plague—the Black Death—that swept through Europe to England in the middle of the century. This catastrophe was almost unprecedented, killing nearly a fourth of the population. The personal horrors were monstrous (bodies dragged through the night to be burned in a futile effort to avoid contamination), and the social effects proved disastrous to the established order. Temporary economic decline was inevitable as production fell and prices rose. The effects of plague were heightened by a series of poor harvests, beginning before the great plague around 1313. Consequently, for almost a century and a half, until roughly 1500, Europe's population growth remained stationary. This was the real medieval decline, the one that affected the majority of the people. Some have claimed that Europe had overexpanded in relation to agricultural resources and was doomed to this demographic recession. In any case, just as an increase in population tended to engender creativity and an air of expansionism, so a decline may be seen as a reason for uncertainty and retrogression in other institutions and values.

But even though a decline in the population reduced economic activity, it did not alter basic economic forms. This was the age of the great Renaissance banks in Italy, and international trade continued, as did other capitalistic practices.

A New Current of Revolt

The fourteenth century was the great century of popular uprisings, the first since Roman times. The obvious impetus to uprisings was the economic hardship that followed the plagues and bad harvests; a companion factor was a desire to continue the trend toward urban freedoms, particularly reduction or elimination of manorial controls. Also contributing was a religious impulse, for popular agitation long had had religious overtones. With the institutional church declining, popular heresies sprang up that promised a return to the true faith and a better life for the poor, in opposition to the overly-rich and overly-powerful pope and bishops.

In the cities, these impulses were translated into the temptation to attack rich merchants who typically also controlled the urban governments. The medieval city had bred two distinct economies based on different principles, and now that times were getting harder these came into conflict. First, there were the capitalists, symbolized by the great international traders. Although few in number, the capitalists dominated society as an economic-political upper class. Second, there were the craft guilds, superior numerically to the capitalists, and with goals that gave promise of individual skill being translated into ultimate ownership of a small shop. In the late thirteenth through the fourteenth centuries, urban craftsmen rebelled because of the gap between the wealth of the few and their own growing poverty, between power and powerlessness. Flemish artisans seldom had a clear program of reform, but they were able to annihilate some of their class enemies and loot their property. Disorder was even more common in nothern Italy. Urban unrest was usually put down, but in some cases it led to new rights under city governments run by middle-level merchants. The squalor of the working class was not quickly corrected, and by the early fourteenth century cities such as Florence and Bruges, with populations of 50,000 to 100,000, saw most of their inhabitants, some of them genuine craftsmen, living in abject misery. Add this, then, to the later plagues and the protracted European economy and one sees the formula for repeated revolt. Roman radicals kicked out the pope in the mid-fourteenth century. In Florence, in 1378, the great *Ciompi* revolt occurred, in which the common people tried to institute direct democracy and briefly took control of the town government. Nevertheless, revolts of this sort, however dramatic and vibrant, almost always failed, and a merchant group, even including capitalists, would regain control. Yet, in spite of this, the guild system was not destroyed but continued to function essentially along medieval lines.

Rural revolts had some impact, too: Peasants defended themselves against incursions from landlords who were hard-pressed for cash. Those who were still in the manorial system wanted out. Peasants who had suffered severely from the plagues saw an opportunity to sell their labor for wages. Major rural uprisings occurred in the Low Countries, France, and England. French peasants in 1358 banded together spontaneously in several areas to attack their landlords and destroy manorial records. One English observer wrote:

These myschevous people thus assembled without
capitayne or armoure, robbed, brent and slewe
all gentylmen that they coude lay handes one, and
forced and ravysshed ladyes and damosels and dyd such
shameful dedes that no hymayne creature ought to
think on any suche. . . .

The most famous uprising was in southern England in 1381, when manorial charters were burned and lords' manors were pillaged, but the rioters finally gave up without having gained many of their key demands. Yet here was the beginning of a recurring feeling that social inequality was unjust and unchristian, and many factions of the masses goaded by economic hardship or catastrophe, such as bubonic plague, would continue to act on this sentiment. In general, the situation in western Europe remained evolutionary; the peasants were no longer under full manorial controls but a powerful landed aristocracy remained, and in France, as well as elsewhere, annoying remnants of the manorial system persisted.

The socio-economic end of the Middle Ages was thus a compromise. There was deterioration from the standpoint of demographic growth, but the *forms* of social relationships continued the medieval evolution—more capitalism in the cities, and decidedly weakened manorialism in the countryside. The medieval spirit would flicker one last time before being snuffed out, and the Reformation of the sixteenth century initially would confirm or revive a host of medieval features, from the religious sentiments of the common people to political trends. The attitudes of the common people continued to change. Even the Renaissance was a medieval phenomenon, part of the cultural and political diversity that had always characterized the Middle Ages. Renaissance, Reformation, and changes in popular culture demonstrate the vitality, the continued evolution, of medieval norms.

Renaissance and Reformation: An Interlude

SOME ARGUE THAT THE RENAISSANCE was a new phenomenon as the name implies. We will contend that it modified yet basically followed medieval patterns. Complicating the debate is the fact that the Renaissance in Italy differed from the Renaissance elsewhere.

The Renaissance began in Italy about 1300. Dante Alighieri, the first major literary figure of the movement, was profoundly religious and wrote elaborate mystical allegories. He knew and used scholastic philosophy and was a devoted Catholic, if often hostile to the political machinations of the Italian church. It is no slur to his genius, best expressed in the *Divine Comedy,* to say that he was essentially a medieval figure except that, unlike most high intellectuals, he did much of his writing in Italian rather than Latin. Following him in the fourteenth century came Boccaccio, who wrote the *Decameron,* which was highly salacious in parts and, again, was written in Italian. Goeffrey Chaucer in England also wrote a bawdy tale, *The Canterbury Tales,* which quite probably, like the *Decameron,* was an accurate description of how many medieval people behaved. But the typical Renaissance successor of Dante was Francesco Petrarch. Petrarch wrote both in Italian and Latin. Petrarch, more than Dante, wrote about secular subjects, although he too was prfoundly religious and often worried that his secular writings were a distraction from man's only proper goal, salvation.

The fourteenth-century Renaissance thus involved new kinds

of writing, on more secular subjects and often in the native tongue. Some have claimed it involved new personal pride as well. Petrarch describes his ascent to one of the Alps as a great personal achievement. Only belatedly does he note that, after all, God created the whole thing and maybe he was guilty of pride. Had this tradition continued, the Renaissance might have been viewed as a real intellectual break in the western tradition. It was not, however, for after the hint of creativity the Italian Renaissance settled down in the fifteenth century to a diligent searching for new classics to copy—rather as medieval scholars had done before. This involved one new element: the search for largely secular authors and these in literature more than in science or philosophy. But this was not an intensely creative period, except in the arts, where classical styles were revived by Michelangelo and others. Writers even returned to Latin and prided themselves on mastering ancient styles.

The Reformation began in the early sixteenth century, its political and theological lines well drawn by 1600. The Reformation bore some relationship to the Renaissance in that persons during each period agreed that one should return to original sources. Luther reread the Letters of Paul in Greek and found signs pointing to a theology very different from that of Catholicism. However, Luther also went to Rome, before he abandoned his role as Catholic monk, and was appalled at the secularism of the Renaissance papacy. The Reformation was definitely a medieval phenomenon, playing on medieval piety, even medieval politics, and it was hostile to Renaissance secularism. The Middle Ages, which had given play to a constantly evolving set of political, economic, and cultural values, produced two final if diverse products in the Renaissance and Reformation.

This is not yet a fully accepted view, and readers should be aware of the debate. Medievalists have tried, correctly, to show that their period was formative, dynamic, and the source of both Renaissance and Reformation. Another group has hailed the Renaissance as the dawn of capitalism (we already know this particular point is not valid but let's play the game for a bit) and of individualism in general. Secular mentalities replace religious superstition. New political approaches follow: Italian city-state rulers, then northern kings, develop a new amoralism—anything goes, so long as one keeps power and wins out. Then comes the Reformation. It has some links to the Renaissance but its causes are not the same, and it largely affects different geographical areas and different kinds of people. The Reformation stresses the individual's relationship to God. It says that worldly success, such as making a lot of money, is a sign of God's blessing. It stresses obedience to the secular ruler (though Calvinists would disagree in part; this was more a Lutheran idea)—and hence furthers the trends of the Renaissance state. And so we have capitalism, modern individualism, the modern state—and a total divorce from the Middle Ages.

Our view is that hundreds of historians can't be wrong—there is some truth in the above argument. But we will argue that change was partly accidental. In the case of the Reformation, the result was growing secularism in the very long run, because religious division and religious wars tired people of the whole subject. But in the short run the Reformation remains a reaffirmation of medieval piety, just as most Renaissance learning follows medieval patterns of where to seek truth. The modern world was born after both Renaissance and Reformation were over, although partly because of their unintended effects.

Let us put our case bluntly, since we have mentioned some names that are familiar. Petrarch would have hated major elements of the culture of the seventeenth century. It would have seemed to him insufficiently classical, too secular, and non-Italian. Luther would have hated the culture of the seventeenth century. He would have seen it as a failure for religious truth—i.e., Lutheranism—to win out, too secular, too defiant of kings, and probably too commercial. Which is to say that the seventeenth century was beginning to be something that neither Renaissance nor Reformation people intended to create or would have liked, even if they unintentionally contributed to it. One other element: one of the reasons the seventeenth century was beginning to be different, although not yet modern, occurred as a result of developments among the common people that were not affected, at least not deeply affected, by either the Renaissance or Reformation.

As an example of the interpretive problem of the Renaissance, consider Leonardo de Vinci—painter, inventor (among other things, designer of prototypes of airplanes), sculptor—the classic Renaissance man of the later fifteenth century, who could do something of almost everything well. His airplanes were never attempted, because nobody cared about flying or believed in its possibility (and also admittedly because Leonardo's designs, while neat, did not include engines). His desire to excel, to be his own man is eminently impressive, but few people could imitate this; in fact most people never heard of Leonardo or were influenced by anything he did, until mass education spread his name and some of his inventions almost four centuries later. Leonardo was *not* a medieval man. He would have enjoyed many aspects of the modern world, though perhaps he would have felt cramped by our tendency to specialize, to build planes or paint but not both. But he was also not a typical Renaissance figure; most Renaissance people, even among the formal intellectuals, were vastly more prosaic and were in the medieval mold. We must distinguish between the famous, who are famous partly because they seem like modern supermen, and the movement, which is the Renaissance as a whole. We must remember how short a reach the Renaissance had in terms of trying to educate beneath the upper classes and in bearing any relevance to the average man who eked out a living on a village plot. The Reformation made more sense to the common people, as we will see, but because it appealed to old values, not new ones. We are then at the creative end of a civilization and only indirectly at the dawn of a new one.

Renaissance Italy

After the great literary trinity of Dante, Petrarch, and Boccaccio, one has to record a century of decline or of assimilation, as the copiers sought Roman and Greek models to imitate. The Italian Renaissance by the fifteenth century retained limited intellectual vitality; it had something of its own political style; and it depended, if not on economic innovation, at least on economic vitality.

In the intellectual sphere, secularism reigned supreme. Few Renaissance thinkers were anti-religious, but it now seemed appropriate to deal with secular wisdom, particularly if derived from the classics. Medieval learning, which was still actively pursued in the universities of northern Europe, was scorned as pedantic and irrelevant. The old faith-reason controversy, for example, died down in Italy. Petrarch had qualms about his secular writing, his love for poems for example, but his fifteenth-century successors, although they might discuss religion, were more concerned with resurrecting every possible aspect of classical learning. The Thomistic concern for reconciliation was gone. Classical writings were good in themselves, though again it was reemphasis, not irreligion, that made most intellectuals stop worrying whether the classics fit Christian truth or not. One could go to church on Sunday and spend the rest of the week in a dusty archive trying to find long-lost versions of Ovid's love poems and feel no conflict whatsoever.

But the result was not very creative, for if Renaissance thinkers avoided narrow scholasticism and implicitly heralded purely secular learning, they retained a key medieval trait, that of seeking learning from the past without thinking seriously of improving on it; this characteristic put them in the medieval cultural orbit. Far more were translators than second-rate philosophers. Even science suffered, although its tradition continued; insofar as Renaissance interest turned mainly to literature, scientific works were copied only because they, too, came from the revered Greeks.

The best term to apply to this approach is "humanistic." Renaissance humanism means roughly a concern for man as the center of intellectual endeavor; and therein the classical influence is genuinely apparent. Renaissance poetry dealt with romance, sorrow—human problems. Choral music treated bawdy themes, love, drink—again, things people did. Renaissance painting and sculpture focused on the human form, often using classical motifs but becoming increasingly realistic in the portrayal of how people actually looked. Michelangelo's mighty statues offered unprecedentedly graphic displays of man's musculature, and Botticelli's painting of a virtually nude Venus rising from the ocean was another departure from medieval prudery. Perhaps most typical, at the end of the Renaissance period, da Vinci actually went to medical classes and painted dissections of the human body with sometimes gruesome realism. What was human was central and should be sung about, analyzed, painted.

All of this obviously reflected and furthered the interest in the classics, but we must remember that the classics were Greek as well as Roman. Italians trading with the declining Byzantine Empire brought back not only Greek art but also literary works in the Greek language, so that, increasingly, intellectuals came to read Greek fluently. Platonic philosophy was revived, but had no enduring influence. Greek influence in art was greater, with sculptors as well as architects copying Greek styles. The typical Renaissance building was an adaptation of the classical style, with the Corinthian-columned form used for churches, palaces, and even marketplaces. Thus in the arts, the Middle Ages seemed over in Italy.

Overall Outlook

Was a new philosophy produced by the humanists? Renaissance thinkers, aside from a few exceptions such as the new Platonists, shied away from too much philosophy as a throwback to medievalism. Specifically, science reveals the worst intellectual side of the Renaissance, ignoring even earlier medieval gains. People loyally copied Greek medical material with the assumption that this had merely to be memorized; there was no reason to do new experimentation. This attitude reflected in part the Greeks' own disinclination for thorough empirical study and in part the Renaissance focus on the arts and letters. There was new work, as the dissection which da Vinci copied indicates, but no major breakthroughs. Renaissance science in Italy was definitely within the medieval culture and if anything showed less advance than earlier research seemed to promise.

What of the view of man himself? Humanism focused on the people. This emphasis allowed the promulgation of the political theory of Niccolo Machiavelli, which would have been impossible in the Middle Ages proper. Like most of the great Renaissance intellectuals, Machiavelli was from Florence, living at the end of the Italian Renaissance when Florentine politics were very confused and the city itself sometimes overrun by French invaders (from the 1490s onward). He believed that he could save Italian civilization if he used the examples of Greece and Rome in fighting wars and administering territory. His political theory was completely secular: Do whatever has to be done, as a prince, to ensure stability; kill dissenters if necessary, but quickly, even en masse, so that the example is clear without the appearance of cruelty. His main philosophy was that the means justify the ends, and the end was to retain power. There was no advocacy of dealing with parliaments or even the church, except insofar as any device might help the prince gain and retain absolute control. And always he referred to the classical example of Caesar or Sulla who had seized power as the Roman republic declined.

By relating to medieval thought in its stress on classical example and emphasizing the power of the central ruler, Machiavelli's political theory has endured. Machiavelli may even have hoped that Italy would be united in a kingdom, as were France and Spain. But the absence of a sense of restraint and of a divine law mark this as something new.

Machiavelli's theories, picked up by later ages, even by such modern rulers as Adolf Hitler, who, it was rumored, kept a copy of *The Prince* by his bedside, cannot be taken as typical expressions of Renaissance thought. Indeed in his own longer political treatises, such as the *Discourses,* Machiavelli, though again citing classical more than medieval examples, writes of the need to restrain the power of the prince, to represent the aristocracy and the common people.

For more typical figures, let us look at two other Florentine thinkers at the end of the fifteenth century, Pico della Mirandola and Lorenzo Valla. Valla was a serious scholar of ancient writings, not a mere copier or antiquarian. He helped found the science of textual criticism, that is, how to determine the authenticity of a document. He proved, among other things, that the papacy used fraudulent materials to base its claims to power. Here, then, was important innovation in technique but not in philosophy. Pico was less impressive. In 1486, at the age of 23, he offered to summarize human knowledge in 900 theses. For all learning was in ancient books—those of "the Chaldaic, Arabic, Hebrew, Grecian, Egyptian and Latin sages." It was assumed all this could be easily mastered. Pico also constructed a ladder to show man's position in God's creation. As in medieval times he stood well above all the animals, below the angels but linked through them to God.

Italian Renaissance culture thus substantially changed artistic styles. It played down some key medieval interests, not only theology but also science. It devoted immense efforts to recover and utilize old texts. Aside from the artistic masterpieces, there were few significant achievements. For all their self-proclaimed newness, Renaissance intellectuals were copying the medieval interest in assimilating past learning. When they waxed philosophical, as Pico did, they repeated a trite version of medieval theology.

Important novelty did emerge. Pico's belief that he could outdo the medieval thinkers was wrong, but the fact that he was boastful reflected a new outlook (though Peter Abelard, three centuries before, came close to the same claim for a time). If little new knowledge was yet produced, if the orientation was to recover the past, enough boasting might produce a potential achievement. This could relate, for example, to the sixteenth- and especially seventeenth-century efforts in scientific innovation.

Italian Renaissance culture tossed up new elements—some,

like the political theory of Machiavelli, really radical by traditional standards—but it did not create a coherent new outlook. It represented the application of selected medieval interests, not the replacement of medieval culture. A clear sign of this is the ease with which northern humanists blended medieval and Italian themes. Finally, even in Italy, Renaissance thought did not remake popular mentality; there was little effort to spread even those elements that were new.

Politics and Economics

Those who claim that the Renaissance created a new man point not only to culture but also to economics and practical politics, attesting that only the whole combination reveals the creative genius of the Renaissance.

Economics need preoccupy us little. Italy remained active in trade: Merchants grew wealthy and loomed large in town politics. Unquestionably Italy was further advanced in these respects than the cities of the North. Renaissance achievement relied on merchant wealth and international, capitalist trade, but the Renaissance did not create this relationship which had proved compatible with medieval civilization previously.

Italian states continued to advance in manufacturing, producing fine silks and metal goods. But technological improvements were minimal. Again we are dealing with evolution from the medieval artisan base. Renaissance Europe was still technologically backward. In 1500 and even beyond, India could produce finer cloth and China finer metal products. This was, after all, one of the bases of European trade, in which the Italians had such an advantage by dominating the Mediterranean. Europe sold raw materials and common, almost semi-manufactured products in return for top-quality crafted materials, plus some special items such as spices.

Renaissance politics is another matter, particularly in Italy. Here one might claim real change. Italy long had been a collection of city-states. During the Renaisssance these states included several types of government. Naples was a small kingdom until the Spaniards took it over early in the sixteenth century. Venice was long known for a balance between a popular voice in government, an executive, and an aristocratic senate—the kind of balance of forces that republican Rome had suggested and that was popular with imitative Renaissance political theorists. Venice offered some suggestions of balance, but drifted increasingly toward rule by merchants-turned-aristocrats, becoming a commercial oligarchy by the fourteenth century. Florence and Milan provided more typical examples. Here a traditional nobility gave way, at least partially, to new men—rich merchants like the Medici family that took over in Florence in the fifteenth century, or even soldiers of fortune, like the Sforzas of Milan. Political disputes, assassinations, and exiles were almost endemic because these new rulers lacked traditional legitimacy for support. By the same token changes were necessary to win support of both the upper classes and the common people. These new ruler not only defended their state and tried to expand it but provided a judicial system, and supported religion—war, justice, and religion being the three functions of the medieval ruler. But the rulers also paid increasing attention to the economic well-being of the city, promoting trade and importing grain to keep prices (and popular unrest) down after bad harvests. This involved massive exploitation of the rural majority, but these were cities and the cities came first. The Renaissance state then suggests new functions. Italian city-states exchanged ambassadors, later sending them to the kingdoms north of Italy. The city-states conducted the first censuses, an effort to determine resources and promote economic advance.

There is another new element in the Italian Renaissance—the forceful personality of an individual city-state ruler—such as the lively but brutal Cesare Borgia, bastard son of a pope who, with his sister's help and papal support, fought and murdered his way into brief control of much of central Italy. Do not this new personality and the new artistic genuises indicate a new sense of individual self-expression against the otherworldliness and traditionalism of the Middle Ages? The Italian Renaissance stressed the word *virtu,* and a man with *virtu* developed his talents and shaped his own destiny.

Yet another Renaissance personality type characterized Christopher Columbus and the Portuguese explorers who pushed Europe's trading contacts to western Africa, to India and to the New World. Europeans were branching out as had no other civilization. The obvious base for this was the long-developing trading impulse, started by the medieval merchants, which had taken them to Russia and, occasionally, to China. There was another medieval base once commercial men helped set the pace: the missionary zeal to convert the entire world to Christianity. But didn't these first explorers and missionaries reflect a new, individual, daring spirit as well—a Renaissance spirit that defied medieval restraints?

Let's try to sort this out, while granting that some fascinating questions remain for the reader to determine. First, we have seen that most achievements of the Italian Renaissance involved a heightening of medieval trends (economics, aspects of politics, maybe even exploration) or at most, as in culture, a redefinition of medieval interests. Second, we can assert that if the Renaissance produced a new man, it remained an atypical development. Whether the Renaissance new man, admittedly exceptional, showed more daring than the medieval merchant who, in the eleventh century, had wandered the dusty, brigand-filled roads from Flanders to Milan, is a moot point. There was a commercial spirit in Europe, resulting from the loosening of manorial ties and the absence of a tightly-controlled central political system. Possibly it reflects a distinctive, though again exceptional, spirit of enterprise. Without question the Renaissance displayed this spirit. What is questionable is whether here, as in other respects, the Renaissance was not just furthering medieval trends.

The Northern Renaissance

Italy, with its city-state organization and expanding trade, had special ties to the classical past which could not represent all of Europe. France, Germany, the Low Countries, and England gained in Renaissance cultural achievements around the middle of the fifteenth century. Their intellectuals did not do the spade work that had fascinated many Italians. There was less grubbing about looking for a new piece of classical verse. But they shared the esteem for the classics. Their artists began, more gradually than the Italians, to build, sculpt, and paint in classical rather than Gothic style, though there are fewer great figures to mention in the arts, indicating a certain tentativeness about novelty.

The classic northern humanist was Erasmus of Rotterdam. We can begin with him to determine the peculiar amalgam which the importation of humanism produced outside of Italy. Erasmus was passionately interested in writing a pure Latin style. He hated scholasticism and was not interested in basic philosophical questions. He was deeply religious, profoundly critical of the corrupt, worldly church, as eager to study the Bible as a text from the past as to deal with Socrates or Cicero. His piety was as much a part of the northern Renaissance as his classicism. From both Christian and classical sources Erasmus derived a belief in an ethic of moderation and renunciation of worldly pleasures. He was, as a scholar, famous throughout Europe. But he obviously does not provide us the personal *panache* of many Italian intellectuals and artists, for he would have frowned on such worldly pride. Erasmus clearly was not a medieval intellectual figure; he would not have shared the theological interests of Thomas Aquinas. But he was attempting in a broader sense to preserve medieval culture, of which religion was the core. His use of Renaissance devices, including the use of original sources and citing classical and Christian ethics, shows an evolutionary state: a new culture was not yet produced even as elements of the old—like scholasticism—were being renounced. Hence the term Christian humanism describes Erasmus and the northern Renaissance culture. As Erasmus demonstrated, the evolution involved new interest in the classics—the Renaissance element—with Christian concern for ethics and piety that obviously blended with elements of the medieval heritage.

Perhaps the Renaissance was shaping up into something new, even outside of a few specific fields like the arts. Perhaps Christian humanism would have provided a new way of life, a new mentality. Even Erasmus was interested in spreading the word to the common people. He had a vision of each plowman working with a Bible in his hand. This implied widespread literacy, translation into native tongues, and a host of exciting new developments. Late in the fifteenth century, the European invention of the printing press (used far earlier in China) made possible extensive production of books, including those of Erasmus himself.

But the new Renaissance culture, the kind that might have caught on because it merged new elements with medieval features, in northern Europe never had a chance. It is difficult to know where to end the Renaissance. Italian Renaissance figures, returning to creative work in the early sixteenth century (and not accidentally abandoning their rather snobbish concern for polished Latin in favor of writing in Italian again), produced histories and literary works of great merit. Shakespeare and Cervantes have been called Renaissance writers because of their secularism and focus on man. But without pretending that the Renaissance strand ended, we must note the obvious: by the time we get to the later sixteenth century another event had occurred, the Reformation. The Reformation cut off the moderate, compromising ethic of Christian humanism. Erasmus himself was personally torn apart by the rise of Protestantism, for while he shared many of the criticisms of the church's corruption he could not go along with any movement so brash and new. Effectively, then, an undiluted northern Renaissance culture had scarcely taken root when the Reformation jolted its basic premises of classical-Christian compromise.

Renaissance politics had clearer durability, since they corresponded so clearly to what the monarchs of the northern states wanted anyway; that is, more power. It was easy to learn to exchange ambassadors and pay more attention to the economy. A typical Renaissance king was Francis I of France. Here was a patron of the arts (subsidizing da Vinci, among others), a man so bent on secular power that he even concluded an alliance with the Turks—not a meaningful alliance in a military sense but the first time a Christian ruler had ever dealt thus with an infidel. Francis was also a ruler with clear interest in new taxes even if he was not possessed of vigorous notions of promoting the economy. Yet Francis was not able to abandon all medieval restraints. He did not shake off parliament. While he quarreled with the pope and took over greater control of the French church, including appointment of loyal bishops, he obviously thought religious functions were vital to his reign. And, like the Christian humanists, his efforts were embroiled in the Reformation.

Like Erasmus, Francis I was not a typical medieval figure in his sphere of activity. But he derived from the Middle Ages more than from the Renaissance, and on the whole he saw in the Renaissance a furthering of medieval goals. Erasmus wanted more ethics and piety. Francis wanted more central power. Their medieval predecessors would have recognized them.

Perhaps, given time to spread, the Renaissance would have created a more completely novel civilization. But in Italy it was cut off by a series of invasions beginning in the 1490s, as France and Spain, particularly, saw a golden opportunity to expand into a politically weak area. Few city-states could retain their autonomy, and cultural activity soon lagged. Added to this was an economic recession. New trade routes to India and gold from the New World changed the center of Europe's economic gravity toward Spain and particularly the states of the North, where medieval civilization persisted. Medievalism was to have its last, ironic flowering in the Reformation, whose cultural and political impact dominated the sixteenth century and overwhelmed any lingering effects of the Renaissance.

Not all of the innovative spirit was lost. Scientific work continued in the sixteenth century, actually with more creativity than the pure Renaissance had produced. It was early in the century that Copernicus, a Polish monk steeped in mathematical training, proclaimed that he had proved that the earth moved about the sun. Medical advances persisted as well. But obviously little of this was picked up until the seventeenth century, again because the Reformation had to be digested before the interests of either intellectuals or common people could depart from the well-traveled medieval paths. For although the Reformation was a thoroughly medieval movement, it ultimately destroyed the Middle Ages. It responded to what was wrong with late medieval civilization, such as the decline of the papacy, by recognizable medieval standards, but it helped end the civilization rather than cure it.

The Reformation

In 1517, a monk and professor at the German university of Wittenberg, Martin Luther, nailed a document containing ninety-five theses to the door of the castle church. Luther regarded the theses as essential for purification of the Roman Catholic Church. His ire was sparked by a wandering salvation-seller who had been authorized by the pope to sell penances. Luther thought that money irrelevant to salvation, so he called selling of penance a false religious practice and demanded reform in the church. He was contesting the validity of sacraments and the priesthood as a source of divine grace. His action challenged centuries of Catholic tradition.

Luther had been driven to his position by several factors, among them resentment of Roman corruption, and perhaps, a nationalistic sense that Germans should not be charged for papal misdeeds. Certainly close reading of the Bible, particularly the Letters of Paul, and of Augustine's writings motivated his belief that salvation was ordained by God before the world began, certainly not to be purchased or earned by worldly works.

Luther's challenge showed a widespread desire for less worldliness, more purity, a return to the original faith of Christ and his disciples. During the previous two centuries, the decadence of the church had prompted many challenges. Ironically most challenges to the church sought formation of new religions. Luther wanted only reform, but soon a religion would bear his name.

Lutheranism evolved as Luther realized that the Catholic Church would not accept his reforms. Most central to it is a contention that man cannot attain salvation through good works—including acts of penance at church; he is saved only by an inner faith granted by God's grace. Faith meant total adherence to Christian doctrine of the Bible. Although a person still sins, Luther emphasized, he will believe. He will be free because of his internal belief, though he be slave or outcast. Once this basic principle is established, two things follow: most practices of the Catholic Church become irrelevant—only two of the seven sacraments, communion, and baptism, remained valid; second, more subtly, Luther's approach had political implications: One should work at his job, obey his ruler, but it made little difference what the job was or how the ruler behaved. The only important factors were, salvation and the inner freedom of faith. Finally, although unintentional, Luther's action had encouraged the establishment of other sects of Protestantism.

The largely abortive strand was Anabaptism. Before Luther posted his scholarly theses, German peasants had been rebellious. They saw in Lutheranism a religion where every individual could see for himself what was right, permitting judgment in this world and the next. Still locked in a manorial system, the peasants rose against oppressive landlords, demanding fair rents and village controls over peasant society.

The German peasant revolt of 1524 was brutally repressed—Luther, himself a social conservative, condemned their rising—but groups continued to demand radical religious and social reform. Some Anabaptists dreamed of a Society of Saints, in which only those saved by God would run society.

Far more important numerically and in terms of durability were the two other strands of Protestantism. Anglicanism, based on the formation of a separate English Church, initially was a pure power play. England in the early sixteenth century was ruled by a strong monarch, Henry VIII, bent on reinforcing the trend toward growing central power. Like most medieval monarchs, he felt responsibility for his subjects' religion. Unlike most, he had a special problem, presumably genetic: he could not easily have a son, and he needed a son for succession of the throne. So he married and remarried, divorcing some wives and beheading others. He finally got two daughters and a sickly son. Unfortunately the pope did not look kindly on divorce, not to mention beheading. So Henry, impatient, named his own leader of the church, the Archbishop of Canterbury, who approved his divorces and repudiated his connection with Rome. Initially this involved no theology at all, just institutional change; Parliament in 1534 acknowledged the monarch as "Protector and Only Supreme Head of the Church and Clergy of England." This was an extreme version of the long medieval fight over power between king and pope, and now the king could easily win. But sincere Catholics retained their loyalties, so Henry was tempted to tamper with Catholic ritual and doctrine. The Anglican church gradually slipped from pure Roman Catholicism. Through the mid-sixteenth century there was great uncertainty. Henry's son, Edward VI, backed a more thoroughly Protestant church with fewer sacraments. His successor, Mary, a devout Catholic, killed Protestant leaders and tried to reestablish Catholicism. But neither had long reigns, and it was Henry's youngest daughter, Elizabeth, who formalized the English Church. It was based on variety— former Catholic priests could become Anglican pastors and continue most traditional rituals. Under Elizabeth, who ruled from 1558 to 1603, membership in the Church of England was required. However, there were many Catholics left, and also more rigorous Protestants, who objected to this compromise church and wanted full religious freedom. Known as Puritans, some survived (like some Catholics) without undue repression, but others feared their position too dangerous. Under Elizabeth's successor, James I, known to be more sympathetic to Catholicism, some went first to Holland and then to New England. But enough stayed in England to create a great fuss there. Their inspiration was Calvinism, the final main strand of Protestantism and the one that really rivaled Lutheranism in importance.

Calvin was a Frenchman who did most of his writing and political work in Geneva. He had read Luther, Paul's Letters, and the other inadvertent inspirers of Protestantism, agreeing on many points. His religion differed in pursuing Luther's objections to Catholicism more rigorously and in avoiding Luther's idea of salvation through inner faith. Calvinism believed in the doctrine of predestination; a person was saved or not, and that was it. And since Calvin was a severe man, few would be saved. Baptism and communion were retained as rituals, but in principle they did nothing for the individual. God had already foreordained the "elect" who would find salvation.

In their hatred of Catholic practices, Calvinists were much more thorough than Lutherans and obviously far more rigorous than Anglicans. This showed, with important effects, in all aspects of affairs from ritual to government to church. A Calvinist minister was no better than anyone else. He hoped he was one of the elect, the saved, but a businessman or a peasant could be saved just as probably. Calvinist worship was naturally stark. No saints' images—for there were no saints—no special people among the elect, no pictures, little music.

But Calvinism did have an interesting twist. If one was of the elect, he had a chance to participate in church governance. The Calvinists were the only ones other than the Anabaptists who disavowed bishops; local groups should run the church. Calvinist-derived churches developed a variety of systems of government by the seventeenth century and even fought over them in England; the main dispute was whether a group of elders should rule (the Presbyterian impulse) or whether the whole congregation had rights (the Congregationalist impulse that won out among Puritans in England and America alike). All these systems suggested some participatory element in church government, and if translated into politics, could prove highly subversive. And translated they were. Calvin, like Luther, initially supported the powers-that-were; princes were divinely appointed even if they persecuted the elect. But whereas Lutheranism spread mainly through adoption by one German or Scandinavian prince after another, and maintained a subordinate posture toward political power, Calvinism won over no major government. Hence Calvin, and his followers, who were minorities in countries like France and England, were inclined to apply the idea of the independence of church from state and even a vague notion of the right of magistrates or even common people to have a voice in government.

The New Religious Configuration

By 1600 the religious map of Europe had been totally transformed, a mere eighty years of upheaval undoing centuries of Catholic unity. The Anabaptists persisted in Holland, the most tolerant of all countries, and its basic impulse has recurred; but the Anabaptists, dealing only with the elect, could not really form large churches. Anglicanism was a creature of the British government, forcibly spread to Ireland (where it won few converts) and imported to North America as Episcopalianism.

Lutheranism won large sections of Germany, particularly states to the west and north but it also spread to eastern France and became the official religion of the Scandinavian kingdoms. Calvinism won Scotland, much of Holland, and parts of Switzerland and Germany (particularly parts of western Germany). It had converts in England and North America. It won perhaps two million people in France. Protestants made gains in Hungary and Bohemia. The new religions had virtually no direct impact on southern Europe where the papal hold remained strong.

This general religious map was pretty well established by 1600. In Germany Lutherans and Catholics in the mid-sixteenth century had agreed on a territorial division—wherever a prince was Lutheran, the state was Lutheran and the people were supposed to be, and, again vice versa. This didn't work entirely, partly because it neglected the Calvinists, and in 1618 the Thirty Years' War began, launched initially by the desire of Catholics to regain Protestant territory and vice versa. The war became a more secular struggle; Catholic France, for example, aided the Protestant princes to weaken the German emperor. Holland was, briefly, another dubious area. Largely Protestant, it was ruled by Catholic Spain. In a civil war around 1600 the Dutch drove out the Spanish (leaving Belgium Catholic and controlled by the Spanish Hapsburg ruling house, later transferred to the Austrian Hapsburgs). France faced endemic fighting between Catholics and Protestants throughout the later sixteenth century, severely weakening the central monarchy. A formerly Protestant king, Henry IV, ended the battles around 1600 by converting to Catholicism, saying "Paris is worth a mass," which obviously meant that he would rather be king than Protestant. He issued the Edict of Nantes, dictating tolerance of the Protestant minority, but this edict, ignored during the next century, was revoked in the 1680s and thousands of Protestants were expelled. However, even before this human tragedy France was clearly a Catholic country, with the king controlling the national Catholic church.

The English situation remained unclear. A minority prayed for a return of Catholicism. Most important in England was the dispute between Calvinist Puritans and the Anglicans, who in Puritan eyes differed from Catholics only in their ignoring of the papacy. Puritans sought control of the government. A new line of kings, the Stuarts, pondered restoration of Catholicism. And the Anglicans, a compromise group, sat uncomfortably in the middle.

The result was the dominance of the Anglican church, some tolerance for Calvinists, and almost no tolerance for Catholics.

Two points emerge from this brief narrative. First, the rise of Protestantism occasioned bloody battles among nations and within nations, reflecting the religious zeal. Also, religion was being employed to cover other motives. Secondly, the entire process discouraged the quest for religious unity. In France, toleration became essential half a century later, lest the nation collapse into perpetual internecine war. Germany's solution was similar. The Lutheran-Catholic agreement to divide territory was sensible, and it was tragic that renewed aggression caused the brutal battles of the Thirty Years' War which decimated this area. Protestant kings from Sweden, calculating French statesmen, and zealous Spanish infantrymen marched up and down the country, leaving it prostrate for almost a century. The only possible solution was at least limited religious toleration as the 1648 Treaty of Munster provided: states were established as Catholic, Lutheran, or Calvinist.

The Thirty Years War also showed that the Catholic Church would not fade away under the Protestant attack. The overall battle with Protestantism revived the papacy. Renaissance interests were relinquished: a Dutch pope ordered fig leaves or loin clothes to be painted or sculpted on nude Renaissance art.

Secular interest had yielded to a new consolidation of the churches as a pious, organized religion. A new monastic order, the Jesuits, arose with the specific mission of retaining Catholic loyalties, training and serving the Catholic kings and princes. The order also served as a missionary force in the New World, converting Indians in Latin America and operating estates in the Spanish and Portuguese empires. Catholicism redefined its doctrines, clarifying its disputes with Protestantism. There was no innovation here, but a vigorous reassertion of Catholic truth, leading to the impossibility of a compromise with the Protestants. The sacraments were valid; a person could participate in his own salvation by his own choice of actions; priests did have special, divinely transmitted powers. This Catholic Reformation, also called a Counter Reformation, strengthened the Church's resistance to further Protestant incursions.

In effect all churches claimed sole possession of religious truth. No one voluntarily gave up the medieval idea that there was one Christianity. They fought and killed to prove the validity of their belief. Thus, the Reformation was at once profoundly medieval in its base and profoundly disruptive in its results. People tired of fighting while kings and princes developed other motives than defense of religious truth. Religion remained vital but no longer under a single church.

But we are anticipating slightly in assessing the impact of the Reformation and Counter Reformation in the century of confrontations. One related question faces us: Why did people accept (or reject) the new religious doctrines and rituals? There are fascinating human problems here, revealing much about persistence of medieval religion and the development of new attitudes. After centuries of Catholicism, how could so many new doctrines make such rapid inroads?

The Cause of Religious Upheaval

For an orderly answer we must begin with three points: Politics played a key role. Firm adherence to Catholicism by the Spanish king made Protestantism impossible. But where a German prince opposed a Catholic emperor, or where a powerful French nobleman saw political gains against the potent central monarchy, Protestantism might win large groups. Even Anglicanism was political.

Often, then, the ruler chose the religion, and people followed his choice despite official edicts; why did Protestantism spread without political rulings? Why did Calvinists appear under Anglican rule or under Lutheran or Catholic princes in Germany? Protestantism offered solutions to defects of the existing church. Add to this a second point: medieval Catholicism, although viciously attacking clear heresies, had been rather tolerant. It allowed scholarly dispute and, for the common people, it accommodated itself to many semi-pagan practices. Hence many people may not have felt a particular jolt in switching religions, particularly when one's former priest himself converted and remained one's pastor (a common occurrence in Lutheran areas, for example).

This brings us to point three. Obviously, Protestantism was not simply Catholicism now split into different churches. The most radical major case is Calvinism. Here was a religion that offered stark, boring church services, a doctrine that virtually told one that one was likely doomed to hell. Why not stay Catholic, where one had elaborate rituals and a chance of earning salvation through sacraments? A partial answer was political forces: One might be pressured into this new conformity by a local political leader who

himself believed or saw gain in converting to a religion which he
might dominate. The gap between late medieval piety and the corruption of the pre-Reformation church also became a factor. And
Calvinism could not be as strict as it seemed on paper. Church services were soon relaxed—more singing was allowed, for example.
But above all the doctrine of predestination could be attractive.

What kinds of people became Protestants? Those obedient to
their converted Protestant rulers, those exposed to a persuasive
preacher, those long worried about the corruption of Catholicism,
and those who preferred a national church to one ruled by Rome
became Protestants. Perhaps some businessmen chose Protestantism because, by eliminating priesthood and monasticism, it
offered equal opportunity for salvation to all. Luther actually
retained the traditional Catholic attitude that business was corrupting; in fact the Church was by now more tolerant of business practices. But Calvin fully admitted the validity of work, so long as it
was the means to an end and not an end.

The Impact of Religious Upheaval

Protestantism's effects definitely differed from the intentions
of Protestant leaders. There was no more universal church, yet the
major leaders still saw a need for a single church. Only after a century of war did a formal concept of tolerance became a political
necessity. By positing a direct personal relationship to God, Protestantism may have encouraged individualism. Calvinism, by refusing allegiance to unholy rulers and admitting the right of revolution
had immense political implications. Let us not exaggerate the
change here. If Catholic popes had not talked directly of revolution,
they had often excommunicated rulers and absolved their subjects
from obedience.

Protestantism has been credited with the rise of capitalism.
This is obviously not so: some Catholics were active capitalists in the
Middle Ages. There was new stress on individual achievement, new
acceptance of work in the world. Certain Protestant
areas—England, Holland—enjoyed unusual commercial success in
the seventeenth century. Yet some Protestant areas, particularly
the Lutheran ones, lagged economically while Catholic regions such
as France were not far behind the commercial leaders. It is dangerous to equate Protestantism with economic development.

However, Protestantism involved change for both Protestants
and Catholics. The Catholic Reformation strengthened and

purified the institutional church. The church became less tolerant, more demanding of its flock. It emulated not the doctrines but the rigorous qualities of Protestantism.

This fact, plus the devastating religious wars and the disunity of Christianity, reduced interest in religion. We can see this in intellectual life most clearly. Montaigne, a Frenchman writing at the end of the sixteenth century, tired of religious struggle, suggested a personal set of ethics to replace theology.

Protestantism had been a blow for the irrational side of medieval religion. Calvin and especially Luther gave no room for human reason: All knowledge depended on faith. Rationalism, however, increased, affecting more than the formal intellectual. The common man might make a similar decision, becoming more secular in his interests. In Protestant countries particularly he was increasingly likely to be able to read, for dependence on faith here meant individual ability to read the Bible. Literacy remained a minority phenomenon; ministers were required to communicate the Bible to illiterate. But with spreading literacy Protestants might read more than the Bible—other religious tracts with, perhaps, political implications, or even purely secular literature. The stage was set for a new intellectual climate.

Finally, Protestantism had an obvious political impact. Where Calvinism loomed, people gained experience in church administration and demanded a voice in the state. Calvinist writers, in France, Holland, and England, pleaded for more formal representative bodies, not just the old Estates-General, which so favored the upper classes. Yet inevitably, Protestantism's greatest impact was in furthering the dominant medieval political trend, strengthening the central state. Lutheran leaders docilely accepted the leadership of German princes who had converted, and Lutheranism became a state church in much of Germanic Europe. It was a decided departure from western Christian tradition of separation of powers, which some have attributed to a peculiar German willingness to obey the state.

The Common Man

Before we tie Renaissance and Reformation together, let us note one final change that may have little to do with either great movement. In the last centuries of the Middle Ages, beginning perhaps in the fourteenth and extending into the fifteenth, common people in Europe, peasants and artisans, developed new attitudes. Let us call this the materialist revolution, which is not to imply that religious interests were dropped. We already have noted that Christianity encouraged a belief that nature's objects are for man's use. The great plagues and bad harvests of the fourteenth century may have heightened concern about protecting one's goods. A reduction in population increased wages. There were fewer people to do the needed jobs.

The Renaissance and Reformation might have aided this movement. We already have discussed how the Reformation tended to approve worldly success; the man of property was most likely to be seen as elected by God. The same impulse, theologically unwarranted, could develop in Catholic areas. We have been more chary about citing Renaissance influence because there is so little evidence of its impact on common people. Obviously material goods had become more abundant with the advance of the medieval economy before the advent of the Renaissance. It was in the Middle Ages, under the influence of Christianity and economic expansion, that diminished pagan superstition. One did not worship his ax, for example, as Balkan peasants did well into the eighteenth century. One used it to chop down trees, with no ritual involved. An average Balkan peasant possessed only three objects (other than food and clothing) in 1500; his western European counterpart owned eighteen or more. Until the Renaissance the only stone buildings were castles and churches; all else was built of wood. With greater wealth, merchants and the more affluent peasants built in stone.

Several factors may have entered into the heightened materialism. It was not a modern attitude. Rather, the medieval and pre-medieval views evolved into a new popular culture which prepared the way for the development of modernity itself. The clearest sign of a new popular culture, whatever its precise causes, was a marked change in family patterns. West Europeans began to marry later. Throughout most of the world and in Europe until the late Middle Ages, most people married fairly young, about twenty. They would produce many children, most of whom died.

By the sixteenth century peasant women in western Europe were marrying around age twenty-five, men, at about twenty-eight to thirty. The immediate reason for the change is clear. Europeans wanted to protect their property for their children. In fact, people without property normally did not marry, which left thirty percent or more of the population celibate. This pattern, it must be noted, prevailed in both Catholic and Protestant countries. Late marriage was a means of birth control, intended to assure new couples property when they began their marriage—hence the delay usually involved waiting for the father's death or retirement.

This family pattern was unique in agricultural societies. It may reflect, and certainly may have caused, any number of sexual frustrations, for clearly Europeans were delaying marriage well beyond puberty. A relatively plausible argument is that sexual repressions led Europeans to seek compensations in economic and military aggression.

The west European family was becoming a tightly-knit unit with property its center. Families in agricultural societies generally had economics as their center: the entire family contributed to survival. It was the concern for ownership that was new.

The End of the Middle Ages

The Middle Ages had ended by the mid-seventeenth century. We have discussed symptoms of the decline four centuries earlier. Renaissance and, to a lesser extent, Reformation, indicated new currents, although they continued the medieval spirit. Taken together, even if they were medieval creations, Renaissance and Reformation destroyed any hope of continuing the medieval fabric. By breaking religious unity and furthering the heightened powers of the central monarchs, the Reformation permitted new secular interests. Here the Renaissance spirit could find a new setting. The new science of Copernicus, the bawdy plays of Shakespeare, the feeling articulated early in the seventeenth century by Descartes that the human mind could grasp the whole meaning of the universe—all were signs of the Renaissance spirit. Descartes indeed was almost a throwback to Pico or even Aquinas in his use of reason to build knowledge. Yet Descartes, in contrast, needed no faith at all, save in himself. He introduced God as a logical necessity and was uninterested in theological detail. Shakespeare owed much to the tradition of medieval urban drama, often vulgar and secular. He borrowed classical themes as had others in the Renaissance. But again, the spirit was different. Shakespeare talked more about man's power to shape his own destiny, to achieve new things.

Reformation and Renaissance in combination, then, both stemming from diverse currents of medieval civilization, broke the mold. Add to this the new popular, materialistic culture developing under the surface of the great men and great events. Again, as we noted in discussing the Middle Ages, there was no collapse. Medieval civilization did not "fall" as did Rome. Hence, even when we turn to the new civilization we will find not just traces or imitations but active, ongoing medieval elements. Newton, the most important figure in science of the seventeenth century, was a mystic who wanted to devote his life and intellect to God's service. His discoveries were basic to undermining the medieval world view, making God seem almost unnecessary. However, he could have talked quite contentedly with Aquinas and might have found Abelard brashly secular.

There was no decisive break; we are unable to say the Middle Ages ended at January 11, 1652. The fact is that we must turn to a new civilization in the mid-seventeenth century, one that was on its way to becoming modern.

Europe and the World at the End of the Middle Ages

Some measure of where Europe stood as medieval civilization drew to a close is essential, particularly because western Europe was already ceasing to be a purely agricultural society. It was a middle-level civilization by 1600, technologically inferior to India and China in agriculture and crafts. Its political structures were obviously less sophisticated, the most coherent product being the nation-state, not an empire. In art, philosophical thought, and science, the Europeans rivaled anyone. Clearly Europe had now surpassed the Arab world in science and mathematics. In commerce Europe had no peers. Explorations during the Renaissance had been interrupted by the religious wars. But at the end of the sixteenth century, as order was partially restored, England, France, Holland, and other countries established gigantic international trading combines such as the East India Company. These companies mixed government backing with a new principle of joint-stock finance, the ancestor of the modern corporation; groups of people could pool their investments. New trade and exploration soon would bring settlement, as existed already in Spanish Latin America and Portuguese holdings in India and Brazil.

It was not just commerce and the beginnings of colonialism that distinguished Europe from other civilizations. Christianity and feudalism had given Europe a distinctive state structure with principles of limitation on outright central rule. The classical heritage, revived by the Renaissance, had stressed human rationality. Christian thought had, on the whole, reinforced this tradition, adding an even clearer statement that the individual was a separate entity directly related to God.

The West developed, in sharp contrast to the classical heritage, a distinctive view of women's roles. Although regarded as inferior, women shared the individuality accorded men. We see this most clearly at the top of society. Strong-minded women indirectly ruled sixteenth-century France, after the death of Francis I, while a female ruler, Queen Elizabeth, extended England's territories and dampened internal strife. Women accepted a leading role in Protestantism, as they had in Catholic piety. How far this trickled to the lower classes we do not know. Artisan and peasant wives worked with their husbands and identified themselves with family survival. They did not suffer the special seclusion and inferiority of Moslem culture. Possibly the late medieval change in family structure, reducing average child bearing, eased the physical burdens of women. We do not know what role, if any, they took in abetting this change.

The West also retained from its feudal past a belief in military glory. As it entered a new age, Europeans did not stop fighting among themselves. They began to fight all over the world in the name of God and king. This and the emphasis on commerce would first mark them off from Indians, Chinese, Mayans, or Senagalese who had increasing numbers of contacts with white-skinned adventurers.

One final point: What was the relationship of western civilization to Europe itself? How far did it penetrate? We have stressed England, France, Germany, Italy, and Spain, all with their peculiarities but all clearly within the western orbit. By the time of the late Renaissance, certain western cultural influences began to push east. Italian architects, for example, were called upon by the Hapsburg emperors in Vienna and ventured even to Russia, helping to create the distinctive, onion-shaped domed church that extends from central Germany into Russia. Isolated east European thinkers were attracted to Renaissance thought. The Polish origin of Copernicus has been mentioned, though he did most of his work in Germany. A significant question, particularly haunting in Russia, would be: How much of the West could be accepted?

But this was not an issue in 1600. Eastern Europe was not in the center of western civilization. Much of it, as with Russia, adhered to the eastern Orthodox church, subordinate to the state and far different theologically from western Christendom. Trading activity was low and mainly in the hands of western foreigners—a sign of contact but not of shared values. Most crucially, in the later Middle Ages the social structure of eastern Europe was moving in precisely the opposite direction from that of the West. Political structures differed. On the eastern fringes of Germany, the House of Brandenburg was establishing a strong, small state called Prussia. Russia freed itself from Mongol rule in the fourteenth century and established a strong central monarchy around Moscow. Poland, on the other hand, was weakened by the refusal of great feudal lords to support an elected king. In Poland, Prussia, and Russia, manorialism was superseding a relatively free village agricultural system. Just as western serfs gained considerable liberty and towns became increasingly important, eastern Europe locked itself in a system of landlord power combined with an absence of urban structures. The dynamic east European monarchs could and would intervene in European diplomacy. As we leave the Middle Ages it is vital to note that western civilization and Europe were not the same entity. Over half of Europe, eastern Germany, the Slavic lands, including the Balkans, was socially and culturally different.

Hence western civilization had a narrow geographical base, open to threats from eastern attack. New outposts of western civilization were being established in South America and, slightly later, North America, though these were modified by frontier conditions and contacts with native peoples, and soon, African slaves.

In 1600, the civilization rested almost exclusively along Europe's Atlantic coast. But this small area already had produced a sufficiently distinctive civilization to push on to an extraordinary new achievement: a total revolution in human life. For we now must turn to the beginnings of the modernization process that would ultimately transform basic human behavior and thought, just as had the transition from hunting to agriculture. This process could only begin in the West because of the distinctive culture and society. The process was only later to be forced upon or sought by virtually the entire world.

Suggested Readings

On the early Middle Ages, Bryce Lyon, *The Origins of the Middle Ages* (1972). Medieval political and social structure are discussed in Christopher Brooke, *The Structure of Medieval Society* (1971); Marc Bloch, *Feudal Society* (1964); F. L. Ganshof, *Feudalism* (1964); Special aspects of social and economic development are treated in Lynn White, *Medieval*

Technology and Social Change (1964); George Homans, *English Villagers of the Thirteenth Century* (1970); Robert Lopez, *The Commercial Revolution of the Middle Ages* (1971). An important discussion of the political heritage is Joseph Strayer, *On the Medieval Origins of the Modern State* (1971).

For medieval thought and art: Etienne Gilson, *Reason and Revelation in the Middle Ages* (1938); R. W. Southern, *Medieval Humanism* (1970); Frederick Copleston, *Medieval Philosophy* (1971); Walter Ullman, *History of Political Thought: the Middle Ages* (1964); P. Francastel, *Medieval Painting* (1967); Otto van Simpson, *The Gothic Cathedral* (1964). On the church: Jeffery Russell, *A History of Medieval Christianity* (1968); Geoffrey Barrclough, *The Medieval Papacy* (1968). On a special strand of religious development: Norman Cohn, *The Pursuit of the Millenium: Revolutionary Millenarians and Mystical Anarchists of the Middle Ages* (1970).

On the decline of the Middle Ages: Johan Huizinga, *The Waning of the Middle Ages* (1967); George Holmes, *The Later Middle Ages, 1272-1485* (1966); Sidney Painter, *French Chivalry* (1957). Science is discussed in the early section of A. R. Hall, *The Scientific Revolution* (1957).

Good surveys of the entire period can be found in R. W. Southern, *The Making of the Middle Ages* (1953); Robert Lopez, *The Birth of Europe* (1967); R. Trevor Davies, *A History of Medieval Europe* (1962).

One basis for the Renaissance is discussed in Daniel Waley, *The Italian City-Republics* (1969). No survey can omit Jacob Burckhardt's discussion of the renaissance man: *Civilization of the Renaissance in Europe* (many editions); a more recent survey is Peter Burke, *The Renaissance* (1964). Karl H. Dannenfeld, *The Renaissance: Medieval or Modern?* (1967) raises the key issue. Important specialized works include: André Chastel, *The Age of Humanism* (1963); Carlo Cipolla, *Money, Prices, and Civilization in the Mediterranean World* (1967); Bernard O'Kelly, ed., *The Renaissance Image of Man and the World* (1968); Johan Huizinga, *Erasmas* (1952); Marc Bloch, *French Rural History* (1966); Herbert Butterfield, *Origins of Modern Science* (1966). On technology: Kingston Derry and T. I. Williams, *A Short History of Technology* (1961); on art, Bernard Berenson, *Italian Painters of the Renaissance* (1952); and F. B. Artz, *From the Renaissance to Romanticism* (1962).

On the Reformation: G. R. Elton, *Reformation Europe* (1964), and H. J. Grimm, *The Reformation Era* (1973) are excellent surveys. Two discussions provided in Lewis W. Spitz, ed., *The Reformation: Material or Spiritual* (1962) and K. C. Sessions, ed., *Reformation and Authority* (1968). See also A. G. Dickens, *The English Reformation* (1964) and *The Counter Reformation* (1969).

On religious struggles, J. H. Elliot, *Europe Divided* (1968). For a psychohistorical study of Luther, Erik Erikson, *Young Man Luther* (1958). Specialized works include T. H. Tawney, *Religion and the Rise of Capitalism* (1926) and Max Weber, *The Protestant Ethic and the Spirit of Capitalism* (1930).

On the great explorations, J. H. Parry, *Europe and a Wider World* (1949); G. J. Fuller, *The Coming of the Europeans* (1962).

Europe from the Reformation to 1750

MOST EUROPEANS DID NOT LIVE or think much differently in 1750 than they had in 1600. Indeed, the life of common people seemed to solidify around the innovations developed at the end of the Middle Ages. Yet in three areas of endeavor major changes occurred which increasingly involved the common people.

The three areas of change were government, science-philosophy, and economics-technology. Because of the degree of change here, some historians have termed this period of European history the first industrial revolution. This is an exaggeration, but when new economic and political forms were added to the concern of the common people for property and material goods, the basis for more dramatic change was set. We will start with the popular base, which in many ways seemed to stabilize during this period; for even though people continued doing what they long had done and expected to do in the future their role was vital.

Capitalists, kings and bureaucrats, and intellectuals were carving out a new world largely above the level of the common people. Actual modernization began when these levels of change merged with the interests of the common people.

Ordinary Life

The common people of western and central Europe had been through a hectic period up to 1600 and beyond. Religious wars disrupted life for many. Some had to make agonizing choices of conscience; others, less concerned with these niceties, simply faced the prospect of armies marching back and forth across their lands. There was another problem as well. Throughout the sixteenth century prices tended to rise as society suffered a new round of inflation. This inflation was due to the import of precious metals from the new world. With more money available—money being based on gold—prices automatically went up. Since the common people, particularly in the cities, had to buy their goods, they were directly affected. The upper classes, landlords and merchants, who depended on money earnings entirely, were tempted to try to squeeze higher rents and more labor out of the masses.

Yet material life improved for the common people. An old English villager in 1577 noted three things "marvelously altered" since his childhood: "One is the multitude of chimneys lately erected . . . ; the second is the great (although not general) emendment of lodging . . . ; the third thing . . . is the exchange of vessel, as of wooden platters into pewter, and wooden spoons into silver or tin." The common people were still desperately poor, but there was new money to make, and with the increased desire for material goods, life began to make sense. There were two accompanying results. One was that in the fifteenth century and until about 1648, population increased again. Cities grew somewhat, and this resulted in great social as well as geographical mobility. Numbers of people traveled long distances to seek work. Smaller numbers rose from humble peasant to urban artisan or even merchant. In other words, beneath the religious wars, this was a time of fruitful change for the common people. The framework of life remained the same. Most people still worked in a family context and married late. This new prosperity merely intensified the late medieval mentality—we should now call it the early modern mentality—that valued property and based life around the possession of it. But within this enduring framework there was great ferment.

Although general prosperity increased, as peasants extended the land under cultivation and artisans turned out more goods for the rising urban population, there was new pressure on the people. Landlords, oppressed by rising prices, either tried to raise rents or buy out the peasantry directly. In England, landlords increased the number of large holdings, seizing church estates—one of the reasons for their support of the Anglican reformation—as well as peasant plots. Poor peasants had to sell not only to nobles but also to urban merchants, who saw land as a way to make money and as a badge of respectability. In one French region at the end of the seventeenth century, thirteen percent of the land was held by urban merchants, twenty-five percent by the nobility—and this in a region where peasant smallholding had traditionally dominated. Overriding all this was the steady effort by the central state to increase direct taxation on the common people. The nobility, still given special privilege by virtue of their birth, paid no taxes; nor did the church. So an expanding central state could only hit the ordinary folk.

We have, then, a mixed picture in western Europe. There was population growth and related signs of new prosperity. But population growth, even amid greater wealth, is disruptive. Fathers have to decide what to do about the extra daughter who needs a dowry. Sons who cannot expect to inherit land must decide how to survive in the world. With rising prices and new efforts from the state and the upper classes to cut into the economy of the common people, confusion inevitably arose. Even the person who moved to the city and made do felt resentful. Add to this the general atmosphere of religious tension and strife, and one had a potentially explosive situation.

In fact, these first decades of early modern times saw an amazing spate of popular outbursts in town and countryside alike. Some occurred in eastern Europe, where serfdom was being imposed with increasing rigor. Hungary and Russia, as well as Italy, France, and England, had major crises. French peasants, both Catholic and Protestant, in the 1590s rose against their landlords "who had reduced them to starvation, violated their wives and daughters, stolen their cattle and wasted their land" while the city merchants, with whom they had to trade, "seek only the ruin of the poor people, for our ruin is their wealth." In other words, as in the earlier round of medieval rebellions, there was a definite sense of the need for social justice which caused this outburst.

The climax came in 1648, when popular rebellions occurred in Spain, Italy, Russia,France, England, and elsewhere. Not for two centuries would there be another such widespread upheaval. Taxes, landlords, and grasping merchants were all attacked. For the first time in England traditional desire for social justice took on a political tinge. Here there was no outright violence, but a petition, signed by almost 100,000 people, known as the Levellers. The petition was written after over a decade of political agitation in which parliamentarians opposed the pretentions of the king to greater power and Puritans fought the rituals and intolerance of the Anglican Church. There was, in other words, an unusually favorable setting for a new kind of popular statement. The Levellers asked for the establishment of a democratic republic in which everyone would have a vote, and for religious toleration. The Levellers were put down and were followed by a smaller group, called the Diggers, who were less active but whose principles called for economic equality—the first modern hint of socialism.

The Meaning of Protest

One could go on describing this fascinating series of uprisings. Let us note the three points of principal importance. First, all were put down; no governmental or social structure was severely shaken. Yet governments sometimes became more attentive to the desirability of preventing the conditions causing such uprisings—keeping bread prices down in the cities, for example. Second, while the uprisings were most clearly directed at immediate economic problems—the rioters in Palermo shouted "Long live the king and down with taxes and bad government"—they did reflect the need for broader changes. Religious enthusiasm and religious confusion created a setting in which people felt more free to attack the established authority or even felt called by God to do so. More important, the uprisings implicitly attacked the new powers of state and the increasingly capitalist economy. Finally, the rebellions, though they died off after 1648, left a legacy which the populace would remember. Ideals of social justice and of proper government were remembered even if the common folk could not afford the energy to rise so powerfully anywhere for another century and a half. Riots for fairer bread prices remained endemic in countries like France. The idea established in England of adding demands for political reform to the traditional demand for social justice could catch on more widely. For the popular mind is retentive; peasants pass on oral traditions. We have seen the medieval origins of this current of popular rebellion, calling on Christianity and village and guild customs for definite rights, definite limits to oppression. This new period of rebellion reinforced the tradition and added a political note. Here was another western tradition that, when revived under more modern circumstances, could provide goals for the oppressed everywhere.

Popular Culture: Its Strengths and Weaknesses

After their great outbursts, the common people calmed down. Almost as if resting for the next round of upheaval, which would be far more profound, peasants and artisans throughout Europe lived a rather stable life for almost a century after 1650. Population growth dropped to almost nothing. Mobility declined, although people still moved from one village to the next, seeking better land or a better marriage. Cities grew, but very slowly. A stable popular society seemed to be reforming, based again on the distinctive western patterns of protection of property.

The typical peasant or artisan married in his mid-to-late twenties, after the man had property of his own or a firm job as a journeyman. The wife also participated in the family economy. She spun thread or did preparatory work for a weaver, and in urban artisan families she kept accounts as well—which meant that in some cases she was better educated, more likely to be literate, than her husband. In peasant households the woman tended garden plots around the house, took care of the animals, and went into the fields at crucial periods to help with planting and harvesting.

There were attractive features to this society, which were soon lost in a tide of change. Families worked together. Religion, whether Protestant or Catholic, provided a social outlet as well as comfort and hope for salvation in the life to come. A solid community, composed of relatives and friends, was available to help in time of need. Periodic festivals, based on community tradition, enlivened an otherwise endless round of work. Even work itself was taken at a leisurely pace, with singing and good fellowship—and sometimes wine or beer—to make the borderline between work and leisure far less distinct than it is today.

But there were unattractive features as well. We do not know the emotional quality of family relations. A man married a woman because she could provide a proper dowry, and he needed her help in running his farm or shop. He had very little time for courtship. He had to wait for eight to ten years after puberty to marry at all, because he lacked the property on which marriage was based; and a significant minority, as we noted, would never marry at all for want of this vital ingredient. Yet sex outside marriage was rare in the century before modernization; around 1700 only two percent of all births were illegitimate. When a man was finally able to court a woman, he went to her house perhaps with a village matchmaker,

and was given half an hour alone with her. If they found each other
pleasing, then the parents took charge. Could the girl provide a
suitable dowry? Was the son's property or job adequate? Affection
might develop later, but this was primarily an economic
relationship and would remain so. The same thing applied to
children. The average couple would produce eight to ten
children—a tremendous physical burden on the woman—and half
of them would die. Infants were an economic drain, so they were
swaddled, sometimes hung up on a wall so that the mother could
continue her vital household work, and fed when the mother—often
exhausted and too poorly nourished to nurse adequately—was
ready. There was an ethic accompanying this, which followed from
economic necessity: infants were not really human, but little
animals whose will had to be broken in order to make them into
human beings. Swaddling and other restraints plus frequent
beatings enforced this view, creating in most cases the ideal child
who would obey his parents and, later in life, the authorities of
church and state. At five or so the child was accepted as human and
put to work, again an economic necessity. In their early teens the
youth were typically sent to work for another family and were under
strict disciplinary control. Wealthier peasant families with few
children could assist poorer families by giving board and room, and
work, to an extra child. But there may also have been an emotional
motive. Discipline was left to others, and the conflict between the
youth entering puberty and the parent was eased by outside
employment.

The same question surrounds the two other popular institution
of pre-industrial Europe, the village or guild. It is easy to see such
groups embracing the individual with care and attention, giving
one a secure sense of place in life. But the counterpart was strict
control. The man who did not come to the village festival was
threatened with the direst calamities—he would break a leg, his
next-born child would die. Rigid conformity was enforced in the urban guilds as well. A colleague died and you not only had to go to
the funeral, but you must stand exactly in the proper order, according to your rank, and wear exactly the established attire. This was
a society which from the modern vantage point seems charming but
in which few modern people could live, for the controls and
emotional tensions would be too great. Even at that time some people left to avoid parental and community controls, heading for the
city, the army, or simply a life of wandering.

Poverty was the underlying problem. Village and family patterns were designed mainly to minimize the chance of economic disaster. Famines still occurred frequently. Many, perhaps most, people were undernourished. The average man in 1700 was about five feet in height, and the average woman about four feet eight inches. Many women lost babies because they were too small and ill-fed to bring them to term, or to nurse them properly once born. It was not the same in all countries. England was richer than France, and France richer than Germany. The average per capita income in England in the mid-eighteenth century was seventy pounds, more than that of India today. Of course, as in modern India, this was unevenly distributed, and England was unusually advantaged. If Europe was by world standards wealthy, this was wealth in terms of an agricultural society, not a modern one. There was money enough to pay the taxes and tithes for support of city folk, governments, and the upper classes. There was money enough for sharp distinctions in property holding within the village itself, for although ideals of equality were remembered, the fact was that there were prosperous peasants, who even employed outside labor; there were middling peasants whose acreage would suffice in normal times but who could not endure a poor harvest; and there were some nearly property-less laborers, who had to work as shepherds, harvesters, and the like. But for all this diversity, poverty underlay rural society, and along with poverty, unpredictability. Even the prosperous peasant could fall with a bad harvest, and the rate of turnover of the "village elite" was rather high as a result.

All of this adds up to two pervasive features of the popular mentality, most prominent among peasants but applicable to artisans as well. First, people felt a definite sense of place. There were few identity crises in this world, for one was surrounded by family and community, told what to do, usually according to the dictates of tradition. One expected to do what one's father and mother did. This means that all sorts of problems—tensions with the parents, grinding poverty—were accepted because there was no sense of alternative. Second, these were fatalistic people—not stupid, not even peasants like those of the rest of the world, for they were freer from landlord control, more conscious of property, possibly more sexually hungup. But this was not a mentality from which change would come spontaneously. These people were convinced that the best one could hope for was to preserve what one had against natural disaster or wars or government tax agents—the popular world held stagnation to be a positive virtue, and change therefore a threat. This is why so little change occurred during the century after 1650. Left to themselves, these people would not produce change.

Economic Development

The leading economic developments of the seventeenth and early eighteenth centuries continued to involve trade, and while capitalists dominated this as before, there was a new direction to their efforts. The inflation of the sixteenth century had given trade a great boost, despite the disruption of the religious wars, so there were more entrepreneurs around than before, and they were ready to cast their nets wider. It is difficult to pinpoint the spot at which medieval-Renaissance capitalism became premodern capitalism, but let us use the late sixteenth century as a benchmark, and note the changes.

First, the worldwide scope of European trade changed from a base of isolated entrepreneurs to the well-organized, state-backed trading companies. Europe now maintained an advantage over the rest of the world in commerce, which meant that, despite the persistence of the aristocracy as the ruling upper class, governments recognized merchants as vital to their own operations. No other civilization had done this. Merchants returned the favor with rich returns from sales with distant countries.

They also began to stake out, with encouragement from explorers, church, and government, actual holdings in other parts of the world. Spaniards and Portuguese had for over a century taken over key parts of South and Central America, seeking gold. Ironically they had only a vague notion of what to do with the mass of new wealth brought back, for they failed to develop an internal banking system or manufacturing network that could use the new wealth to develop a profitable internal economy. Individuals gained fortunes, but the bulk of Spain's gold and silver passed to Holland, England, and elsewhere in the North where there were bankers ready to invest and pirates ready to seize the Spanish gold ships at sea. So while Spain and Portugal established a durable empire in South America, they did not make a great economic success of it. Aspects of the operation were successful. Spanish Jesuits found new fields for conversion of natives. At the same time, they profitably raised sugar and other crops on huge plantations where slave labor was freely used. Younger sons of Spanish or Portuguese

nobles got administrative posts in the vast new empire, and significant numbers of common people migrated, many benefiting from
the ability to set up larger farms or to work in the freer atmosphere
of new cities like Buenos Aires.

But it remains true that the first colonial empires established
by European countries did not directly transform the economy
back home. This was not true, however, of the ventures from
northwestern Europe in the next century. The Puritans went to
New England for religious reasons, but they had to make an
economic contribution to their English sovereign. More important
were the English colonies established explicitly for money-making
purposes in the West Indies and the central and southern Atlantic
seaboard of North America. Here, well into the eighteenth century,
was the economic heartland of England's American operation.
England sent settlers to North America and the Caribbean islands.
This was not just a trading post operation. England got timber and
pitch for ships, sugar, tobacco, and cotton from the colonies, which
were supported by African slave labor (introduced first by the
Dutch in the seventeenth century).

Holland and France also developed international trade and
organized trading companies. Holland bought Manhattan, and the
Dutch settled throughout New York and northern New Jersey during the seventeenth century. The French swept into Canada and
from there down into the Mississippi valley to New Orleans; their
economic rewards were mainly furs, though they sought gold. Both
Holland and France also got a share of the Western Indian islands,
where they developed the sugar economy.

England, France, and Holland staked out Asian trading areas,
although here it was not a matter of conquest and settlement but of
control over seaports. France and England, like Portugal earlier,
had holdings in India. Political chaos there, plus mutual rivalry,
drove them to fight for greater control of the Indian subcontinent
during the eighteenth century, a simultaneous occurrence with
their juxtaposition in North America. In both cases the British,
with a better fleet and no distractions with rival armies on the
European continent, got the upper hand. Holland established firm
contacts in Indonesia, Taiwan, and even dented Japan's historic
unwillingness to trade with foreigners. Indeed, until what is inac-
curately termed America's opening of Japan in 1853, the Dutch enjoyed a neat little trading monopoly there.

The third innovation in European capitalism was a growing interest in developing a home manufacturing base. All three changes affected ordinary people—the first two mainly by bringing in more money, which raised the stature of the merchant class but also modestly improved the general standard of living. This third innovation involved lots of people. And it brought with it, logically, an interest in technological change on the part of a growing minority of western producers.

We must not exaggerate the extent of economic change affecting ordinary people or the basic economic system during this period. Most people were still not involved in an elaborate capitalist network. Economic motives were not dramatically altered. There were eager merchants, bankers, and European slave traders willing to do anything to make the pre-modern equivalent of a buck. But most merchants preferred secure investments, even at low return; one study shows that in Paris aristocrats were more venturesome than merchants. Most merchants, even in England, got out of their operations quickly or encouraged their sons to do so, buying land and becoming respectable gentlemen if possible. The capitalist ethic had not won over even the capitalists.

The desire to make money, however, did spread, and Europe's total world economic dominance created a new field of operations. The next logical question was what to sell. Europe had long been marked by a distinctive trading instinct but held an inferior manufacturing position, raw or crude materials were exchanged for the technologically and artistically superior goods of the East. By 1700 this had changed. Europe extended its manufacturing base and improved its technology so that by 1700 it was largely importing raw materials, and had the most advanced technology in the world. Both of these changes involved many people, even part-time workers not fully drawn into the capitalist system but simply supplementing a traditional peasant economy.

Capitalism and Production

The principal method of spreading manufacturing occurred through the putting-out or domestic system. Take the raw materials to the cottage door, have them spun, woven, or hammered into finished products; pick them up and sell them to urban capitalists. A few factories were developed with division of labor, but these were not typical. The domestic production system was not new, but it was now greatly extended in countries like England, which supplied finished cloth and metal goods to the colonies, as well as internally, in exchange for food and raw materials. This was basically a capitalist system, in that the supplier-seller provided funds for the raw materials and did not have personal acquaintance with his labor force; but it was compatible with peasant values as well. The workers labored in a family setting. The merchants running the system might make considerable fortunes, while at the other end of the scale, workers had to deal with strangers, make products for distant markets, and operate within the framework of a money economy. Of course, most of the peasants did agricultural work as well, but periods of unemployment when a product was not selling or when raw materials prices went up could be troubling.

There were also urban industries that had to be expanded if not reorganized. Growing armies required weapons in greater number, and this spurred the metals industry. For the most part, guns were supplied by hosts of individual artisans. But because of the number needed, the artisans, while still working with traditional methods and in small units, were often directed not by a guild master but by a capitalist who could provide the investment for mass production and negotiate the sale. The same development occurred in the production of military uniforms. Here, again without significant technological change, was mass production in its earliest form.

Mining was not a new industry, but with new use for metals and coal it took on added importance in the sixteenth century. Again, it had to be organized on a capitalistic basis, for no ordinary laborer could afford the funds to dig pits, seek markets, and so on. Many mines were tiny, employing only six or ten people, but they were not guild enterprises and were designed for regional or national sales. Printing, on the other hand, developed a guild structure. But here too sales expanded, causing problems for the individual craftsman who could not afford a printing press; so an element of capitalism was essential. Shipbuilding boomed with the steady growth in trade, along with the manufacture of cannons and muskets to protect the precious cargoes.

In sum, an increasing number of people were involved in a market economy as capitalist employers or as paid workers. In every western country, particularly in Holland and England, the guild system declined under the impact of new economic opportunity. The artisan master found it extremely tempting to set up as a capitalist employer, which freed him from the dirty work of laboring with his hands and opened the door to greater earnings. If the guild objected to his self-assertion, he would either leave it or, with other masters, take over and run it as a kind of employers' association against the interests of the journeymen. Not surprisingly, in response, a number of strikes began as journeymen printers or weavers, seeing that they were now a separate class, used withdrawal of labor to seek better wages and conditions. Domestic workers in the countryside were calmer, because they were closer to tradition, but they too were being drawn into new forms of enterprise.

The key result of the new economic system was a vast increase in production. There were technical improvements. In France new looms were developed that, although still run by hand, produced fancier cloth at lower cost. Techniques of shoring up mine shafts to allow deeper penetration were greatly improved. In the early eighteenth century the first steam engine, the Newcomen, was invented in England to pump water from deeper shafts. Here was a foretaste of things to come. These were incremental developments, not an overall technological revolution, but they set the base, well before formal industrialization, for further change.

There were also promising developments in agriculture. Holland, a heavily populated country, threatened with flooding of its low-lying fields, sought to increase production. Peasants introduced new crops such as the turnip, which restored nitrogen to the soil and allowed them to use land every year rather than leaving a portion fallow. They also improved methods of drainage which increased the available arable land.

Developments were still tentative, however, and did not fundamentally change the lives of most people. Dutch agricultural advances were the forerunners of a massive agricultural revolution, but they had not yet spread beyond Holland and eventually caught on only in the early nineteenth century among agricultural producers. Only a minority of people were involved in urban commerce and industry, and most of these still worked in traditional artisan and merchant guilds. The rural economy was not shaken by the spread of domestic manufacturing which served as a supplement rather than a replacement to standard peasant agricultural production. New economic measures were extensions of older patterns to new areas and new people; they were not revolutionary. At most they whetted new motives, such as the desire to earn more money and build up capital or purchasing power, providing a background for the real industrial revolution of the next century.

One final note. Economic development—capitalist trade and manufacturing—took place in this period under the aegis of mercantilism, a special form of government intervention in the economy but also a distinctive conception of the economy itself. We noted earlier, with the Renaissance state, that governments began to take on specific economic functions as part of their growing secularization; now they did so with a vengeance. Governments organized trading companies, supported colonial ventures, and introduced new industries, as in the case of France where silk production was brought in from Italy. Barriers to internal trade were reduced. It was generally agreed that the government's business included the promotion of economic prosperity.

But mercantilism was not as novel as it might appear. In the first place, governments in countries like France supported economic development in order to increase tax revenues toward a more effective base for war—new methods for old purposes. This was less true in England where the merchant spirit was freer, but governments were not undertaking economic measures solely for the good of the people. Second, mercantile controls could hamper economic development rather than encourage it. Colbert, the economic Minister of France in the late seventeenth century, provides a classic case in point. He introduced new industries, but his main impulse in manufacturing was to use state officials to enforce guild restrictions and *prevent* technological change. England was not so rigid, but even so a basic trading system was set up that could have been self-defeating. English merchants cried out for protection against foreign goods, such as cotton cloth from India, and they won their point. Finally, mercantilism involved the belief that there was only a limited amount of wealth in the world, and the only means of advancing your own power was to take it away from someone else—hence high tariffs, rigidly defended colonial systems, and efforts to keep out foreign goods. Countries that were most mercantilistic because of their effort to control their economies, were ironically less likely to advance rapidly than those with looser controls. Hence France or Prussia, with heavy state involvement, moved ahead less quickly than England or Holland, because there was less room for individual initiative and experiment. The whole mercantilist movement demonstrated that even at the government level an economic revolution had not occurred. Economics was less a goal of the state than an adjunct of military aggression. Colbert built his system not only to provide taxes but to rob trade from England which was, in his mind, as good as sinking her ships or killing her troops. Economic development was proceeding but without a major shift in techniques or motives on the part of government, workers, or most merchants.

Absolute Monarchy

The key political development of the seventeenth and early eighteenth centuries consisted of another round in the strengthening of the central state. This is now such a familiar theme in western political history that it may seem ridiculous to cite it as a source of change. In many ways, absolute monarchy, which is what the new state form was called, simply continued the medieval-Renaissance-Reformation trends we have already noted. Central states got stronger at the expense of competing powers, and they expanded their concept of what their functions were. But while this ongoing trend must be recognized, at some point the historian has to jump in and say that, however gradually, this has become a different animal. Louis XIV of France had powers and ambitions that Henry II of England never even dreamed of. Hence the rise of absolute monarchy is a new development, if in a familiar mold.

Let us look at a key example. Louis XIV was king of France between 1643 and 1715, although in the early years of his reign, when he was a mere child, affairs of state were directed by powerful ministers. He is the prototypical absolute monarch because of what he bragged about and what he actually achieved. Under a rationalizing minister of state, Louvois, Louis built himself an army that simply would have been unrecognizable to feudal monarchs, even to Francis I. Though generalled by aristocrats, there were no vassals in his army, and officers were recruited with some regard to their ability to teach and act upon successful tactics. The bulk of the soldiers were trained mercenary troops, paid by state tax funds and signed up for long terms of service (up to 25 years), or dragooned by state recruiters into the same dubious fate. Well-trained, they were also, for the first time in post-Roman European history, given adequate supplies. When they marched, provisions were sent along with them. They did not depend, like feudal bands, on pillaging the countryside. This may have reduced local opposition to their incursions, and it certainly increased their efficiency. To reward military service, Louis set up hospitals and pensions—the first time the idea of retirement was ever formally presented. This constituted the outlines of a modern army. All it lacked was professionally trained generals. Louis fancied himself as a great strategist and made some horrendous blunders; some of his followers did the same. There was no officers' training school open to those with talent rather than aristocratic birth. (However, some new types of men were used, like the fort-builder Vauban, whose massive constructions have resisted even twentieth-century bombardments.) And the French army missed all-out recruitment, the great modern achievement that proclaims that every able-bodied man can be called into service. The state was not strong enough to compel this—although it could drag off a random number of peasants under the king's name—and the economy could not afford it. While this was not a modern army, it was definitely not a medieval one, and this is a major reason that we can talk of a new kind of state.

Though we mark a political break here, the medieval heritage remained strong. Louis continued to think he had religious duties, to the detriment of France's strength. More important, the term "absolute monarch" should be taken as relative. These rulers were not absolute. They got rid of a number of medieval restrictions but not of the basic notion that the state is and should be restricted. Louis, as everyone knows, said, *"L'Etat c'est moi,"* ("I am the state.") This is a ringing phrase which sounds good in history books and on exams but it simply was not true. Louis did not have the technology or even the desire to maintain direct contact with his subjects. He was still formally restrained in many ways, including by provincial parliaments, like that of Normandy, that solemnly ruled as to how much he could tax their province and for what return benefits. This was no dictatorship, no total departure from the western tradition. In fact, less than a century after a ruler like Louis, France rose up to proclaim once again the western tradition of limited government and representative institutions. Louis and his predecessors had maimed some of the institutions. Most notably, the medieval Estates-General did not meet on a national basis from 1614 until 1789. But the spirit was not dead, and new political theorists would cast the role of legislatures in a new guise. Hence the French Revolution of 1789 began with the calling of the Estates-General on a medieval format but soon found that the medieval tradition could be transformed into modern form, linking the old and the new in the distinctive western tradition of government.

The Rise of Eastern Europe

At least as important, however, was the fact that absolute monarchy could be copied. Rulers in central and eastern Europe could see a clear purpose in what someone like Louis XIV was doing. Prussia began to spread her eagle's wings. Russia, free of Tartar control, became more saucy. Austria, having defeated the Turkish threat in the late seventeenth century by turning back the final attempt to invade Vienna, began to push eastward into Hungary and the European lands the Turks controlled. The Austrian case was always a bit confused, because the Hapsburg monarchs, rulers of the land, were by now regularly elected Holy Roman Emperors, giving them a sense of power over the whole of Germany and, to an extent, Italy. But even so, from the late seventeenth century onward, absolute monarchies developed in all three of the new east European powers. Here, too, absolute must be understood with some qualification—these were *not* areas with a real western tradition of medieval constraints on central rule. Russia, indeed, as an Orthodox country, was accustomed to the complete subservience of church to state.

So we have three themes. The most obvious, illustrated first by France, is the extent of development of new state forms. The second, illustrated by the eastern powers, is the possibility of new countries coming into the western political orbit, indeed doing so directly in terms of diplomacy and war, but without a full western political background. And the third, applicable most obviously to France but also elsewhere, is the continued limits on the monarch's central powers.

The Sun King and His Heritage

France dominated Europe from the mid-seventeenth century until 1815. She suffered defeats from overambition, but no single power could match her military, economic, or cultural influence—an overwhelming combination. Her population, at about twenty million, was largest in Europe, her total (though not per capita) wealth greatest. Her cultural influence was unrivaled. Dramatists, particularly—Racine, Molière, and others—blended classical and Renaissance styles to create plays whose power and humor remain compelling. Art and sculpture also flourished. The style was basically classical, but with increasing flourishes. It was officially called Baroque, but for historical comparison a better word would be flamboyant classical, suggesting that maybe Renaissance styles were undergoing the same decadence as medieval Gothic did earlier with a passion for detail and gimmicks. But whatever the style, if France did it, it was all right. Nothing more clearly illustrates the French dominance than the effort of one monarch after another to imitate, even with reduced funds and on a lesser scale, Louis XIV's monumental, ornate palace at Versailles. The Nymphenburg in Munich for the kings of Bavaria, the Schönbrunn in Vienna for the Hapsburgs, Potsdam near Berlin for the king of Prussia—all were basically of maximum grandeur, classical design, and ornate Baroque decoration to mess up the whole image. Finally, French became the language of culture. Aristocrats in Russia into the nineteenth century might refuse to speak anything else—some did not even know Russian. All of which adds up to saying that any French developments would have wide repercussions.

What was done in government certainly had such repercussions, particularly since it corresponded to what any ambitious prince would want anyway—power. Beginning even before Louis XIV, particularly under the ministry of Cardinal Richelieu, who ruled on behalf of a weak king, traditional restraints on the monarch were torn down. Nobles were reduced in power. Richelieu destroyed many of their castles, particularly those surrounding Paris, so they could offer no independent military resistance to the monarch. Louis continued this policy by building up an elaborate court ritual that compelled the aristocrats to stay at his new palace at Versailles, where they played stupid games such as: who could sit closest to the king, who could watch him dress or even go to the bathroom. The old aristocracy, save for a few key generals, was thus separated not only from military but also from administrative functions and spent their time and huge sums of money rivalling each other in fancy costumes and parties at Versailles. And, as noted, they no longer sat in the Estates-General, the key medieval institution designed to preserve their aristocratic role as formal advisers to the king. Most seemed too busy with their posing and their games to care, though Louis faced a major uprising of aristocrats early in his reign, and his weaker successors found that the sweet life of Versailles had not completely sapped the desire to have an active voice in government. But during most of his reign Louis seemed to have effectively neutralized one traditional barrier to state power.

He also abolished the other traditional restraint, religion. He would permit no religious opposition to a Catholic France whose king was the religious as well as political leader. Hence he banned Protestants, revoking the Edict of Nantes. The result was that tens of thousands of Protestants, many of them talented businessmen and artisans, went to England or Prussia, making France's economic loss the gain of rival states. But Louis was no lackey of the pope. He steadfastly resisted papal interference, continued to name his own bishops, and even resolved theological quarrels. His main religious advisor, Bishop Bossuet, encouraged him to believe in a special religious mission in which the French, or Gallican, church, under royal leadership, could steer its own path.

No parliament, de-fanged nobles, a docile church—what would Louis do with his new power? It was all very well to keep the nobles busy at Versailles, but someone had to run the country. Here Louis, building again on what his predecessors had begun, made three essential innovations. The most durable was to increase the size of the bureaucracy under royal employ. France was a big country, and it was difficult for the king to know what was going on in the far corners, much less exercise any control. Louis began the practice of installing centrally-appointed officials, *intendants,* throughout the country to report to him but also to exercise controls over economic activity—road-building, recruiting, and so on. These were not, like their medieval predecessors, wandering officials. They were responsible for an area but rotated periodically so that they would not develop dangerous local attachments. The second innovation followed even more obviously from the past, and this was to increase the specialization as well as the size of the central bureaucracy. Military affairs, finance and economy, and justice were all clearly defined. This development, too, would continue as part of governmental rationalization.

Finally, Louis unwilling to rely on aristocrats, brought in "new men," mainly from the merchant class, to staff his government. These were people of great energy and talent, like Louvois in the military post, or Colbert, who set up the mercantilist apparatus. Here was a principle of great importance, involving talent rather than birth and drawing on the merchant group as an alternative pool of ability and a political counterpoise to the aristocracy. But this innovation did not last. It served Louis well, but he and his successors found it logical to make these new ministers nobles, which meant that they or their sons might side with the aristocratic tradition against undue central power. Also Louis, and his eighteenth-century successors even more so, found they had to sell a lot of staff offices, either for life or in perpetuity, because they needed money. This created more instant aristocrats and in no way guaranteed high quality bureaucracy.

This leads to the central point about absolute monarchy. Its purposes changed less than its structure did. Justice and prevention of internal disorder remained vital. Some new methods were introduced here; intendants, for example, administered regional systems of courts that further reduced the judicial powers of manorial lords. Rudimentary police forces were developed, even in villages, to reduce disorder. We have already mentioned that importation of grain to key centers like Paris during famines was vital for preventing riots, though Louis faced major internal unrest during the 1690s when harvests failed. The state's economic activity obviously increased; this was what mercantilism was all about. This system, combined with the desire to inhibit disorder, led to some rudimentary welfare measures. The state set up homes for beggars, horrible places whose main purpose was to keep the potentially dangerous poor, ill, and insane off the streets. Somewhat more humanely, the English monarchy, in its period of greatest strength at the end of the sixteenth century, passed the famous Poor Law which required each locality to take care of its poor. It may have aided some needy people, but it also bound them to their locality, for if they moved they would not qualify for aid. The point of all this is that new economic activity on the part of the state was not primarily intended for the benefit of the state's subjects, but rather to improve the state's tax base. And the state's tax base had to be improved so that the king could maintain his role as cultural sponsor, backing the famous playwrights or the new dance form called ballet, and building expensive baubles such as the massive palace at Versailles. But above all, the tax base had to be improved so that the king could make war.

Louis' expenses were as immense as his girth and his ambitions. He tried with limited success to tax the nobility directly, but here privilege of birth restricted his opportunities. The nobles would have rebelled if he had pressed them too hard. His only recourse was to add new impositions on the common people, which is why rebellion became increasingly frequent.

Though Louis left the royal coffers empty, he had enough money to carry out his main ambition, the very traditional ambition of the absolute monarch. He made war. He expanded French territory to the north and east. He invaded Germany; his troops destroyed every castle down the Rhine in a power play that could only be rivaled by the bombers of two and a half centuries later. He hoped to control Spain by putting a relative on the throne and another major war resulted. Louis got his relative on the throne, so that the house of Bourbon actually ruled Spain longer than it ruled France. (One of its scions has returned as the Spanish king.) Peace was restored right before Louis' death in 1715 by the Treaty of Utrecht. France had gained most of its modern boundaries. It had kept Germany weak and divided. It had broken an ominous dynastic alliance between the Hapsburgs and Spain, which potentially threatened France on the east and south simultaneously. In fact Spain, though its new ruler successfully introduced a few of the measures of absolute monarchy, was knocked out as a diplomatic threat. Ironically, Louis' gains must be counted against the great drain in France of money and morale. They must also be counted against the failure to use a really new government structure to more constructive, novel purposes.

What hemmed Louis in was a diplomatic-military combination that was not new but was to become increasingly important, a combination called balance of power. Beginning in Renaissance Italy, states had discovered that when any one of them threatened to become too powerful, an alliance by the others was an essential countermeasure. This policy did not work, of course, when the big powers broke into the confines of Italy, for no balance could pit city-states against France or Spain. But then the big powers themselves began to take over the strategy. It was first used against the Hapsburgs, when their dynastic alliance united Spain and the Holy Roman Empire. Lesser German princes (particularly Protestants), France, Sweden, and to an extent England, opposed this threat, which was one of the chief causes of the Thirty Years' War. But then France was the threat. Holland, Britain, several German states, and others allied against Louis, and again the system worked. France made some gains but was not to flex her muscles toward overthrowing the balance of power for another century.

The balance of power encouraged the development of Europe as a diplomatic entity—not united, indeed with its powers at loggerheads, but with the whole array of powers involved. Even though Italy and Spain were weaker and played lesser roles they were still in the system or liable to be touched by it. More novel was the increasing involvement of the Hapsburgs as rulers of Austria, Prussia, and ultimately even Russia. By the eighteenth century the old rivals, France and England, were at it again, fighting from North America to India. This time they sought continental help as well, allying with Austria or Prussia who in turn fought each other. Russia, in the meantime, was attacking Swedish holdings on the Baltic with such success that Sweden receded, placidly enough, into small-power status. Details of wars during this period need not delay us. They remained quite bloody in eastern Europe, where states like Prussia were fighting for basic power positions after having been insignificant duchies for centuries. In the West they were calmer, even langorous, and since the stakes were not too high, relatively few people got killed. But whatever the style of fighting, two points remain: First, war persisted as the basic function of the state, and states built their new structures of government primarily so they could make war more effectively. Second, the balance of power, triggered by France's rise and the receding of Turkish strength, brought eastern Europe into the regular diplomatic orbit of continental conflict for the first time.

We must reemphasize that diplomatic contact did not involve deep cultural or social contacts even though the upper classes could speak French and ape French fashions. Some western ideas were absorbed, although there was also suspicion of foreign influence. Artistic styles might be copied, and ballet, for example, soon became a Russian specialty, far from its origin in France. The East produced few painters or writers recognized in the western mold; this would await the nineteenth century. Fundamental differences persisted. Eastern Europe remained locked in a manorial system, with tiny cities and little manufacturing; its trade was largely confined to raw materials, grain, and timber, sent to the West and often handled by western merchants. But the eastern governments could and did copy the new western political model, which is what allowed them to enter the European diplomatic game. Absolute monarchy proved natural in Prussia, Russia and, with some hesitation, Austria.

Eastern Monarchs

There are several key examples of the political westernization of the East. As early as the sixteenth century under Ivan the Great, the Russian emperors, or tsars (caesars), had not only expelled the Mongols but had won control over the nobility. A belated but surprisingly effective system of vassalage was established. The nobles held the land on a hereditary basis, but in return for administrative and military service to the tsar. By the early eighteenth century no European monarch so effectively controlled his nobility as the Russian, and this excused the absence of any independent bureaucratic class. The nobles could serve to rule in the tsar's interest, and given the fact that Russia barely had an urban merchant group the tsar was fortunate that this system worked so well. There was, of course, no independent church to control the tsar, and tsars freely introduced changes in church ritual and liturgy. By the sixteenth and seventeenth centuries tsars were ready to open contacts with western traders—reviving a tradition of the Dark Ages—and a foreigners' quarter was set up in Moscow. Many disapproved of these innovations; one man wrote, brashly, "You feed the foreigners too well, instead of bidding your folk to cling to the old customs."

But the tsars saw strength increasingly in western terms. Their policy reached a height under Peter the Great (1689-1725), who had traveled to the West, working as a shipwright in Holland, and knew western ways thoroughly. He built the first Russian navy of significance. He introduced the western calendar and western styles of dress; he also required that beards be shaved off. He improved the legal position of women. These were measures designed deliberately to attack traditionalism, even if they were in many ways superficial. More basically, Peter enlarged the central bureaucracy and raised taxes. Like Louis XIV he further reduced the nobles' power, abolishing their Duma, or traditional council, and simply setting up advisers whom he appointed. Many new nobles were appointed on the basis of their bureaucratic service, while the old nobility was further pressed into military or bureaucratic duties. Many foreigners were imported to aid in administration and in trade and industry.

The comparison cannot be pushed too far, however. Peter was attempting a government-imposed alteration of popular mentalities as well as government reform per se—far beyond what Louis XIV had to do. Many of his efforts failed. Russians did not adopt a western commercial mentality; serfdom was not modified. Even among the aristocracy, groups opposing western influence arose, setting up a tension that still marks Russia.

Peter did resemble Louis XIV as an absolute monarch in his

organization of the state, in his primary reliance on taxing the common people, forcing many into deep misery, and in his belief that the primary purpose of the state was war. Peter's wars were directed at pushing the Swedes out of the continental Baltic coast. Here, for example, he built Russia's new capital, modestly called St. Petersburg. He also took over such Baltic states as Estonia—all of this representing Russia's first push to the West. With less success Peter also pushed southward against the Turkish empire.

The rise of Prussia involved less enforced westernization, for although a manorial country, Prussia was Protestant and Prussian intellectuals had long participated in western intellectual life. The Prussian rulers' formation of universities during the seventeenth century confirmed the link with the West. By 1700 the Prussian king was a patron of intellectual life, his star being the great mathematician and philosopher, Leibnitz. The court at Berlin was even known as the "Versailles of the North." But if the Prussians were at least partially westernized, their territorial base was far different from that of Russia. They began the seventeenth century as a small duchy, and it took a steady combination of diplomacy and war to build this into a European power. To provide a foundation for expansion, Prussian rulers promoted economic development in agriculture and industry alike. They were more diligent and successful here than any of the other absolute monarchs, because they had to be. By the eighteenth century, under the famous Prussian ruler Frederick the Great, the state was importing model factories from Britain, promoting the potato as a staple crop among the peasantry, importing iron plows, and improving roads and canals for trade. But while this had potentially beneficial side effects for the common people, the purpose was always the same: better economy meant a growing population and a larger tax base, and this meant more means for war. Prussia had the largest army per capita of any state in Europe, and great attention was given to its supply and training. Finally, Prussia developed a specialized central bureaucracy, with trained, honest personnel—indeed the best civil service of any European state. Prussia, through several monarchs, thus developed the typical apparatus of the absolute government.

All this paid off in the expansion of the Prussian state. In a war against Austria in the mid-eighteenth century, Frederick the Great gained the territory of Silesia. There followed a second war in which Austria was backed by Russia and France, neither of whom wished to see a new power in central Europe. But despite great losses among the troops, Frederick held onto his new territories. With a firm governmental base, Prussia was on the road to a century of successful expansion.

The Hapsburgs in Austria, having beaten back the Turks, found themselves rulers of a multinational empire including: Austria; Bohemia, which was largely Slavic in population; and Hungary, conquered in the late seventeenth century. Under the Empress Maria Theresa in the early eighteenth century, typical absolutist measures were taken. Noble power suffered as local aristocratic assemblies (called Diets) were deprived of their power to regulate taxes. Her son, Joseph II, who was far more radical, took over control of the Catholic church, appointing bishops himself and confiscating much church land and property. As in Prussia, a school system was begun for the common people, and laws were codified.

The basic principles of absolutism should by now be obvious. Reduce the power of the aristocracy, setting up a bureaucracy loyal to the monarch. Make sure the church is under control. Extend the economic functions of the state, usually through an essentially mercantilist system whereby the state intervenes to encourage and direct economic development and always imposes high tariffs on goods from abroad. Embellish the culture and pomp of the royal court. And always build up the army and have it ready for action. Even Joseph II, who more than most monarchs really took to heart the good of the common people, wanted to construct a huge army ready to add territory by beating Prussians, Turks, or anyone around.

Enlightened Despotism

By the mid-eighteenth century absolute monarchs were beginning to be called enlightened despots. This new term involved some significant changes in policy. As Joseph II's actions already indicated, the enlightened despot had no concern for enforcing a single religion. In both Prussia and Austria, and even in eighteenth century France, Protestants and Catholics alike were tolerated and even legal discrimination against Jews diminished. Several Catholic states expelled the Jesuit order as an insidious agent of papal power. The enlightened despots—Frederick, Joseph, and Catherine the Great of Russia—read the writings of the new philosophers and scientists, often inviting them to their courts.

They were genuinely interested in advancing knowledge and doubtless thought in terms of justifying their rule, not by traditional principles of divine right, but by their benefits to the people. But we need not take their enlightenment too seriously, save perhaps in the case of Joseph II. When Catherine the Great saw the first results of the French Revolution, out went the philosophers and in came rigorous state censorship. The enlightened despots, believing in reason, were more likely to codify laws and reduce excessive punishments for crime. And there is no question that their reading differed, and they fancied the enlightenment label. But the key word remains "despot." These people were only slightly modified versions of the absolute monarchs, and their fundamental definition of the state remained unchanged. The state was to serve to dispense justice, maintain internal order, and be ready to make war whenever opportunity presented itself.

Despite these traditional motives, absolutists and enlightened despots had gone a considerable way toward the creation of the modern central state—economically active; possessed of a larger, more specialized, and usually better-trained bureaucracy; and increasingly secular in purpose. But none of the states was modern yet. Louis XIV's ministers had to deal with provincial estates-general everywhere save in central France. His successors faced a law court called the *parlement* that claimed the right to approve or disapprove any law passed. Staffed mainly by nobles, the *parlement* won considerable popular backing. Frederick the Great made no attempt to cut into his nobles' control over their serfs. In this sense he not only failed to better the lot of the common people, which was of little account to him, but failed to put the central government in any direct contact with them. Taxation, military recruitment, even appointment of local pastors and teachers were done by the nobility. Frederick could not develop a bureaucracy separate from the nobility, so he had to confirm their powers to rule the country. Catherine the Great actually extended the power of her nobles, giving them new rights of punishment over their serfs, though Russian nobles remained more dependent on the central court than in Prussia. None of the absolute monarchs or enlightened despots really wanted to change the social hierarchy. They simply wanted fewer aristocratic restrictions over themselves as central rulers, but they did not always succeed even here. In central and eastern Europe, where manorialism was pervasive, this ob-

viously meant reliance on aristocrats for all local administration.
And since there were few towns and little trade, there was no substantial merchant class from which to draw new bureaucrats even
at the central government level. So here, too, aristocrats ruled.
They might be loyal as in Russia, specifically trained and efficient
as in Prussia (though there was a deterioration even here at the end
of the eighteenth century), or sloppy and inefficient as in Austria.
But they were the only ruling class available.

France had briefly faced a different opportunity, for there was
a different potential ruling class. Here manorial powers were
limited, and there was a large merchant group as a pool of talent.
But Louis XIV had exhausted his country and his budget. His
successors were weak and kept getting deeper and deeper into trouble as eighteenth century wars, though not bloody, increased the
national debt and usually ended in defeat at the hands of England.
France alone had to maintain a land army against threats from the
eastern powers, and sea power to be able to fight England; or at
least she thought she had to do this. The division of effort was expensive, and it made any war hard to win. France's participation on
America's side in the 1776 revolt against England finally brought
victory. But France gained nothing save the pleasure of seeing
England's nose tweaked, and her treasury was still further drained.
The moral was: in a system of absolute monarchy one had to have a
strong monarch and a string of successes for otherwise the system
wouldn't stand up. Nobles in France were soon demanding the calling of a new Estates-General, the first one in 175 years, to discuss
the state's need for new taxes. This in turn led to revolution and a
modern state. It proved that the representative tradition was not
dead. In combination, it was to show that absolutism, if put in a
different social context, could become a vital political motor for
change.

One ends with a mixed judgment on absolute monarchy. Vital
new structures were created, as in the bureaucratic innovations.
Broader popular change was stimulated, as in Prussian encouragement to economic development. But neither the purposes nor the
social context of the state was new. It took revolution to establish the
new social tie by which the central state could develop new contacts with subjects or citizens directly. And: even with revolution,
there is still a question about the extent to which the *purposes* of
the state change. Remember the list of functions: medieval
state—religion, internal order, justice, defense; absolutist

state—religion, justice, internal order, war; modern state—justice, internal order—and what? This we must explore further.

The Parliamentary Alternative

Two countries, England and Holland, did not follow the absolutist model during this early modern period. England, with only about 3100 government bureaucrats in the late eighteenth century, had a third the number of central state officials per capita as France (military excluded). Most administration was local, and these states simply did not do some things others regarded as normal. They did not, for example, provide police forces; this was up to localities or private groups. Most important, while England and Holland were monarchies, sovereign power rested in the hands of elected parliaments.

These were not typical government forms. The parliamentary states would soon find, in the nineteenth century, that a much more elaborate central governmental apparatus was essential. In this sense the absolutist model, besides being more common in the seventeenth and eighteenth centuries, is genuinely more important in pointing toward future political trends. But few countries today are without parliaments as well, even if many are shams. In western Europe and North America, the parliamentary and central state traditions were reunited in the nineteenth to twentieth centuries. In a sense, continental Europe (aside from Holland) followed one extreme of the medieval tradition in the early modern period, while England exaggerated the other one. In both cases, an uncomfortable remerger became essential, reviving the basic western political tradition. But of course by the time of this remarriage the central state and parliament alike had vastly changed. With England, from the later seventeenth century, we must talk of the partial, tentative beginning of the modernization of parliament, away from purely medieval forms; just as with absolutism we saw a tentative break from traditional monarchical growth.

England had had strong monarchs and a docile, though not inactive, parliament in the sixteenth century. In the early seventeenth century new rulers, the Stuarts, and a more awakened parliament broke this peaceful relationship. The Stuarts claimed divine right to rule; parliament thought that it controlled the basic right to rule and must pass on all laws. The Stuarts leaned toward Catholicism, terrifying the Puritans (who were well represented in

parliament) and many Anglicans. With religious and political conflict intermingled, it was not surprising that blood was spilled. The
second Stuart king, Charles I, got his head chopped off by the
parliamentary faction, and for a time England was without a king.
Vicious Civil war reigned in the middle of the seventeenth century,
with partisans of the king fighting parliamentarians in one definition of the war while in another Catholics and Anglicans fought
Presbyterians and Congregationalists. (The opposing groups were
similar but not always identical). Some historians have tried to
make this into a social revolution by showing that the rebels were
mainly merchants fighting royalist aristocrats, but this does not
work out so neatly as the result indicates. Civil war was followed by
the return of two Stuart kings who made the same mistakes their
predecessors had in attacking parliament and leaning toward
Catholicism. The final one, James II, was deposed in a bloodless
coup, the Glorious Revolution of 1688. This is what set up early
modern English government.

The new English government was a monarchy whose powers
were strictly limited primarily by rights of parliament; rights of ordinary citizens were not spelled out. There was a restricted degree
of religious freedom. The Toleration Act of 1689 granted freedom of
worship to all non-conformists (i.e., the various Calvinist sects),
although Roman Catholics and non-Christians were pointedly
omitted. But the king still ran the Anglican church, and this
remained the official religious body of the nation. This was, then, a
less complete religious settlement than occurred under the
enlightened despots a few decades later. Even the Puritans, for example, while free to worship, could not attend universities or hold
public office. In contrast, in more despotic and Catholic France a
Protestant, Necker, was chief minister during the last years before
the revolution. In other words, the ordinary person under the
English government had no more formal rights than his counterpart under absolutism, though here as elsewhere there was enough
religious tolerance to defuse this issue.

What was distinctive was the power of parliament. The new ruling
monarchs, William and Mary, had been designated by parliament. So
much for divine right or hereditary succession; though in fact kings
and queens continued to ascend to the throne by their birthright,
parliament made it clear that it, not the monarch, was the sovereign
body. The crown could not suspend laws, levy taxes without parliamentary consent, or maintain a standing army in time of peace.

But parliament itself remained a largely medieval body. The House of Lords, with full coordinate power, was still composed of hereditary aristocracy and top members of the Anglican hierarchy. The House of Commons was mainly aristocratic also, although here one had to run for office. Voting was restricted to those with substantial property, which let the better-established merchants in London and other key cities have representation but gave greater voice to people with land—not necessarily great landowners, but at least titled gentry. There was no clear class division in the Commons, though parties formed in the eighteenth century. Tories (a word derived from the Irish phrase meaning "live, o king") tended to back the monarch toward greater authority, while Whigs defended parliament's power. But neither party disagreed strongly, and there was more political jostling than political dispute. Elections were highly corrupt, since in any district there were very few qualified voters (and some districts, given the uneven population distribution, had almost no voters at all). It was easy to use personal prestige and bribes to win office; the position of election manager was created to make sure the bribes went to the right places, with a share for the manager, of course.

This was not, then, a modern government or a modern parliament. It worked for a century and a half. England was quite calm, after the storms of the Civil war, until the 1760s, when certain radical agitators and elements of the urban common people began to wonder again if they, too, should have political rights. The relative calm lasted until the 1790s. If a measure of good government is stability, England did at least as well as the efficient absolute monarchs and much better than the inefficient ones. This was also a government capable of evolution; if parliament was not yet modern, in the sense of being representative, neither was it purely medieval, in that it depended on elected personnel rather than designees of old regime estates or orders.

It can be argued that England's government, even without guaranteeing clear or equal rights to citizens, worked better than the absolute monarchies because of what it did not do. It was true, as noted earlier, that the central bureaucracy was small. Mercantilist practices were adopted in the levying of tariffs on imported goods and developing a colonial empire. Within this empire, colonials, even of English origin, had no rights of representation and were discouraged from commerce and manufacturing that would compete with the home country, being directed instead toward provision of raw materials. This would soon cause grievance and, in one colony, the future United States, revolt. But at home English mercantilism lay lightly on the people. There were no officials regulating how one made new goods or how much money one could earn. Without anything like a bill of rights, with only the vaguest hint of a constitution, England's people were freer than most of their continental counterparts. The English government did not enforce guild restrictions, like Colbert in France. It did not encourage potato planting, like Frederick the Great in Prussia (although potato growing spread widely by the spontaneous efforts of farmers themselves). It did help merchants, through the colonial system and by banning competitive goods, via tariffs— indeed the English cotton industry flourished in the early eighteenth century as a result of the new, prohibitive tariff. Although we must acknowledge that the government played a positive role in economic development, it was mainly through regulation, not active intervention. Hence England lagged in road and canal building, police protection, and a host of other activities which continental governments were beginning to take as a matter of course.

What this adds up to goes as follows: by historical accident, including religious divisions, a strong remnant of feudal restraints over the king, perhaps some sense even on the part of the ordinary Englishman (as expressed for example by the Levellers) that there were rights the state could not violate, England took a very different political course from that of the absolute monarchies. She could also afford this because of her island status. She did not need a land army. She did need a navy, and her navy recruiters, boozing and beating potential recruits until they were literally and figuratively at sea, were as ruthless as any French or Prussian army men; but the numbers involved were smaller, and these practices escaped general attention (at least until American colonials, subjected to similar treatment but conscious of rights by birth as Americans, began to howl). Without need for a land army there was less need for taxation, hence less need for massive bureaucracy. Perhaps here lies the key to parliament's success in winning control over the kings. France, with a strong parliamentary tradition, lost it for a century and a half and has been fighting about the proper legislative-executive balance ever since. Spain, with another strong parliamentary structure in the late middle ages, saw only brief returns to legislative rule; in Spain, if there is to be a balance struck, we must wait for the future, for all modern parliamentary efforts have failed.

England should not, however, seem the winner in all this. Her governmental structure was partly accidental, however much it would be admired by French, German, and other reformers later on. Like absolute monarchy, her parliament constituted a way station between medieval tradition and modern structures. Enough people, particularly those with property and clout, were able to vote to give a show of representativeness. Unquestionably the monarch was restrained, and unlike any of his continental peers he could not rule by fiat. But a modern constitution, modern rights of the individual, modern notions of representation were all absent, and would have to be fought for about the same time the absolute monarchies were being attacked at the end of the eighteenth century. In the meantime, corrupt parliamentarians could play their game of getting elected and switching from one meaningless faction to another. To most people the only advantage of this whole system was that it cost less than absolutism and implicity set forth areas, such as technological innovation, out of which the government would keep its nose. Add to this a sufficient dose of mercantilism and colonialism to protect the trading interest, and one has a legitimate picture of a happy kingdom for at least three-quarters of a century, which is not a bad track record.

Even so, the English parliament was unable to control a mad George III who probably needlessly precipitated war with the American colonies in the 1770s, where concessions would have sufficed, and ran the war so badly that a ragtag colony of less than three million people won its independence. But, this example aside, let us not forget that the tradition of the growing central state, named absolutist but not free from constraints and controls, was the more powerful current. We must jump ahead here, by way of suggestion; it is obvious that the English system, deliberately or not, worked marvelously until about 1870, and it was still being copied by new states like Bulgaria (or, even later, by India in 1947). Then it began to break down, because the central government tradition had not remained strong enough to deal with the exigencies of a modern, developing society.

To return to the late seventeenth century: if England and Holland, which actually had an even fuller parliamentary setup than England, were oddities, both they and the absolute monarchies had a long way to go. We talk of absolutism but then immediately recognize that however much Louis XIV claimed full power he was hemmed in by all sorts of restrictions. The same applies to the English parliament, for instead of representing citizens it represented upper propertied groups. It was based on documents signed by a king but not on a constitution which assured quarrels over who had what power in the future. But if its system was not modern, at least England was not dependent on the quality of a given ruler, which was fortunate, because her eighteenth century kings were on the dull side. Kings chose their ministers in accordance with the latters' ability to get majority support in parliament, and this system worked fairly well. As one measure: French kings were no worse than English in the eighteenth century in terms of qualification of rulership, but this was not saying much, and because the French system depended on hereditary traits it was in trouble. A system of ministers subject to the king but responsible to a wider group was England's greatest informal governmental contribution at his time.

From the two main strands of political development in the early modern period come two main conclusions. First, neither strand touched the common person deeply; neither revolutionized society or intended to. We must look elsewhere for sources of basic change, even though new political forms had evolved. Second, the obvious: if we recall the persistence of both strands, plus the qualifications within each, we can realize that the western political tradition was being preserved. Strong parliaments, if not typical, existed as powerful examples, and the more pervasive trend of centralization could be modified by this tradition. The West retained political flexibility with political options.

The Cultural Revolution

The seventeenth and, to a lesser extent, early eighteenth centuries were busy periods in the arts. We have mentioned the baroque style, the modifications of Renaissance classicism, in architecture and sculpture. As in so many periods, one can see some correspondence between politics and culture, in part because the absolute monarchs became the leading art patrons. Monumentalism was obvious, from Versailles to its later imitations. On the stage the classicism of Racine was a link with the past in its copying of Greek themes and Aristotelian rules of drama. Put on for the court of Louis XIV, drama, like architecture, caught some of the spirit of absolutism, stressing themes of human power and the ability of great men to control their destiny or fall into deepest tragedy. Painting was similarly grandiose but less original. Classical themes were stressed, along with flattering portraits of monarchs and idle aristocrats.

This was a rich culture in many ways, and the French continue to cherish the seventeenth century as a founding period in their literary development. We see the cultural-political link very clearly here, as governments established academies to standardize the French language and reward particularly prominent and accept- able writers in all fields; these academies still exist. One result is that literary French has changed less than any other language since the seventeenth century, which is a debatably desirable result of absolutism in culture. For all the variety of this period, it is dif- ficult to pinpoint durable new styles or modes of thought expressed in art or writing.

The same goes for theology, save that religious writers, though often brilliant, were definitely on the defensive by the century's end. Actually, even apart from the impassioned writings of Puritans during the English civil wars and other embattled Christians, who were sure they knew the path to salvation and equally sure that everyone who disagreed was doomed to damna- tion, the seventeenth century was by many cultural standards a religious period. It produced in the Catholic Church a great number of saints, both male and female. The monastic-conventual tradi- tion endured. Christian humanism was revived by St. Francis de Sales, a bishop who was both mystic and organizer of charitable works. In France, mysticism, the belief in personal contact with God in a fleeting emotional experience, underwent unprecedented revival. In France also was St. Vincent de Paul, founder of a variety of orders, most notably the Sisters of Charity which aided the poor at the time and have survived to the present day. There were even throwbacks to the most extreme Christian traditions, like the new Trappist order that opposed the secular society of Louis XIV and whose members were forbidden to utter a single word except during specific periods of prayer. Catholicism, in other words, was alive and kicking. Blaise Pascal tried to combine scientific work with a set of personal confessions that stressed man's need for divine guidance. But perhaps more typical and equally brilliant in his own way was Bishop Bossuet, advisor to Louis XIV, who urged the rights of monarchy while sternly lecturing the king on his holy duty to defend the true religion (i.e., drive the Protestants out) and also on obeying Christian principles in his rule. Bossuet also attacked the new science and spirit of skepticism, and he was right from the religious standpoint, though powerless to stem the tide of interest. We have politicized prelates, mystics, and Christian philosophers—a rich yield for a century not known for its religion.

Western society was becoming wealthy enough and urban enough to afford all sorts of cultural activities. Trappists deliberately recalled early hermit-monks. Racine, although creative in his own right, would have been pleased to be linked with Euripides in a classical drama series. English drama was actually more innovative after the tradition of Shakespeare and the dour, repressed period in which the Puritans had ruled the country. Bawdy plays, known under the general heading of Restoration drama, drew aristocratic audiences. Aristocratic costume increasingly became an art in itself, and displays of men's legs in stockings and silk knickers, powdered hair or wigs, and of women's elaborate gowns with maximum *décolletage* all showed that tastes were ranging freely and widely and that the upper class enjoyed a variety of entertainment.

Even though much of this culture was episodic, we must not forget variety. We must not forget the perpetuation of classical traditions in literature, or hedonism in aristocratic taste. (After all, even a century later, somber New England revolutionaries would carefully powder their hair, although, admittedly, they abandoned wigs.) We certainly must not forget the ongoing strand of Christian thought—in popular belief, but also high-level theology. People like Bossuet and Pascal would produce clear, convincing arguments against the leading intellectual innovation of the day.

The Scientific Revolution and the Enlightenment

8

THERE WAS NO QUESTION that the intellectual innovation, now the coming trend but soon to be the dominant trend, was the scientific revolution. We must realize that precisely because there *was* a revolution, the majority of intellectuals were still doing things related to tradition, as in classical art, theology, or bawdy drama. Well into the eighteenth century most intellectuals ignored or opposed the change going on around them. Science did not automatically convert the cultural world. What happened in the seventeenth century is: first, that the older tradition of interest in science came into its own, without so much competition from theological interests; and second, that amazing new discoveries were made within the scientific world. The contrast with the earliest age of science, the late Hellenistic period, is obvious. Then, rising interest in religion made abstract science suspect; here, ultimately, the reverse occurred, and scientific advance began to put the theologians on the defensive.

The key point was new discovery, for in contrast to most medieval and Renaissance science, scientific leaders were able to break away from the classical tradition and make their own findings, often at complete variance with inherited wisdom. The classical tradition of interest in the empirical investigation of nature had been continued from the Middle Ages. Here we have one of the key strands of western intellectual endeavor. But this was a new age, which is why we use the word "revolution." Science and the attitudes accompanying it began to take pride of place for the first time in any period of intellectual development, and the implications of science were quickly applied to a new world view in subjects as diverse as politics and criminology.

Empirical Scientists

The origins of the scientific revolution were complex, partly because science was not entirely new, partly because diverse approaches were possible. Let us take three figures to illustrate what was going on.

In Italy, Galileo Galilei (1564-1642) first applied both the telescope and microscope to scientific work and experimented with an early type of thermometer. Here, then, was an empiricist, ready to experiment and observe directly, and also a man who illustrates a key principle of the new science: the steady improvement of investigatory instruments. Air pumps to measure the weight of gasses, barometers, pendulums for clocks, and reflecting telescopes (this latter the invention of Newton much later in the century) indicate the range of technical advance now possible. But Galileo was no mere technician. On the basis of his own observations, he accepted the half-buried conclusion of Copernicus, that the earth moved around the sun and not vice versa. He proved experimentally that Aristotle had committed an elementary error in saying that heavy bodies would fall in a vacuum more rapidly than light bodies. In other words, he moved toward a proper understanding of gravity. Discovering also that a pendulum of fixed length, whether it takes a long or short swing, consumes the same time for its swing, he anticipated even further the Newtonian laws of motion. So we use Galileo as an example of an empirical scientist, inventor of new technical means of investigation but also applier of mathematical principles to his observations. Unfortunately we must also recognize him as victim of the new toughness of Christianity (in this case, the Catholic Church) against departures from accepted methods of learning. Needlessly, the principle of the earth as center of universe had been taken into Christian doctrine; if this aspect of accepted truth were attacked, what else might be? So Galileo was brought before the Italian inquisition as a potential heretic and compelled to renounce his belief. His actual sentence was light: three days in prison and recitation of seven penitential psalms for three years; a threat of torture was never carried out, nor meant to be. But it remained true that Catholic countries were not the productive areas of scientific inquiry.

However, Galileo (and hosts of fellow scientists, from Scandinavia south) gradually made it impossible to believe in the old Ptolemaic theory about earth as center of universe. This was vital to further astronomical knowledge. It was also a major new intellectual principle in itself: the ancients might be wrong, and provably wrong. Galileo's further empirical work only confirmed that there were new ways of getting at truth, and this was really the foundation of the scientific revolution.

A slightly different approach was taken by Réné Descartes, also in the early seventeenth century. Descartes was a rationalist, and although he conducted some experiments on anatomy and such, his main weapon was reason. Of all the pioneers of the scientific revolution, he was the most direct heir of the Greek and the medieval approach. For with him, one begins with material constructs and reasons out the whole nature of the universe. His first construct was: "I think therefore I am." This meant that human beings, himself included, really existed. God's existence was proved soon after, as follows: human beings exist, and they can conceive of a perfect being; no perfect being can be conceived of unless he really exists, because otherwise he would not be perfect; therefore an omnipotent God has to exist. This kept Descartes out of trouble with the church and allowed him to forget about God in most of the rest of his philosophical constructs.

All of this may sound a bit silly, but Descartes has to belong among the founders of the new scientific revolution precisely because he continued the tradition of using logic to create elaborate generalizations. Social scientists today, heirs of this intellectual tradition, do much the same thing. (One of the most famous twentieth century economists, the Austrian Joseph Schumpeter, regularly read Aquinas and Descartes to improve his logic). Their data are vast, but when they come to apply them they assume that they can be ordered into simple logical principles, so that when a government does X the result economically will be Y. We are still part of the rationalistic tradition of the West, and logic is our first tool of reason. Maybe this is unfortunate, but it's a fact.

Descartes is more famous for his approach to past knowledge than any positive conclusions, such as how to please the church by showing God is a logical necessity. He started with doubt, a departure from the medieval tradition, and went on to define modern rationalism, adding up to four rules for his method: "The *first* was never to accept anything for true which I did not clearly know to be such . . . the *second* to divide each of the difficulties under examination into as many parts as possible, and as might be necessary for its adequate solution . . . the *third*, to conduct my thoughts in such order that, by commencing with the objects the simplest and easiest to know, I might ascend little by little . . . to the knowledge of the more complex. . . . And the *last*, in every case to make enumerations so complete, and reviews so general, that I might be assured that nothing was omitted."

Descartes' followers, the Cartesians, were legion in France. Their collective innovation was to continue this new spirit of boastful doubt, in which if an individual was not convinced that a bit of inherited knowledge was true he would simply start afresh. This was what Galileo had done in principle, but the Cartesians translated it into a whole manner of philosophy. Thus not only medieval theology could be torn down but also classical scientific learning. The Cartesians, from Descartes onward, also made major strides in developing mathematics, the obvious tool of the rationalizer. Ultimately, the mathematical approach, combined with greater empiricism, such as Galileo's, produced the modern scientific method.

Our third figure, whose main work was published in 1620, is Francis Bacon (no relation to Roger). Bacon, like Descartes, made few actual scientific discoveries; in this sense he is not in the same league with Galileo and other experimenters of the same era. But Bacon for the first time set forth a philosophy of empiricism. The way to knowledge was not through abstract reasoning, but through repeated experiments which, when they produced a predictable result, represented new truth. One had to pile up data before one knew anything. And one set of conclusions would prepare a new set of experiments leading to more advanced conclusions, and so on. This was the *inductive* method, as Bacon named it, opposed to Descartes' more traditional, if potentially explosive, *deductive* method. Bacon, like Descartes, said that all the old conclusions and established authorities had to be set aside. Scientists must begin anew but by experiment. He also added other vital points. One was that scientific advance would steadily expand the boundaries of human progress. Less egocentric than Descartes, he nonetheless set out a clear idea of advancing knowledge, the most direct, early statement of a belief in progress. Next, he said that expanding knowledge could lead to progress in other aspects of human life. New science could bring technological improvements that would raise production and make the whole human lot easier to bear. It was a long while before this idea was accepted, for aside from a few contacts in navigation, where mathematics and new compasses could link, scientific advance had little to do with technology. Ultimately, Bacon was right, and his pragmatic approach was in use before much real progress was made. French philosophers by the mid-eighteenth century for example, prided themselves on scientific knowledge but were also interested in the workings of machinery and craft techniques, even though most ordinary people had never heard of science and were working as they had for centuries. Finally, Bacon wanted scientists to get together in institutes where they could cooperate and communicate with each other. Here his ideas bore fruit, for from England to Italy by the mid-seventeenth century there were state-supported organizations, like the Royal Society in London, that held regular meetings and received communications from members too distant to attend.

The interest in science boomed from the mid-seventeenth century onward, which is not the same thing as saying that it always progressed. Clergy and landlords, with time on their hands, fancied themselves major contributors to this new stream of knowledge and wrote papers on the latest new butterfly they had seen or a rock formation that to them was unique. The new societies served as much for upper class showmanship as for serious science. But the trend was important. It showed that science was the new thing, spreading beyond the genius level. And the new discoveries, if sometimes silly, could be assembled by a superior intellect into useful knowledge. In the eighteenth century, the Swedish scientist Linnaeus began a vital scientific process, that of labeling biological specimens, both plant and animal. The earlier work of amateurs was essential to him.

This was well after the initial steps in the scientific revolution. Galileo, Bacon, and Descartes do not add up to a neat picture of intellectual cohesion. But they do indicate a mutual scorn for received knowledge. What had previously been said about the physical universe needed to be re-reasoned (Descartes) or exposed to direct experimentation (Galileo-Bacon). This was an immense break with the medieval-Renaissance approach to knowledge. The new emphasis on empiricism also broke with classical tradition, despite the credit that must be given to those ancient scientists who conducted direct observation or experiment. There was already, in the combination of the new approaches, the budding of a new intellectual outlook which would blossom more explicitly a

century later: knowledge could expand; man could fully understand the world about him; man's reason could stand alone. This
was revolution, but like all such upheavals, ties to the past, were
maintained such as: the stress on reason, logic, and a man-centered
universe.

Later Advances in Science

The later seventeenth century saw steady advance in scientific
knowledge. Biology tends to be shortchanged, but the gains here
were great. Microscopes allowed new knowledge of invisible, uni-
cellular organisms. The English doctor, John Harvey, first
demonstrated the circular movement of the blood in animals and
humans, together with the role of the heart as the "central pump-
ing station." This was literally the first major advance in
anatomical knowledge since the Hellenistic period. It did not lead
to new medical practice, for here again the gap between theory and
application was considerable. But amateur scientists, collecting
specimens and examples from China to the New World, did add
new drugs to the ordinary doctor's pharmacopoeia. One new drug,
quinine from Peru, was of immediate use. Furthermore, knowledge
from Turkey and China concerning inoculation for smallpox, using serum from infected animals, was tested in the early eighteenth
century and was soon spread widely. Formal vaccination awaited
the end of the century, but limited inoculation reduced the in-
cidence of the epidemic disease even earlier. Once the new mental
set was achieved, major new experiments could be made with resultant advances in knowledge. More humble practitioners could test
what had been known elsewhere, with a lot of resulting disasters
but some major gains. The unworkable theories were gradually
separated from the workable.

The great developments in the later seventeenth century in
astronomy and physics became the basis for calling what happened
an intellectual revolution. Advances from Copernicus and Galileo
accrued steadily, as observation showed elliptical instead of
circular orbits of planets about the sun. In such work telescopic
observation was combined with mathematical calculation, the
classic scientific method. The *pièce de résistance,* the culmination
of previous theory and methodology, came with Isaac Newton at
the end of the century. Through his study of falling bodies, balls
rolled on inclined planes, and also through telescopic observations
of the behavior of planetary bodies, Newton had an empirical basis
for his work. But he was even more open to the older western scien-

tific tradition, that of applying logic, in this case mathematical logic, to his observations. Hence his statement of three basic laws of all physical motion: every body preserves its momentum in a straight line unless forced by outside pressure to deviate; change of motion is proportional to the impressed force and takes place in the direction to which the force is impressed; and to every action there is always an equal reaction. Newton added a full statement of the workings of gravitation—traditionally he was first impressed with the force of gravity when, while he was sitting under a tree, an apple fell on his head. Newton showed not only why not to sit under apple trees but how gravitational pull kept the planets in their orbit around the sun, and the moons around their planets, for gravity varies with mass, and the same laws of attraction and motion apply throughout the universe as well as in humbler spheres such as bouncing balls or falling apples.

These discoveries were of fundamental importance. They were largely correct. They erred, as Einstein was to show in the twentieth century, in their continued assumption of undue rationality and what one might call, solar-centrism. Newton assumed that the whole universe behaved in a uniform fashion and that, even within the solar system, more uniformities existed than is the case. There is no reason to take cheap shots at Newton. His theories are great and mostly accurate with respect to the solar system. The only reason to mention that there were some inaccuracies is because of the continued assumption of complete rationality in the physical universe in our own world view. For Newton, planets might not move in neat circles, as had long been recognized, but their motion was entirely calculable mathematically. All matter moved according to the universal law of gravitation. Newton, although not claiming to be a philosopher, set down these statements: all laws governing the physical world are simple and consistent; they are absolute, and will apply to bodies which we cannot experiment with as well as those with which we can; and they can be determined by a combination of inductive and deductive reasoning, that is, by conclusions from observed phenomena that can then be made into rules applicable to phenomena that cannot be observed.

This was all new in terms of the specifics demonstrated, but straight out of western tradition in its use of logical reasoning. It was easy to believe that the same methods were applicable in other areas of study; and this was to be the principal work of the next century. Newton's world was non-mystical, graspable by human reason. Why could not everything be thus?

John Locke

To translate this scientific revolution into other areas of knowledge, we must add another figure, actually consonant with Newton although not a scientist: John Locke. Locke (1632-1703) was an important political philosopher, hostile to absolute rule and a defender of toleration and individual rights. He believed that government owed duties to its citizens and even assumed the right of revolution when these duties were not fulfilled. Sovereignty, in other words, went beyond parliament to the people themselves. In nature people had been free and equal; they formed civil society only to protect themselves. They did not have to elect a parliament directly—Locke was not a literal democrat—but they did have ultimate powers to defend their life, health, liberty, and possessions. Here, obviously, in combination with the political settlement of 1688 in England, was inspiration for limited government and popular rights. Locke's philosophy would be copied almost word for word in the Declaration of Independence and would be widely noted in France and elsewhere.

But Locke's basic philosophical contribution went deeper than this. We can start with the political aspect. Men were basically good and rational. For Locke, man was born without original sin, with a blank mind (a *tabula rasa*). Man learned by experience, plus some rather vaguely spelled out principles of internal reasoning. The result, normally, would be a rational man, capable of understanding the world around him and possessed with freedoms through which to exercise his abilities—natural rights, Locke called them. All of this relates to the science of the day. The scientists showed that the world was rational and that they, at least by observation and deduction, could fathom its workings. Locke translated this into a general statement of human nature, that men could operate by their experience-*cum*-reason to get along without faith or any outside aid. The invocation of natural rights was not new—medieval theologians had used it, as we have noted—but it took on new connotations when nature was seen as predictable and benign. What Locke and other seventeenth century political theorists did was to give natural rights the place previously given to divine rights. What was previously man's due because he possessed an immortal soul was now his due because he possessed, however humble his state, a spark of reason. In both cases there were laws and rights with which the secular state could not interfere. For the modern political theorists, now that the church could not be counted on to protect these rights, constitutions and limits on central state action, such as parliaments, were essential for a proper policy.

In all this we have continuity of tradition in a radically different setting. Limited government, not a new idea, was to be limited in new, purely secular ways. But we still have not reached Locke's central contribution, not the one he was most famous for, but the principle most indicative of a really new way of thinking. This principle was enunciated not in his political writings but in his discussions of how people know what they know. We have already indicated that Locke rejected the medieval approach which posited knowledge by faith, which might then be followed by reason. He also rejected Descartes' idea of innate knowledge. Hence the idea of the newborn human mind as a blank sheet of paper, to be filled in by rational experience. There was faith here that the world around man was so ordered that experience would lead to a rational mind; Locke himself had no doubt of this. He went one vital step further, breaking with the past more decisively even than in his rejection of faith as a means of knowledge. He said, explicitly, that there were things men could not know and did not have to know. How was the world created? There was no way of knowing. Locke professed belief in God and would have been willing to grant divine creation, but this did not really come under the scope he attributed to human knowledge. Locke was making explicit what people like Newton had kept implicit. Newton could explain how gravity worked but not why; indeed Newton attributed this sort of thing to "occult qualities" and left it at that. The point was to understand how things worked, not why, for concentration on "occult put a stop to improvement" of science.

All this, Locke noted, was in a way profoundly pessimistic. Aquinas would have been quick to agree. Whole areas of inquiry were being abandoned because man's reason could not encompass them. Locke, and certainly Newton, would not have disagreed with Aquinas about the limits of human reason, but they would have disagreed that there was anything else, such as faith, to add to it. More important, the overall tone of the scientific revolution, and of Locke's work, ignored the theory of human limitations in favor of a resounding statement of how much man could know. He could understand the physical world, which operated in harmony with the rational principles of his own mind. He could grasp a proper political order, for natural rights were based on rational understanding of what one person should do with another—hence an officious government did not have to butt in all the time.

The scientific revolution then, consisted of: immense new discoveries in physics and biology; of a related belief that nature was orderly and that human reason could progressively grasp more and more of its workings; of a denial of the necessity of faith. God might still be around, but he was just part of the rational order, a clockmaker, as would be said in the eighteenth century, who put the works together and then let them run. Divine intervention, miracles, and faith were nonsense. And finally, the scientific revolution resulted in the statement that there were things that could not, but also need not, be known. Fundamentals of theology as well as trite angels-on-pins debates were abandoned. Learning was rigorously secular, with science as the primary course and the study of human affairs of growing concern. By the 1680s, thinking was redefined, though within a western context. What we are supposed to think about, how deeply we probe into creation or an afterlife, were radically altered, despite vehement resistance from theologians who saw how subversive this all was.

Do you wonder how the universe got started? Probably, sometimes. But can you imagine taking courses that have this as their central subject, as opposed to something that will get you a job, like ceramic engineering, or even history? Medieval universities would see a course dealing with the first question as the capstone of knowledge. They may have been right, but they no longer preside. This was part of the knowledge revolution.

The Impact of the New Intellectuals

The new science and related philosophy made little difference to most people for many decades. A growing band of thinkers, like Locke, who were not formal scientists, used new knowledge to attack Christianity. Pierre Bayle, a French Protestant by origin, used rationalist techniques to claim that many Biblical miracles and other claims of the Catholic church were frauds. The Renaissance principles of textual criticism were vital here, as well as the kind of intellectual self-assertion that had been building up for centuries. All of this created great fuss and furor, because governments and probably most ordinary people liked their truth simple and the way they first learned it. Bayle was driven out of France to more tolerant Holland.

There was some movement toward popularizing the new

science per se among literate groups, mainly aristocrats. This was done in a way that would not explicitly disturb established beliefs: isn't it interesting that the earth revolves around the sun, or would you care to take a peek through my telescope? This was a new fad, and while it spread widely and even made some popularizing authors a good bit of money, it did not add up to a change in the mentality of even the upper class. A few individuals might understand the basic principles of what was being taught and be subverted from traditional belief, but by 1700 this was still rare. Among the popular classes, even merchants whom we assume had an affinity toward science, there was no time for the new stuff. After all, the Reformation had just been assimilated. The spreading of the new principles was the work of the next century, the age of Enlightenment, not the revolutionary century itself, when a genuinely new science and mental outlook was born.

One final point. There was no simple, automatic link between a new science and a new technology. We have noted that technological developments still took place slowly. We can now add that they were mainly the fruit of artisans, people working with their hands. In 1733, James Kay, a British weaver, invented the flying shuttle for a new loom. Previously two weavers had worked a loom, one shoving the thread one way, one the other. Kay's device allowed the transverse weaving to be done by foot pedal; hence one weaver per loom and a massive increase in productivity. This invention, which could ultimately be linked to steam engines, had important economic implications for ordinary people. It resulted from the boom in domestic manufacturing we have already described, and it furthered the boom. But this technological advancement had nothing to do with new science. Kay may or may not have been literate, but he certainly derived no benefit from Newton or Locke. In other words, while the early modern period offers us new business and production forms, new means of government, and a real revolution in knowledge, we must beware of linking the innovations. There had to be felt a need to think about the world in new ways before new knowledge would spread very far, and this involved further changes on the part of governments and common people alike.

The Enlightenment

The Enlightenment was primarily based in France, but original thinkers from England and Germany contributed to it. Its influence extended not only to those countries, but to Italy, Spain, and as far east as Russia, where a few aristocrats took Enlightenment principles seriously—Catherine the Great, as we have seen, played at being a new kind of monarch until her absolutist principles were challenged. The Enlightenment is, then, the first intellectual movement since Christianity to be able to claim European-wide scope. For that matter we must now include the Americas, for North American thinkers made notable scientific contributions throughout the eighteenth century, sending all sorts of data to the Royal Society in London, and at the end of the century offered adaptations of political and ethical theory as well through pens such as Franklin's and Jefferson's. There was serious interest in the Enlightenment in Latin America as well, particularly in the more urbanized areas of Columbia, Venezuela, Argentina and Brazil.

As with Christianity, degrees of penetration varied. Russian aristocrats, though seriously rethinking their society and deciding that the Enlightenment principles of technical improvement and material progress were good ones, did nothing to better the condition of their serfs. They did not even change their methods of production, meeting in solemn agricultural societies that discussed new agricultural advances but never went further. Italian and Spanish interest was more serious, but did not penetrate as deeply as in England or even Germany. North American intellectuals were fully ready for the Enlightenment, whereas in Latin America there was less interest, because urban concentration was smaller and the hold of the Catholic Church greater. Nevertheless, the Enlightenment's greatest contribution, given the attractiveness of its principles and the growing political contacts among European and New World states, was its ability to create a sense of shared cultural values.

When we say shared cultural values, we mean among intellectuals and related aristocratic or priestly dilettantes who were interested in formal thought. We must emphasize this point, which is crucial to the question of how much of the world, defined in terms of the common people, was really western. Unlike Christianity, the Enlightenment started with formal thought and upper class backing. Countries like France, with a big merchant class and relatively free peasants and England, with a proportionately larger merchant class, freer peasants, and artisans as well, would obviously differ from East Prussia in its reception of Enlightenment ideas. The question of literacy is involved, for in western Europe almost a third of the people could read by 1800. In eastern Europe a seven percent figure would be generous; even many Orthodox priests could not read.

The Enlightenment created a common set of values. We probably still live within the value system the movement produced. Most modern science, modern social science, and modern political theory (from western capitalist-liberalism to Russian Marxism) are Enlightenment derived, even though they differ. This is not the same thing, however, as saying that the value system was universally accepted, even by intellectuals. Even early on, the Enlightenment produced formal intellectual opposition. Some Russian intellectuals suspected it as a form of western subversion. In the West, movements arose by 1800 that contradicted everything the Enlightenment stood for. One such movement was called Romanticism. We still have intellectuals fighting the Enlightenment, and maybe they are right. But the point is that in some areas such as science and the rational nature of man, they have to deal with Enlightenment problems. The Enlightenment did not create uniformity. It did create a common base of argument.

So we have two points about the Enlightenment before we have even tried to define it. Point one: along with politics, it pulled Europe and the Atlantic fringe of the New World together more than ever before into a common western civilization. In America, where literacy was higher than any place else in the world in that century, intellectuals and many common people could understand the principles of British politics and the ideas of the Enlightenment; they were part of this world, which is obviously why they fought a revolution in the name of these goals. Europe was more tenuously spread to the East, from the standpoint of a common cultural language. But absolutist could talk to absolutist; an aristocrat from Russia (who often toured in France for the cultural gains) could talk to his Italian counterpart, both speaking French, about some aspects of science or political theory. Western civilization, then, had grown at one key level. Point two: the Enlightenment's hold must be understood as non-universal, as traditional Christians or newer kinds of critics took aim at its basic principles. This debate has continued, and we stress the Enlightenment only because, on the whole, it continues to define the nature of the debate.

And, of course, the Enlightenment evolved. Thinkers even in

the eighteenth century varied widely, though we will not go into great detail here. The Enlightenment tradition in the nineteenth century was subjected to even greater alterations. So when we say the Enlightenment set our ongoing world view, we mean this in very basic terms. We have found out, or think we have found out, that some Enlightenment principles were overly simple though we may reach the same conclusions about man's rationality by different means. We have, one must admit, become a little more uncertain than the optimistic eighteenth century thinkers about the rationality of the universe and the inevitability of progress. But Enlightenment thinkers were not stupid. They knew there was tragedy in the world; they knew that some people, at least, were not rational and had to be treated in special ways. We must simplify their thought to get at the main points, but the reminder that they were subtle, sensitive philosophers is truly in order. Voltaire, hearing of a Lisbon earthquake that killed thousands, wrote a poem of despair about nature's cruelty to man and man's inability to control his own destiny. A Christian could have written much the same. But Voltaire recovered some of his optimism, believing that most people most of the time could plan on progress by understanding the workings of nature and using their own minds. Furthermore, even in despair, Voltaire lacked the dubious comfort of turning to a God who might cause earthquakes but some how would make things all right. Voltaire, though he professed what was called deist belief in God as a first principle, a God who set things going and then butted out (deism was a tactful transition to outright atheism), did not believe that there was a God to help man. We, too, having changed various specifics of Enlightenment philosophy and added a great deal of knowledge, can modify, perhaps permanently doubt, the optimism that characterized the movement as a whole. But most of us retain its intellectual framework.

Twentieth-century sociologists, defining "modern man or woman" (they would admit that many do not qualify as fully modern, even in advanced industrial societies), use the following characteristics: rational, believes in science, open to change and confident in progress, materialistic, politically conscious and insistent on at least a potential voice in government, confident that education will improve people. The test could have been drawn up in the eighteenth century; indeed it was drawn up by the Enlightenment philosophers who collectively defined the new intellectual outlook. Most people, the ordinary peasants and artisans, did not share this mentality then, but one of the aspects of any new restructuring of intellectual world view is the study of its effect on the people. This permeation of a new outlook which would, like Christianity, undoubtedly be mixed with a host of ongoing popular traditions, constitutes much of modern cultural-social history.

So we have a major movement here, in its essence quite simple. The Enlightenment consisted, first, of an effort to spread understanding of the principles of the scientific revolution to a broader public. Voltaire, for example, studied in England and then wrote to his countrymen about the discoveries of Newton and Locke. The Enlightenment, in other words, was not in itself a revolution but the application of a revolution; the new world view had developed the century before, through science. But the Enlightenment did not just spur the popularization of science. Its second contribution was to apply scientific principles to the study of man and society. Here, it created its larger view of the world.

Most obviously, the Enlightenment began to experiment on man. Scientific advance continued in the eighteenth century, spreading steadily to new areas. Chemistry joined the lengthening parade of sciences; for example, Lavoisier discovered the functions of oxygen. There was more work in biology. But most interesting to us is the beginning of the scientific study of man's mind. Early psychologists speculated on how man learns, how his mind could go astray, what made him tick. In medicine proper, although many doctors continued to mouth the learning of the ancients, there was new understanding of improved means of child delivery (even though the germ theory was decades away, an English doctor properly noted that the doctor with clean hands would be much less likely to create disease in mother or child, though too few of his colleagues heeded his advice); and there was new, experimental study of gout, the characteristic disease of the overfed upper classes, and how to cure it. The eighteenth century offered no breakthroughs like those of Newton, but science remained the key to the intellectual approach of the age. Respect for its ability to penetrate the orderly laws of the universe was basic to the whole Enlightenment movement. And growing interest in applying science to people in terms of theoretical understanding of human functions, showed the Enlightenment's desire to make new knowledge relevant to man.

The Enlightenment figures in France were called *philosophes,* which literally means philosophers but can be taken here to have a broader connotation, for many *philosophes* were not formal thinkers or scientists. Respect it but don't do it, constituted their approach, and it saved them a lot of work. They were translators of the implications of the scientific revolution into societal terms.

This translation involved several basic principles. First, and least surprising, it was secular. God was no longer needed, though most *philosophes* professed the vague deism we have already described. Some, inconsistently, also believed that religion was essential for the masses who were not yet enlightened and maybe never could be, to keep them obedient with the promise (which the *philosophes* themselves did not believe) of better things in the world to come. But, particularly as the Enlightenment gained momentum in the later eighteenth century, there were professed atheists as well. Even before this the Enlightenment was fiercely hostile to the church and its teachings. The church filled men with superstitions. Priests talked of miracles that offended the orderly workings of nature. They told man he is evil, when in fact he is good. And politically the church was part of a system of privilege and intolerance that was unacceptable. "Clericalism, that is the enemy," shouted Voltaire, and few would have disagreed. The Enlightenment was not, then, just secular, but was militantly against established religion, particularly in France. In Protestant countries, with a less ritualistic religion and, often, some degree of tolerance, this vehemence was absent, but here too the Enlightenment focused attention on this earth, on man's power. God might be allowed to exist, but he had no active role; heaven, priesthood, and faith ranged from irrelevant to downright dangerous.

Equally important, in terms of setting new ground, was the firm belief that knowledge could steadily advance. In a way this seems of lesser importance than secularism, but it was just as fundamental. It distinguished the Enlightenment not only from Christianity but also from Renaissance humanism. Enlightenment figures might use Greek examples, but only as examples. They knew that they knew more than the Greeks did. Man's reason could steadily build greater knowledge. And the way to start this was by looking at recent advances, doing one's own experiments, and above all using one's own reason. At the end of the eighteenth century, a particularly optimistic *philosophe*, Condorcet (who ironically was to have his head cut off in the French revolution for not being radical enough), wrote while in prison a statement of man's steady progress. Of course there were achievements in classical times, while the Middle Ages represented a church-caused retrogression. (Religion was the tool used to escape the logical dilemma of why man had not progressed steadily; it wasn't too solid as historical explanation, but evil priests somehow had deceived a rational people into a dark age.) The Renaissance was an improvement, but look what's happened since. And above all, look what will happen in the future. Things will get better and better. The whole human breed may improve. We can expect more knowledge, more comfort, better political systems, more of all the good things. This is a sharp break from classical thinking, which believed that history moved in cycles, and obviously from post-classical thinking that had constantly looked to the past for truth. The belief in progress was indeed fundamental to this whole intellectual movement.

The key to progress was man himself, who was rational and perfectable. The means of progress was education. Take a criminal, said the noted Italian penologist Beccaria: don't just torture him or tie him up, but teach him. And, with some lag, new prison systems were built that did not just incarcerate but pretended to offer reeducation through work and moral lessons. Children obviously should be educated. So should native peoples. For all men were basically alike in their sharing of human reason. Again, as the Enlightenment took hold and became more radical, some, like Mary Wollstonecraft in England in 1792, wrote about equality for women. Hence systems that kept people unequal were evil. Aristocratic privilege, slave-holding, and the like were bitterly attacked. A few minor *philosophes* in the 1780s were outright socialists, wanting equality of property, but this was not typical. Elimination of legal inequality was the major focus.

Since man was rational nothing should restrict his liberty. He should be free to believe in a religion or not, to try a new technique or not. Voltaire was a particular devotee of tolerance, rousing French opinion in defense of Protestants condemned to death or torture for their beliefs—and he often won his point. By the mid-eighteenth century this current of belief was becoming too strong for a troubled monarchy to ignore. The enlightened despots of Prussia and Austria avoided the problem altogether by granting outright religious freedom. Claims for freedom of economic activity drew less notice. But *philosophes* attacked barriers on trade, guild restrictions, and manorial systems that prevented workers from leaving and working where they chose. Mercantilism generally was disapproved because it limited free economic activity, and therefore protected inefficient operations that cost people more money. Let people compete freely and the result will be the best products at cheapest price; this was the preaching of Adam Smith, the Scottish economist. A general dislike of mercantilism also stemmed from the *philosophes'* internationalism, their belief that as all people are basically alike and good, the evil of war can be avoided. Liberty, equality, fraternity—the French revolutionary motto was all ready.

Underlying the *philosophes'* social and political views was not only faith in man's rationality but also a related belief that the social as well as the physical world operated by simple, orderly laws. Set up a clear constitution, as the Americans did after their revolution, and you have all you need for an orderly social world in harmony with nature. We have already discussed the fact that this concept was not new. What was new that was the faith now put in the idea that just a bit of tampering with existing evils, a bit of reordering on simple, natural lines, would make things all right.

The Enlightenment outlook was completed by one other interest: an interest in material as well as moral/political progress. There was no reason for man not to advance technically, as he applied his rational mind to improving the procedures of the past. Wealth was good, material pleasures and comforts to be desired. The most ambitious publication of the Enlightenment, the *Encyclopedia,* masterminded by Denis Diderot with hosts of collaborators, gave great attention to the current methods of manufacture and agriculture (mainly of the craft and village type) and, to a lesser extent, how they might be improved.

The thinking of the Enlightenment can seem pleasantly uncomplicated, though as we have indicated this would ignore the serious wrestling that the major philosophers did with problems of injustice and misery that went against their basic beliefs. But it did have a basic flaw that was to be pointed out in the later eighteenth century, first by David Hume, a Scotsman, and then, more complexly by Emmanuel Kant, a German. For all its innovation, and probably precisely because it was so new, the Enlightenment had retained a vital element of the past that made no sense when exposed to the scrutiny of the movement itself. This was the faith (and faith it was) that society could be ordered on the same principles as nature. Said Hume, scientists have shown us that nature operates according to simple natural laws, but who has done more than assert that society does so or can do so?

This was really a rather fundamental attack, and opponents of the Enlightenment have used it for almost two centuries just as people in the Enlightenment tradition have sought various ways to patch things up. Two approaches were obvious. Political theorists could stop talking about "natural law," and justify freedom and equality in terms of the good of the individual, the good of society and so on. By the late eighteenth century this was precisely what a new school in England, called utilitarians and headed by Jeremy Bentham, was doing—setting up society rationally according to what fit the good of the greatest number. Abstractions like natural law were needless. One could, in fact, study society directly; the late Enlightenment spawned the beginnings of sociology, economics, and other means of figuring out how society worked. Most, in fact, assumed that order could be found, so that the social-scientific tradition and the Enlightenment remained closely intertwined; the difference being that the Enlightenment naïvely assumed society was orderly whereas that social scientists insisted that society must be studied before they could assert the orderly laws by which it operates. In any event, however criticized and modified, the basic faith of the Enlightenment went forward. This may make it seem simplistic and philosophically indefensible, but most great belief systems, like Christianity, have gone forward with huge logical flaws—one thinks of the Christian problem in reconciling an omnipotent God with any belief in human free will. The point is not logical consistency so much as the overall cast of mind.

The Spread of the Enlightenment

Enlightenment writers were keenly conscious of publicity. They wrote for as wide an audience as possible. People like Voltaire were the first writers, in fact, to make a living (in his case a fortune) selling books to the reading public, as opposed to depending on a noble sponsor who would subsidize part of the effort. A biting style, a keen sense of the issues of the day, and the obvious basic faith in man's reason—all account for the Enlightenment as a dissemination device. The great Encyclopedia, almost the equivalent of a *Summa* in bringing together all the knowledge of the day, was a compendium destined for the information of a wide public. Successors, such as the Encyclopedia Britannica, first published in 1771, have continued the belief that the spread of factual knowledge is good in itself, because it gives man's mind the information required for rational thought and further study.

In those days, reading ability was limited. And we must not forget that some who could read were actively hostile to Enlightenment principles. If a number of bored priests joined new discussion groups, most of the Catholic hierarchy was opposed. Indeed the Enlightenment faced active censorship in many areas, though ironically this may have called more attention to its ideas than would otherwise have occurred. There is no question that key Enlightenment publications received unprecedented sales and went through numerous editions; no question either that a given book was often read by many people. Many aristocrats, some merchants who were not too busy making money, others in the middle level of society, such as lawyers or doctors, learned of the Enlightenment through books and accepted the ideas they read.

Books were not the only means of dissemination. Enlightenment thinkers did not go out on the stump; this awaited a more radical generation, from the 1790s onward, who wanted to speak directly to the people. But there were a number of informal gathering places where new ideas could be discussed. Salons, or receptions in houses of fashionable hostesses, were used for meetings. The new ideas were so clever, some of the authors so witty, that these social gatherings were often intermingled with the spread of the Enlightenment. And while most of the guests were aristocrats or upper class merchants, a clever but poor young fellow might gain admittance—and new ideas—as well. Gatherings in the salons, particularly common in France and Italy, varied in seriousness. They ranged from the largely social, where a serious idea would be almost a *faux pas,* to formal discussion groups focusing on politics, science, or a mixture of subjects. Shading off from this were the flourishing scientific academies; these obviously dealt with new ideas, though ironically they served a social function as well and remained, like the salons, largely an upper class preserve.

In England, and to a lesser degree on the continent, coffee houses were new meeting places for discussion of ideas. Here, the latest pamphlet might be read even to illiterate businessmen or artisans. Some coffee houses had regular meeting days to discuss science, others focused more on literature, but few could avoid some comment on political ideas.

Newly created periodicals and weekly newspapers combined the discussion method with the dissemination through publication. Most of the periodicals were fairly expensive, though they sought to explain new scientific and philosophical discoveries in layman's terms. But a "penny press" burgeoned as well, particularly in England and America where literacy was particularly high. Franklin's "Poor Richard's Almanac" was a famous example. Here up-to-date news, summaries of scientific articles, along with gems of homely wisdom were mixed in an Enlightenment brew.

In east central Germany and in Spain and its colonies, the new ideas did not reach below the aristocracy and the occasional merchant or professional man. Literacy was too low, discussion was too strictly confined to highly fashionable salons and scientific societies. But for western Europe penetration remains unclear: aristocrats and educated priests had access to the ideas, and although the Enlightenment attacked privilege and religion, there were some who wanted to show off or who lacked a vigorous sense of class interest and toyed with the notions anyway. A smaller number, such as the Marquis de Lafayette who, although not terribly bright participated in three revolutions, acted on their beliefs. It was the priest, the abbe de Siéyès, long a participant in a provincial discussion group, who wrote the pamphlet *What Is The Third Estate* before the French Revolution, attacking privilege and defining what would become the basic principle of middle-class politics—that those who worked and produced should run the country.

Obviously, by reading and through coffee-house groups, important elements of the middle levels of society grasped the new ideas. Some businessmen, lawyers, and middle-rank state bureaucrats found real attraction in the new principles. Few would oppose them, but we must not assume that a united middle class was aroused by the Enlightenment to new kinds of behavior. Some thought the present order was acceptable (some even hoped to gain an aristocratic title); still more, active innovators in business, simply remained apathetic to formal thought. The Enlightenment was to help define the middle class and its political interests; most, although not all, Enlightenment thinkers were from middle-level social backgrounds. But we do not know the precise equation between class and intellectual movement.

We have mentioned the uncertain link between new science and new technology. It becomes no less complex as the eighteenth century wears on. Few inventors were educated. Scientists tended to learn more from inventions like the steam engine (which taught much about the behavior of gasses) than inventors from Enlightenment ideas. James Watt, the steam engine's inventor, was an artisan whose firm made precision instruments for scientists at the University of Glasgow. His engine owed nothing to existing science, but maybe he had picked up some sense that nature could be harnessed, that material progress was desirable and possible; this is as close as we can get to a link. The *Encyclopedia* described craft procedures; it rarely speculated on how they could be improved beyond the most up-to-date existing techniques, and certainly suggested no forthcoming technological revolution. As to the businessmen who exploited the new machines (for actual inventors rarely had great business acumen and either formed a partnership or went broke), they might trumpet their belief in material progress after they had made their fortune, but it is difficult to see that they were motivated by the new ideas to be profit-seekers. The same goes for the merchants making new money in the expanding slave trade or other forms of commerce. The ethic of self-improvement and material progress would motivate more people in the nineteenth century when the example of success through innovation was clear in practice. Enlightenment ideas would become the expression for the new industrial middle class; they did not create this class or cause its activities.

Enlightenment impact on politics was much more definite. Aristocratic reformers in France, like Turgot, chief minister in the 1770s, sought to apply Enlightenment principles to remove barriers to economic development, reduce noble privilege, and urge a tax on the noble class. Certainly many lawyers, disgruntled that they could not get good jobs in the state bureaucracy, found Enlightenment attacks on the established order appealing. Or, conversely, even if successful they might be motivated by these attacks to criticize the existing system. On the other hand, there were businessmen who had no interest in political change and seemed oblivious to the world the Enlightenment projected. In other words, Enlightenment political impact was not to any one social class. In the first days of the French Revolution a minority of Enlightenment-inspired nobles, plus many priests, joined middle-level representatives in asking for reforms. The latter were, with rare exceptions, far from being radicals by the standards of the Enlightenment. Only events of the Revolution itself helped equate Enlightenment and middle-class politics.

Finally, how far below the merchant and professional levels of society did Enlightenment ideas reach? How much influence did a strolling speaker, a heated discussion in the local tavern, or a cheap newspaper passed from hand to hand or read aloud, have on artisans and peasants? We can safely say the influence was nil on peasants. They might be discontented, but their discontent did not need ideological inspiration or expression. Even artisans were rarely reached by the new ideas, though here there would be individual exceptions, not only in the political sphere but where a craftsman might take great interest in reading of the latest advances in, say, astronomical knowledge. But there clearly was some contact. Enlightenment political theory became increasingly explicit concerning what was meant by the equality of man, and with writers like Jean-Jacques Rousseau in the 1760s and 1770s, not only privilege of birth but undue inequality of wealth were coming under attack. Rousseau's own political solution was a bit idiosyncratic, calling for an almost mystical *general will* that by definition could never err; but popularized, it looked like Rousseau was invoking a general right to vote. Here, along with earlier Enlightenment principles, was something that could make disgruntled artisans articulate, conscious of new rights. There were clear signs by the 1780s that some craftsmen had done their homework, not only in revolutionary France but also among groups urging popular rights in Holland and England. Even among lowly American seamen, during this same decade, came articulate expressions of Enlightenment philosophy. An American sailor escaping from a British prison during the 1790s shouted "Kiss my arse," to his former guard. The prison commander shouted back: "Do you know that it is a great crime to break one of His Majesty's locks?" Which elicited a less pungent but Enlightenment-like reply from the successful escape: "I told him that I did not regard His Majesty nor his locks. What I was after was my liberty."

Was this unknown sailor influenced by new ideas? Were the craftsmen who circulated petitions for new rights aware of philosophy or expressing traditional popular ideas of equality which we have seen in earlier uprisings and which had taken political tone as early as the seventeenth century Levellers? The 1790s provided a new revolutionary setting. The radical ideas of the Enlightenment provided ammunition for the more articulate elements of the lower classes. It is doubtful that many had been aware of the ideas before or were motivated by them in early actions such as the storming of the Bastille. But this is open to endless debate, and Enlightenment ideas definitely spread to elements of the lower classes after the French Revolution began.

What Caused Change?

We have identified three currents of change in the century-and-a-half after 1600. Governments altered functions if not purposes. They seem the least likely agents of broader upheaval, for they also enforced the existing social hierarchy and might even strengthen it. But we cannot discount the possibility of unintended effects. The spread of domestic manufacturing and of capitalist trade brought new wealth and new contacts to many sorts of people. Here is the more likely source of broader changes in popular behavior. Finally, the Enlightenment deliberately sought change; our problem with it has not been intent but role, as we do not know how far the new ideas spread or how deeply they were absorbed to serve as motives for action.

Which returns us to the point made earlier. Most people lived in 1750 about as they had in 1650, and a good bit more calmly than their ancestors had in 1550. The peasant mentality had not been dented. Artisans expected to make things by the tried and true methods of old. Most businessmen—though there was an innovating group—were really not capitalists at all, but simply hoped to live respectable lives at the same level their fathers had. Hence they shunned risk and innovation.

By 1850 we see a western world bursting with change. In some countries half the people had moved to new areas to live, mainly cities. Industry was becoming the major source of wealth. A new middle class was bent on further innovation. Enlightenment ideas were being used to justify this material upheaval, and also to urge political change against the established institutions of monarchy and even the traditional parliamentary structure of Britain. The United States was independent with an Enlightenment-style government. Even here there were pressures for further change as state governments were forced to become democratic, and there were growing stirrings against the continuation of slavery in the South. Revolution after revolution occurred throughout the western world fostered by groups with diverse goals, some wanting to turn back the clock and others going forward—but unprecedented by any measure.

By 1850 a large, growing segment of the population of western civilization was modern in outlook. This is why Enlightenment ideas—belief in science, progress, individual reason—now made sense. The premodern period, in its intellectual revolution, its economic and political changes, was vital in setting the stage for the transition to modernity and in giving it direction. But we need at least one other ingredient or else we cannot understand how a society that, like all agricultural societies, still valued stability, accepted an unprecedented current of change.

Suggestions for Reading

A number of textbooks cover the period 1500-present. The most durable has been R. R. Palmer and Joel Colton, *A History of the Modern World* (New York, 1971); for a different approach and a more up-to-date bibliography, Eugene Weber, *A Modern History of Europe* (1871).

For diverse approaches to the life of the common people in the period, Peter Laslett, *The World We Have Lost* (1965); Pierre Goubert, *Louis XIV and Twenty Million Frenchmen* (New York, 1969); Philippe Ariès, *Centuries of Childhood: A Social History of Family Life* (1962); and David Hunt, *Parents and Children in History* (1970).

A general history of the seventeenth century is G. N. Clark, *The Seventeenth Century* (1947); see also A. L. Moote, *The Seventeenth Century: Europe in Ferment* (1970); General coverage of the next period is found in M.S. Anderson, *Eighteenth Century Europe* (1966).

On political structures, E. N. Williams, *The Ancient Regime in Europe* (1970), and Max Beloff, *The Age of Absolutism* (1954). On revolts early in the period, and social-political development generally, (1550-1660), Henry Kamen, *The Iron Century* (1971). On specific countries. J. B. Wolf, *Louis XIV* (1968); B. H. Sumner, *Peter the Great and the Emergence of Russia* (1950); Christopher Hill, *The Century of Revolution, 1603-1714* (on England) (1963); Sidney Fay, *The Rise of Brandenburg-Prussia* (1937). On enlightened despotism, Geoffrey Bruun, *The Enlightened Despots* (1967) and J. G. Galiardo, *Enlightened Despotism* (1967).

For general coverage of intellectual development, Jacob Bronowski and Bruce Mazlish, *The Western Intellectual Tradition From Leonardo to Hegel* (1960); see also G. H. Sabine, *A History of Political Theory* (1955). The new intellectual mood is brilliantly captured in Paul Hazard, *The European Mind: The Critical Years (1680-1715)* (1953); see also Peter Gay, *The Enlightenment* (1967). For the scientific revolution, Marie Boas, *The Scientific Renaissance, 1450-1630* (1962); Herbert Butterfield, *The Origins of Modern Science* (1965); Thomas Kuhn, *The Structure of Scientific Revolutions* (1962); and Alfred Hall, *The Scientific Revolution, 1500-1800* (1954). On art, V. L. Tapié, *The Age of Grandeur* (1960). Concerning economics and European expansion, Eric. E. Williams, *Capitalism and Slavery* (1944); C. H. Wilson, *England's Apprenticeship (1603-1763)* (1965); E. Hecksher, *Mercantilism* (1935); C. E. Carriggton, *The British Overseas* (1950).

The Industrial
Revolution

9

THE INDUSTRIAL REVOLUTION consisted of roughly a century of transition and upheaval. Old ways of thinking and behaving showed remarkable tenacity. The new society, prepared as it was by intellectual and politico-economic change, took a full hundred years to solidify. The most convenient label for this period, the early industrial revolution, is misleading in one respect. Most people, even at the end of the period, were not involved in factories either as owners or workers. Most were still peasants or artisans. Their lives had been changed by a conversion to a market economy, in which one produced goods to sell, sold to strangers, and had one's work controlled by strangers. This was truer for artisans than for peasants, but a commercialization of economic relationships touched countryside and city alike. Factory industry was simply the most extreme form of this process. The early industrial revolution also embraces a century of protest against change, which is one of its defining features. After about a hundred years, people seemed to settle down or give up. Protest by no means ceased, but it took new forms and was directed mainly toward gains within the system, not against the system itself. In the process of revolution political structures had been profoundly altered; the changes involved in the development of absolutism or parliamentary government were minor in comparison. Enlightenment ideas had been refined to serve the variety of groups spawned by the new society.

The dates of the early industrial period must be flexibly

stated. Western Europe, where the common people had already developed a distinctive society, was the source of change and therefore the chronological leader. From 1750–1850, give or take a decade or two, will fit France, western Germany, the Low Countries, and the United States, as well as Britain. Southern Europe, though firmly in the tradition of western civilization, had not made the adaptations in popular culture or political structure of the North. Their economics were far more backward at this time. Italy went through her century of transition from about 1850–1950; Spain and Portugal, like the Balkans, are still locked in the process. For eastern Europe, ready to copy the West even if only superficially, the bulk of change occurred during the century after 1850. This is a messy chronology, but there is no help for it. Basic social developments simply occurred at different paces. Of course, the precise process varied from place to place, as we will see. Countries industrializing late, like Russia, could copy earlier western developments and change on a more sophisticated basis, at least from a technological standpoint. Finally, as the obvious final preliminary, industrial society even once formed was not a homogeneous product. Differences in the process of change combined with various pre-industrial traditions to produce various government structures, economic forms, perhaps even popular outlook. And here, for later consideration, is a vital question: Is industrial society "western" no matter where its geographic location? Early industrial society was a western product. It could only have happened in the West (which does not of course mean that we must judge the West as being a superior place; for maybe we'd be better off without industrial society). The causes and early results of industrialization corresponded to western tradition. But what of the later imitators, Russia, even Japan, which industrialized successfully without question but which had not previously been part of western civilization? We will hope to find out, but must begin by showing what the process was about where it first occurred.

Causes of Change: Demographic Revolution

Remember that there are three pieces on the board already, toward the mid-eighteenth century: intellectual revolution, and significant political and economic evolution. We add now another piece: the population revolution. Between about 1750 and 1800 population in most western countries doubled, a staggering increase without precedent in human history. Population rose massively in other areas too, such as most of Asia, but without the same effects. For in the West, population revolution created new attitudes and economic structures derived from the earlier peculiarities of western society.

The causes of such a huge change have naturally received extensive analysis, and there is still no agreement. Some old chestnuts have been tossed on the garbage heap. Population revolution was not the result of better medicine—an early explanation popular among doctors—because there wasn't better medicine around. Medical care and sanitation improved in the nineteenth century, though the rapid growth of cities could slow the process; this helped keep the revolution going but did not start it. Smallpox vaccination may have helped a bit, for this was introduced in England in the eighteenth century, but this is at best a minor factor.

There are four elements intertwined in the population revolution in North America, Europe, and Asia: weather, disease, food, and for Europe/North America at least, sexual habits. The weather in the northern hemisphere was unusually warm, the warmest since the eleventh century. This helped population growth by encouraging good harvests and the possibility of growing a greater variety of crops—such as peach trees in Scotland, to use an extreme example.

There was a cyclical decline in plagues after about 1730. This happens from time to time in human history as people build up immunities to certain germs and viruses This was one of those times. In Europe, stronger government controls in countries bordering the Mideast, the traditional center of plague, may have helped a bit. The germs regrouped, and there were new plagues (cholera in the 1830s and 1860s, for example), but by this time there was better sanitation and the population surge was not deterred by short-run epidemics. Food supplies increased. This was particularly due to the introduction of the potato from the New World. The potato had been known to Europe since the Spanish brought it back from the Andes in the sixteenth century, but peasants had long feared it as a novelty, because it was not mentioned in the Bible, and for a host of other good peasant reasons. But governments pushed it. More important, it produced more calories per acre than any other crop. When peasants faced a bad grain harvest it was tempting to convert, or when they had unusually large families and wanted to give everyone a bit of land (the potato could support a family of parents, three children, and one animal on a single acre) they might convert. Once the potato was adopted it could support an immense number of people that even cheap grain like rye had not previously maintained. Countries such as Ireland that converted massively to potato growth had huge population increases. In Ireland's case this brought tragedy, for the potato, too, proved susceptible to disease. In 1846-1847 millions of people died in Ireland or emigrated during this disaster, and the country's population has never recovered its peak size. But England, France, Prussia, and later Russia, switched to the crop without abandoning grains, so they were hit but not decimated. Overall, the potato is the most important single factor in northern Europe's population surge. In the south—Spain, Italy, southern France and Germany—and also in Asia and Africa, American corn provided a similar new food and supported new population growth.

Finally, the element of fertility affected the population revolution. An old calculation held that in England, eighty percent of population growth was due to fewer deaths (less plague, less famine) and twenty percent to more births. Recent historians have urged more attention to fertility, some even claiming that people having more babies accounted for the majority of new population. Why should people have more babies? The argument runs that the spread of domestic manufacture (part of the "first" industrial revolution and the expansion of commerce) freed children from traditional northwestern European restraints on birth. Children who could earn money on their own as spinners and weavers didn't have to wait for papa to die or retire in order to have sexual intercourse and/or get married. Hence more babies and more population. Actually, there were other reasons for fertility to increase. Better nutrition increased female regularity of ovulation, so conception was more likely. We know that the age of puberty began to drop in this century. Boys' choirs, for example, were harder to recruit because voices began to change at sixteen instead of eigheen, and girls' menstruation occurred earlier as well. So fertility undoubtedly did rise.

But decline in the death rate was still the key. We know that fertility had increased by the 1780s, because marriage rates had risen and the age of marriage fallen while illegitimacy rates rose as well (beginning from about two percent of the total, in a prudish peasant society, to a peak of eleven percent of the total around 1870, when they leveled off until the 1960s). With less famine and disease more people lived to reach childbearing age. There was a crucial reduction of deaths of infants from fifty percent to about thirty-three percent by the early nineteenth century. More people living to childbearing age meant more children born; more children born meant still more children born in the next generation, and on and on for over a hundred years in Europe.

Population growth and its causes have raised three additional questions. They can all be debated, but here we'll be arbitrary and simply offer answers. Question one: was this simply a growing population living in increasing misery (until 1850 or so, or later in places like Russia, after which everyone admits that things got better)? One sees the Irish peasant with his acre, surviving on the potato; not dying, but in far worse health than his ancestors. No question that most people were badly off by modern standards, but all the evidence is against the picture of comparative decline, except, of course, in special calamities such as the potato famine of the mid-nineteenth century. There is evidence that not only did more people live to childbearing age but that the life expectancy of adults went up, though slightly, in this period. Declining ages of puberty and higher fertility both suggest better nutrition. This was a stronger people than Europe had produced before, and new vitality in turn played a role in economic innovation and political upheaval alike. By the early nineteenth century, in fact, people began to get bigger. Breast size increased, but foot size grew even more rapidly. The average male Frenchman, five feet in height in 1800, was 5 foot 6 in 1900.

Question two involves mentalities. Here, while not agreeing with the fertility advocates on their precise statistics, we can accept some of their conclusions about new attitudes involved. Western Europe created, four centuries earlier, a society of sexual restraint and late marriage. Obviously, this involved a great deal of self-control and authoritarian upbringing, plus ongoing supervision by the village. These were now loosened. With more sex, at earlier ages, people began to develop a greater sense of personal independence and a desire for sensual expression of self. Here, indeed, was one of the first signs of popular modernization of personality. Rising illegitimacy was a sign of this, though many a girl must have expected a purely traditional relationship to result only to be cruelly deceived. Within marriage sexual intercourse became more frequent. Previously concentrated in the spring months, May and June, it now spread out more evenly throughout the year (though we still retain traces of the traditional conception cycle). One side effect was, again, stronger and brighter children, for babies born in

February—March, the traditional glut months, receive poorer nutrition and less parental care in their first crucial six months of existence, and so are on the average, in peasant society, smaller and dumber. The traditional cycle was based on economics, for women had little economic function in late winter and yet could be ready to help with the planting after giving birth in late winter. Now, with domestic manufacturing, work was spread more evenly. And very gradually, marriages began to be based on emotional attraction as well as economics; family culture began an evolution that is still continuing today. The clear point is that there was more sex, probably with increasing pleasure for both partners, which reflected a new sense of self, and perhaps a new need for love and pleasure in a period of immense change. The development occurred within marriage as well as outside it. Without a doubt, the major direct result was the birth of more children.

The Impact of More People

Finally, what of the effects on society of a population boom? With growth rates of one hundred percent every half century, institutions and individuals were faced with unprecedented choices. People could, quite literally, have rolled over and died, claiming that there were no new means of support and that the population had to shrink back to its previous size. But the expanded food supply and the new attitudes developing forbade this approach. Yet the pressure was immense. An aristocratic family counting on sending one son to military training suddenly found new competition, for there were far more sons in the aristocracy as a whole. Some would be tempted to try new things, such as monopolizing still more state positions. A businessman suddenly found himself with twelve children. It was not surprising to have had such a number born, but raising them all to maturity was an overwhelming prospect—a spur to change. So the businessman might expand his operation, and bring in new machines, to be able to bring up his sons and daughters in middle class fashion. Even at the lowest levels of society, where population growth could bring suffering, there was a new incentive for peasants to accept the domestic manufacturing system or go to the city to seek new kinds of work.

Previous changes in western civilization had prepared most levels of European society to accept this massive challenge by further innovation. Hence the spread of domestic manufacturing and new inventions, designed to improve the system—Kay's flying shuttle is an early example. These advances led gradually into a technological revolution. With governments ready to undertake some new functions, with an Enlightenment ideology that would back any move toward progress and freedom from tradition. Europe could absorb the demographic revolution and, though with great anguish, turn it into a creative step toward a whole new way of life. This, then, was the final push to modernity.

Commercialization

The commercialization of western society stemmed from elements of every social group. They might be pushed into the system against their will at every level also. Aristocrats commonly hated the necessity to produce cash crops for a distant market and profited little by it. Many lost their estates, and gradually the class declined. Traditional lawyers and merchants were faced with the need for new practices or suffer a relative decline compared to rising industrialists. They might choose respectability in the old sense, and so decline with dignity. But the real burden was on the poor, who had to endure new taxes, rate hikes from the local miller, dependence on shops for bread; they could easily be victimized. With the average family growing, the push to adopt new money-making practices was intense, and people were forced to involve themselves in a commercial network they might heartily disapprove of.

But there was a "pull" factor as well, given the fact that innovation might mean not only survival but success. Western society had long been property-conscious, things-conscious. This was the basis of the popular culture that arose in the late Middle Ages. The culture had been combined with the traditional peasant stability ethic. But stability was now gone, given the population revolution. So some could take the other element of popular outlook and work to build a modest little empire that would take care of a growing family and also meet some older culture norms. Population alone would have been a purely push item, as it was in Asia. Given peculiar western values, it could create some pull factors for some people too.

Hence, the spread of new business practices was not simply a matter of governments or aristocrats forcing the common people into new ways of doing things, although governments did impose new taxes and individual aristocrats did try to make their estates more efficient. Nor was it simply a matter of merchant-capitalists taking a greater whack at the common people. Indeed, many merchants disdained new practices, though it is true that the number of money-grubbing capitalists increased. But modern commercialization was not simply a singular phenomenon imposed from above, or else it would have been resisted more firmly. Ordinary types participated. Four common examples, briefly stated, were: peasant, artisan, domestic manufacturing worker, and servant.

With a growing population to feed and with expanding cities, it was not impossible for an alert peasant to realize he could improve his lot and better secure his family's future by producing more for the market. This normally involved greater specialization in a few crops particularly suited to the area, replacing the effort to grow everything one's family needed. It might involve new tools, such as the use of a scythe instead of a sickle for harvest, which increased labor productivity by fifty percent. Above all, it meant, to the peasant mentality, acquisition of more land. The pushier peasants began to press their poorer neighbors to sell out, and some did because they needed cash and thought they could do better elsewhere. The expansionists also farmed on village common lands, to the great anger of most peasants. Economics in the villages had long been unequal, but now they became more so, as population growth created a landless class. At the other end successful peasant farmers carved out a spread that would produce crops to sell to the city and require the employment of labor. The middling peasant still existed, defending older ways of doing things, but very slowly he would be squeezed out.

By 1850, the countryside of western Europe was increasingly divided between owners and non-owners, a gross violation of village tradition but a logical response to the market. And while this meant loss of status and sometimes dire poverty for the non-owners, it showed that some owners could hang on and others really make a go of the new market economy. They could deal with urban merchants and employ labor while enhancing the traditional esteem for landed property. Another way to "make it" in the new economy was to become a tenant-overseer of a large estate, running it on commercial principles. This occupation developed in Prussia, in the rich wheat fields of Normandy, but was particularly prominent in England. Here, landlords in the eighteenth century, via acts of parliament, got permission to enclose, or fence in, their estates. As ordinary peasants could not afford to do this, they were bought out, and most of them had to work as estate laborers. A minority was ready to take charge as overseers for the aristocratic landlords; though eager to make more money, these latter did not want to fuss with details. Again we have a sign that a minority of peasants were, under the pressure of changing circumstances, ready to innovate. The overseers proved capable of running the estates on an efficient basis, introducing technological changes and attending to the needs of the market.

Commercialization in the artisan economy consisted of the following: an artisan master with a bit of extra greed, or ambition if you prefer a nicer term, decides that with growing markets (and, perhaps, with his own growing family) he needs to expand his operation. Ignoring guild rules, he takes on extra apprentices and maybe cuts down on their formal training. He stops working alongside his journeymen, spending his time instead arranging for new supplies and sales. He becomes, in short, a small manufacturer, producing according to market demand and treating his laborers not as fellow craftsmen but as people with whom he has an essentially commercial relationship—paying them a wage and that was all. Obviously, as with the peasantry, this process took time. As late as 1900, over half of all German barbers lived with their masters and expected to become masters in good time in the old artisan tradition. But the system faded demonstrably from the mid-eighteenth century onward, particularly where goods were in high demand, as in metalware, luxury cloth, and the like. The transformation allowed the introduction of some new techniques, for now that making money was the game the old restraints were gone. It allowed for new pressure on workers to step up their pace and take less time off for drinking and festivals. It definitely decreased traditional mobility. As small businessmen with growing families, artisan masters tried to reserve their positions for their own sons. Hence, although the number of artisans grew rapidly, the number of masterships stagnated.

The basic similarity between artisan and peasant adaptation to the market should be obvious. In both cases a minority of quite ordinary people proved capable of taking advantage of new opportunities. In both cases the majority were progressively deprived of their traditional access to land or masterships—they might improve their lot materially, they might enjoy new sexual relationships, but they were propertyless. This was a new category in western civilization, indeed, in terms of any large group, except slaves, in agricultural society generally.

Domestic manufacturing had its own long tradition in Europe, but hundreds of thousands of newcomers entered the field in the eighteenth century. Population pressure provided the spur, but again we note quick adaptability on the part of ordinary people. In the first place, it took not only capital but a certain sense of risk-taking to invest in a loom or spindles for one's cottage. Whole villages in fact converted to this new system, abandoning agriculture except for home gardens. The market was the key, and here were the most widespread proofs that its impulses were not totally foreign to the western mentality. A minority of individuals used the domestic system to rise. They started as simple workers, but impressed their employers so much that they, or their sons, became foremen, distributing materials and orders and collecting finished goods. This work in turn provided some savings, so that the foreman, or his son, turns up as a capitalist in his own right, either in the domestic system or as a small factory owner. Here was the new mobility procedure, based on openness to innovation and a realization that making money brought one up in society.

But this again involved a minority vital to Europe's develop-ment and it was proof that innovation did not simply come from above. Equally interesting is the behavior of the ordinary worker in the system. Although not literally propertyless, in that he or she owned the producing equipment, domestic workers were in-creasingly controlled by merchant capitalists; in this sense they shared in the general trend for society to divide between those with enough property to make them employers of labor and those who were simply labor. Resentment against exploitation was common in this group as it was among journeymen and poor peasants. But, as we have already suggested, the group also demonstrated com-pensatory behavior on a more day-to-day basis, at least when wages were adequate. They married earlier than peasant tradition dic-tated and were key figures in the sexual revolution. They wore more urban styles of dress, bought new products like coffee and sugar. Coincidentally, village festivals, though not disappearing, began to bring in urban talent—jugglers, popular singers, and the like. A new popular culture was beginning to emerge, though it had links with the intermediate, late medieval taste for material things and the attraction of the city.

Commercialization and Women

The domestic manufacturing system was particularly important for women. It preserved enough of a traditional aura to be respectable, for the work was in the home and earnings were put into the family savings. Women were widely used as spinners and weavers. Their work gave them new importance in the family. It broke from purely traditional patterns. It could expose them to strangers, dealers from outside the village. This could disturb traditionalists. It could lead to sexual immorality, as strangers exploited or attracted simple village maidens. But it was new, and women were active in the system throughout the early industrial period. Along with continued work in agriculture and massive employment as urban household servants, domestic manufacturing indeed constituted the main female occupation in the period.

The domestic servant is another example of the new role for women. It was not a new job but it rapidly increased in scale as cities expanded. Many men worked as servants, but the occupation became increasingly female. It has been estimated that by 1850, about a third of all women would spend some time as a servant, usually working alone or with but one other servant in a middle-class household of modest means. Here again, for men and women alike, we see the common pattern. Servanthood, like all the other popular occupations thus far mentioned was traditional; this doubtless gave it respectability and recognizability. But two changes were now apparent. Most servants had previously worked for bed and board. Now they were given a wage in addition—not a very good one but enough to place their relationship to their employer on a partly commercial basis. Second, increasing numbers worked in the city. This involved choice—where to go, how far to travel. So, as in the other main jobs taken by the common people, there was change and partial commercialization. As in the other cases also, responses varied. A minority of servants were abused and so exploited that they were driven to prostitution or even suicide. Another minority used servanthood as a means of learning new skills, from reading to fancy cooking. Male servants might become hotel keepers and women might marry substantial shopkeepers. Another minority became part of the urban working class, living in a new culture but not demonstrably better or worse off than their forebearers had been.

In sum, commercialization was not foisted on the common people. It changed their lives immensely, and it brought some to misery and degradation. But it gave others a chance to rise and helped create a new style of life—new clothing, a wider array of personal relationships—that could be pleasing even for those who did not soar toward the top. Women, still linked with tradition but able to marry earlier, had new contacts and job experiences, and were often able to benefit from them. Teenagers might be confused as parental controls and traditions waned, particularly if they drifted to strange cities, but they could benefit from freedom also.

If commercialization had caught the common people completely closed to its values, it simply would not have worked. Western culture had been prepared earlier for innovation in economic method and personal life style. Positive adaptation is not the whole story, but it must not be forgotten as we turn to other elements of commercialization: the compulsions placed upon the common people; the suffering as age-old traditions were broken; and the positive effort to defend old ways against new. In the not-too-long run, the adaptive element, visible from the first, triumphed.

Compulsions to Change

We have dealt with the most obvious cause of commercialization, the population revolution. Other factors must be added. Some seem almost laughably accidental. England ran short on timber early in the eighteenth century and had to turn to coal for fuel. This meant expansion of mines and new attention to other possible uses of coal. Hence, in fairly short order, there were new inventions using coal, notably the steam engine. On the continent new laws were essential for commercialization, and these stemmed particularly from the French revolution of 1789 and imitations of it by other governments who saw that economic expansion required innovation. Guild restrictions were abolished, save in a few areas. Artisans could operate as they pleased toward their workers and with regard to technology. Manorialism was abolished fully in France and modified even in Prussia by 1815. This movement would spread to Austria in 1848, southern Italy and Spain in the 1850s, and Russia in the 1860s. Here, it would seem, was a vital gain for the peasantry, for they were now free to leave the land for more profitable work elsewhere, free to farm as they wished (Russian emancipation imposed some village limitations on these gains, but this was not the general pattern). In southern and eastern Europe, particularly, the growing peasant population with no place else to go created greater poverty. Emigration to the New World provided some outlet but not enough. Furthermore, abolition of manorialism rarely meant that the peasants got the land they had farmed. They had to give over at least some of it to their lords in compensation for their freedom; some were turned into outright laborers as a result. Now that they were "free," governments imposed new taxes on them, which meant they needed cash. Some sold out to richer peasants or to the landlords and became sharecroppers or laborers. This was a particularly tragic pattern in Spain and southern Italy. But those who hung on, like the many peasants who kept modest plots in France or west Germany or, later, Russia, had to commercialize to keep alive. Otherwise taxes could not be met, and holdings would prove insufficient to support growing families. Law, then, as well as demography, prompted conversion to a commercial economy. Law confirmed the tendency of aggressive artisan masters or peasants to press their workers or their neighbors toward new market relations that all too often involved a transformation from villager-villager to owner/laborer or master-journeyman to employer/worker.

All of this occurred amid immense material confusion. Population was growing faster than rural opportunities, and the same trend would soon occur elsewhere in the world. City growth, just keeping pace with the population explosion, put immense strain on traditional urban facilities. Open sewers and unpaved streets had been horrible enough in the Middle Ages; they now became unbelievably foul. The pollution of drinking water, for example, was never greater; even the twentieth century has not duplicated this first urban shock. Crime rose. It was definitely more dangerous to walk in London in 1800 than it is today. Although overall wealth was rising rapidly, it was unequally distributed, and the new division between propertied and unpropertied was potentially menacing. What was a landless laborer to do when a harvest failed? Famine was not new, but its horrors were concentrated and more visible as cities grew and more people depended on shops for their food. Agricultural production rose, with new specialization, new tools, and the general desire for exploitation of the market. But it was still very uneven, so prices of food fluctuated widely and starvation remained a real possibility. Material conditions for the poorer classes in general may have deteriorated in England for the two decades when cities grew fastest, between 1820 and 1840. With more developed urban facilities, France and Germany fared a bit better.

But there was great poverty everywhere, as new economic forms struggled to keep pace with population growth. Even if most people were slightly better off than before on the average, they faced the recurrent uncertainty of economic crisis, which was unimaginably harsher than later depressions in that prices rose dramatically while unemployment went up and wages fell. Only the very recent industrial economy has approximated this foul combination, and then at a much higher level of general well-being. In the early industrial crises many artisans and workers had to sell tools and furniture, avoid paying rent, and reduce diet to a minimum; and some died of starvation. All this happened while people were making status adjustments, whether toward success, defined as greater wealth and property ownership, or the new condition of propertylessness—not necessarily materially miserable, but definitely not provided for in the old hierarchy of things.

Material confusion and status change account for the most obvious features of this first industrial age, particularly violent collective protest. But we have argued that status change might be accepted, for very good reasons, not only by the obvious winners who rose in society but also by people who had been kept down in pre-industrial times. A case in point: the pre-industrial family was a tight economic unit, yet not only was marriage delayed, but also thirty percent or more of the total adult population never married. By the early nineteenth century this percentage was down to fifteen, and by the twentieth century it was scarcely seven percent. One might be propertyless, but one had the status and possible emotional and sexual satisfactions of marriage far more readily at hand. We have argued that overall material conditions improved, which is not at all to ignore oscillations and huge segments of tormented paupers. This is why, in outlining commercialization, the adaptive qualities of owners and even non-owners are stressed, particularly in western Europe where the grip of the large estates was not dominant (or in England, where people fled the large estates for the cities). All was far from rosy. The wave of revolution and protest, still to be discussed, demonstrates this amply. But most people did not sit around plotting revolt or even wanting revolt when they were not actually in rebellion. This is clear when we look at the groups involved in the most drastic change of the period, the rise of factory production itself.

Mechanization in the Industrial Revolution

The growth of factories really represented an extreme of commercialization. Indeed, many journeymen who realized they were doomed to being wage earners forever entered the factories as the skilled echelon of labor because they could earn more money.

Many successful domestic manufacturing merchants set up a factory as a logical extension of their operations. And we must remember that while commercialization touched almost everybody to some degree in this first phase of economic change, the factory system was a minority phenomenon.

Yet it was revolutionary, part of the greatest change of human economics and life style since the Neolithic revolution millennia before. The latter brought people from caves to villages, the former brought them from farm to city. Attitudes, social relationships, and political structures had to change.

The revolution was technological in the first instance, and here we offer a short but vital definition. Industrialization featured the application of non-human, non-animal power to production. Initially, this occurred in textiles and metallurgy. Devices to speed up domestic spinning and weaving involved sufficient automatic processes to make them adaptable to new power sources. Spinning jennies wound fiber into thread, and in weaving there was the flying shuttle. Both were initially designed to be propelled by hands and feet, but hands were already less necessary for guiding the process; hence the possibility of mechanization through water power or new engines. Hammering and rolling of metals were mechanized as well. And, of course, the key invention, developed around 1770 in Scotland, was the steam engine itself, the new transformer of power. By the late 1780s British cotton spinning was fully mechanized (though some of this still involved use of water power instead of steam). Spinning of other fabrics, like wool, soon followed. Weaving of the coarser kinds of cloth was mechanized by 1820. Application of steam engines to metallurgy began about the same time. Soon thereafter steam was applied to transportation, via the railroad. Initial rail transport usually involved horses as sources of power serving the prosaic but vital purpose of getting coal out of mines, for with the steam age coal production had to soar. But in the 1820s, rail lines were built to transport goods and people as well as coal. By 1850 Britain and Belgium and the German states had elaborate rail networks; France was well on the way to a full national system; and other countries had at least short lines, if partly for show.

Still later the principles of mechanization would be applied to other branches of manufacturing ranging from shoemaking to food processing. The production of machines themselves, initially a semi-artisanal operation involving much hand labor, was increasingly subjected to non-manual power and the automatic production processes that accompanied this. Agriculture, too, was affected. Areas like North America, Argentina, and Australia—the outlying areas of western civilization—were quicker to pick up this aspect of industrialization. They lacked a peasant culture to resist machines in the name of old ways. They had vast acreage and a shortage of labor, the reverse of the traditional village where land was scarce and hands abundant. But Europe, too, would gradually be forced to mechanize its agriculture, if only to maintain some semblance of competition. Industrialization, then, ultimately involved at least partial mechanization of almost every productive operation. Even office work, as it expanded, was soon performed with typewriters, cash registers, and in the twentieth century still more sophisticated devices.

Following from the proclivities of mechanization we can trace some inevitable results of industrialization. First, productive groupings tended to become larger. Early factories often had but twenty workers, but some increased quickly to several hundred. The basic principle was that workers had to be gathered around the power source to make production efficient. Factory organization had the further advantage of greater specialization of labor, more discipline—indeed, an effort was made to inculcate a whole new style of labor involving getting to work on time and putting out maximum effort during the work day, under careful rules and supervision. Mechanization demanded capital; the machines cost money. So new groups of owners arose, often building up their operations gradually. They were a dynamic addition to the propertied class. Needless to say, the contrast between their fortunes, if they were successful, and workers' wages represented an extreme of the new gap between owners and non-owners. At the same time, mechanization inevitably raised total production and therefore total wealth. This was the whole point. With a spinning machine, around 1800, a worker could turn out 100 times the product of a manual spinner. Other machines were less productive, but the general principle was clear. This meant that society could increase its wealth in such a way that while the gap between lower and upper classes became greater, large segments of the lower classes could also gain a better material existence.

New wealth, for owners and many workers alike, cushioned the shock of this new way of producing things, but shock there was even so. There are a few vital qualifications here, which we tend to forget when we use a dramatic word like "revolution." Mechanization did not hit all branches of production at the same time; some branches were only gradually mechanized; some, like housing construction, are not substantially mechanized even today. Early factories were dangerous, dirty, and noisy, but they were not usually the impersonal horrors we might imagine. In a thirty-man shop, workers knew each other and the owner. The latter might be hated, but he could also be liked; it was a question, in part, of personal style. Early factories, and indeed the whole industrialization process, did not destroy skill. Making machines, setting them up, working as a miner or even a master cotton spinner all involved skill and usually years of training. Efforts to make employees work harder did gradually change the pace of labor, but only gradually. Human beings are very inventive, and workers quickly found out that they could take days off, change jobs, and simply keep their output below maximum levels, which they thought would also help protect their jobs against overproduction. A radically new work ethic, involving intense labor for maximum gain, has never completely won the working class, and it certainly did not do so in the first industrial century.

By 1850, at the end of the early industrial period in the West, most people in factories retained important elements of traditional work habits. Many persons could claim a definite skill. They were not slaves to an assembly line; many could even sneak naps during the work day. This is not to argue that no change occurred but that we should not exaggerate its speed or extent.

Middle Class and Working Class

There was strain, however, in any kind of operation this novel. We are not accustomed to associate strain with the factory owners, but it was very real. New and unfamiliar techniques, risky investments, the stark fact of approximately fifty percent rate of business failure—all could unnerve even a bold industrial entrepreneur. One very successful iron magnate wrote in his diary: "Every day I make decisions that terrify me, whose results I cannot foresee." The bulk of manufacturers in fact did not innovate in the early industrial period. They remained small artisan masters, simply exploiting their labor a bit more harshly and escaping the traditional camaraderie of the guild system; or they ran domestic operations where innovation was even less necessary. Of course many failed, because the larger operations with the machines could out-compete them. Nevertheless, there were so many areas where machines were not yet developed or were inefficient that a large traditionalist business group remained.

The new men, at first a minority in the business world, brought a new ethic with them which, if it did not always reduce personal strain, at least explained what was going on. The ethic owed something to older capitalist values and something to the Enlightenment, but it was partly new and had never before found such a wide audience. Material progress was good and manufacturers were its chief sponsor. New methods, including machines and new organization of labor, aided material progress, and so they were good. Production, and indeed society itself, including government, should be *rationalized,* that is, rethought so that maximum production resulted and talent was rewarded. Man should be able to control his own destiny. This principle caused great harshness to the poor, who could be blamed for their poverty as a personal failing; though, like most new principles, it was not carried through consistently and both charity and paternal controls persisted. The principle justified suport for universal systems of education, which were, again as a throwback to older ideas, partly designed to keep the poor in line by teaching them that the existing system was divinely ordained, but which also taught some new skills and even let a few rise to new status levels. The rationalization principle could be applied to the household, where the middle-class woman devoted increasing energy to adoption of new techniques, such as account books, and new machines to maintain her complicated daily work. It could be applied to health, as the new middle class saw less and less reason to accept traditional diseases and high child mortality as inevitable. The world was made to advance, and this new middle class, manufacturers and their wives foremost among them, was determined to make sure that it did. This attitude inevitably spilled over into politics, for the new middle class proved vital in the next stage of the modernization of the state.

Joining the new manufacturers in a new outlook were many professional people. Here claims to special knowledge rather than property were the key base, even when knowledge advanced rather slowly. Doctors and lawyers formed associations and licensing procedures to enforce certain educational levels, and medical knowledge began a gradual improvement. New professions joined the old: engineering, surgery, pharmacy, and, later, accounting. The new professionals had a distinctive way of adapting to change and not all got along well with businessmen. But they shared a belief in change and rationalization. When, as often was the case, particularly with lawyers, they were civil servants, this had obvious political consequences.

The workers in the factories offered no such clear pattern of reaction. Some enjoyed their relatively high earnings, using them to buy fancy clothes or marry early—in other words to enhance the new self-expression of the lower classes. Individual workers might appreciate the new machines, because they were interesting or simply because they lightened the traditional physical burdens of work. Overall, however, the initial adjustment of the factory working class was traditionalist, which is not really surprising and certainly not stupid, for tradition, properly adapted, provided real comforts. Indeed, the many workers who refused high pay to become foremen because they did not want that kind of middle-class regimen or responsibility, were saying that they too had a culture that they did not wish to violate. Traditionalism meant not working too hard, quitting jobs often to get a bit of leisure and a change of scene. It meant forming a family and expecting children to work at an early age—sometimes at six-years-old, more often at eight—as part of the family economy. It meant expecting sons to follow fathers into their job and protecting rights of entry for one's own. It also meant some adjustments to preserve the essence of the traditional family economy. Married women, after a brief period in which they could work with their husbands, were supposed to stay at home. They might engage in domestic production or take care of a lodger and thus aid the family economy. They certainly were now the consumer agents of the family and expected to make the best deals possible with the local stores. But it was inappropriate for them to work outside, unless the husband was dead, drunk, or disabled. Other relatives grouped around the working-class wife. But this enhanced the emotional support the family provided in a period of change and served the very practical purpose of economic aid. If one member of this extended group lacked work, perhaps another could find him a job or tide him over until times got better. Workers faced strangers on the job, a boss or a foreman who might or might not be friendly but whose main task was to get as much production as possible. They faced strange machines, noisy and dangerous (to save money, employers did not even put up available safety devices). Some, disabled or aging, suffered great material misery as their wages ceased or declined. Even some good earners, in the prime of youth, felt that their life was bewildering in its novelty, and took to excessive drink or went back home to an impoverished countryside.

While not forgetting class distinctions, another group commands consideration. This was a period of great change for women generally. Most obviously, married women were rarely employed in a formal sense in the growing cities, and in the middle class even girls did not have jobs. To work, at least once married, was undignified. So said the "culture of the time," and so people seem to have believed. As a rapidly-growing percentage of women did marry, home-centeredness, by no means entirely new, became increasingly prominent. But the home was not a changeless place. Women might work informally there. They might surround themselves with their relatives to form the vital, protective family network. These were reactions particularly notable among workers. Women generally won new prestige as mothers, for careful, loving attention to children was a vital new outlet. They were also budget managers, stretching meager resources, as among workers, or managing the complex operations of a middle-class home, with still too few resources and too little help to make the task simple. Women were not functionless. They did not idly grace a pedestal. But had they gained or lost from this first round of industrialization? To many feminists, home-centeredness means loss of status. But others point to new diversions and roles. As women adopted sewing machines and washers, for example, they became technological innovators in their own right. Led by the middle class, they also won greater control over their bodies. Birth control methods, sponsored mainly by women (sometimes without their husbands' knowledge) spread widely by the mid-nineteenth century and penetrated substantial segments of the working class after 1870. Laws improving married women's legal status, as in property rights, tends to confirm the notion of growing importance for the sex. The debate is still hotly joined, but it seems clear that the range of choice for women was widening overall, even if a distinctive culture still prevailed.

Political and Intellectual Reaction

10

WE HAVE RANGED BROADLY over a century-long period, to 1850 or so in western Europe and the United States in which everyone's economic life was being altered, in some cases drastically. By the end of the first century of industrialization forty or fifty percent of all people lived in cities, working in factories or as artisans, servants, and casual laborers. Never before had this level of urbanization occurred in human history. And the urban pattern itself was changed. Traditional cities had been scattered about the country. Now many old centers declined, while the wave of the future was the city with hundreds of thousands, even millions of inhabitants. In 1800, Europe had twenty cities with more than 100,000 people; by 1900 she had 122, representing over a tenth of the total population of the continent. In countryside as in city social structure had been altered, with a basic division between property owners, not a new group per se, and propertyless, whose proportion exceeded that tolerated in western custom since the fall of Rome. And while many of the property owners remained highly traditional, a new group among them was talking about innovation, progress, new ways of dealing with everything from the treatment of the poor, to health care, to manufacturing methods.

All this added up to a challenge to existing governments and existing intellectual traditions. We must recall here the three strands of change suggested for the post-medieval period. Clearly, now, economic change had gained pride of place. It had

231

transformed the lives and at least modified the outlook of the common people. It had created a new social structure. How would semi-modernized governments—the absolute monarchs or the British parliament—react? Would Enlightenment-derived doctrines suffice for intellectuals in this period of social upheaval? Economic change prompted a clear new stage in political development. It dispersed the off-shoots of the Enlightenment without destroying the tradition. It also helped create an intellectual countercurrent which has warred with the Enlightenment to this day, in a modernized version of the old conflict between reason and faith.

The obvious pressure on governments came from the amazing series of revolutions and revolts. At the base of these was a desire by many common people to resist the new economic trends, to go back to old ways or to ways that had been idealized in the popular mind. But the modernized middle class participated in the major revolts also, and almost always gained the upper hand. This meant that the common people either lost or, if they seemed to gain their demands, actually furthered the development of the new industrial society.

Of all the revolutions, the French upheaval beginning in 1789 is the most important because it alone can claim major success and because it provided the precedents for all later efforts (though it borrowed from the earlier American revolution, this latter was more a war for independence than a social upheaval). The French revolution offers one initial variant on the pattern suggested above, for the middle class had not yet been formed. France had undergone substantial commercialization, but it had no factory industry to speak of. However, after the first two crucial years of revolt the middle class was defined, and from then on the pattern suggested above holds true. We can now move from the abstract to the concrete.

France had been inundated with Enlightenment propaganda urging liberty, perhaps democracy, perhaps even socialism. It had an inefficient, bankrupt monarchy. A really enlightened despotism would have prevented the revolution by taking the necessary measures to keep the populace moderately contented and by repressing dissidence. Revolutions, in other words, cannot succeed and usually cannot begin unless the government is played out. The French people had a variety of grievances over commercialization, like the peasants who resented the richer farmers taking over the common lands. There was population pressure as well, though less than in other countries. The trigger to the revolution in France (leaving aside the earlier American example, which showed that a radical new kind of government was possible) was the combination of weak government and, ironically, an attempt by aristocrats to return to semi-medieval forms of control. The aristocrats wanted the return of the Estates-General so their representatives could regularly advise the king. They were pressed by their own population growth and by inflation. They had already succeeded, in what is called the "aristocrat resurgence," in imposing some new dues on their peasants, in capturing all the high offices of the church, and in preventing new ennoblements for successful merchants—all of which made the bulk of the population extremely angry. But it was the aristocrats who seized on the government's financial plight to insist on the calling of the Estates-General. In preliminary meetings to discuss grievances, aristocrats typically dominated. But gradually, before the Estate-General actually convened in 1789, middle class people became more assertive. They saw that their interests differed from those of the aristocracy; some were inspired by Enlightenment ideas. The first concrete result of their new political awareness was the king's permission for the Third Estate to have twice as many representatives as either the First or Second. The second result, once the Estates met, was insistence that voting be by head, not by estate. In other words, the middle class, joined by some others, was asking for a modern parliament, representative of property owners at least, and not a medieval Estate system. Further, they wanted this parliament to draw up a constitution. France was to have a different government before the king would get a *centime* of new tax money.

These efforts were resisted, but the king steadily backed down. This was not simply due to the firmness of the middle-class representatives but also to popular riots in Paris. The two years prior to 1789 had seen bad harvests and high grain prices. Given the example of middle-class leadership, the people of Paris gladly pitched in against royal troops and the aristocracy. There was no sense of conflict at this point between their interests—which on the popular side were mainly for cheaper bread and a fairer government—and the interests of the middle class.

Finally, in the summer of 1789, the peasants rose in various parts of France, again inspired by the sense that things had to change. They attacked their lords' castles, burned records of manorial obligations, and in general threatened chaos for the whole country. In October, the new parliament responded by abolishing all remnants of manorialism and proclaiming equality under the law. Because many peasants had basically controlled their plots of land even if they owed a bit of work service or rent to the lord, this act made France mostly a small-holding area of peasant farming. No longer could there be annoyances such as a lord claiming the right to hunt over the peasant's field. Manorial courts were also abolished. Peasants, having got what they wanted, largely dropped out of the revolution, for they had no directly political goals on a national scale.

The legal change they had triggered was an immense victory for the middle class. Aristocracy was now virtually meaningless, entirely so in law. A commoner could compete for a job in the bureaucracy on theoretically equal terms. The whole legal system of the old regime had been destroyed, for no longer did birth count for anything. In its place the revolutionary government installed the class system which had existed beneath the legal orders: property was now the key. The Constitution of 1791 confirmed a wide variety of rights for all Frenchmen—right to equal justice, freedom of speech, religious toleration, and so on—but the voting system for parliament was carefully placed in the hands of those people who had a good bit of property.

In the first phase of the revolution the church was also attacked. Church lands were seized to pay outstanding government debts. To compensate, churchmen were put on salary and soon required to pay an oath of loyalty to the state. From Rome the pope resisted this incursion, and most French priests obeyed him. The result was a century-long split between church and modern political principles, probably inevitable but tragic, for although Catholic resistance could retard modernity, as it did in the French revolution as loyal Catholics staged civil war against the new government, modernity would win out and the church would only be diminished as a result.

The revolution, finally, attacked the traditional economic structure. Manorialism was already gone. Then guilds were abolished and along with them any right for working men to associate in defense of their rights. Here was open running room for further capitalist development even though revolutionary chaos kept France economically stagnant for some decades. Here, also, was a clear sign of the split in interests between middle class and urban workers. Artisans did not necessarily lament the passing of the guilds, for these had not worked well for some time and were largely the creatures of the masters alone. But they did want their traditional right of collective protection, and this was now gone in the name of capitalist individualism.

What the first phase of the revolution had done, overall, was to tear down most of the traditional buffers between individual and state. This is its key role in political modernization. Church was reduced in power; guilds were gone; traditional provincial assemblies were abolished, and even provinces themselves were destroyed as political entities lest they disrupt national unity. Manorialism was gone, so there was the state, on the one hand, and the people on the other. The people had guaranteed rights, as individuals; this was part of the new constitutionalism. A few could vote for the representatives of the government. All this in one sense completed absolutism by eliminating all competing powers to the state; but it revived the other medieval tradition too, of elected bodies to monitor the actions of this state. But, while tradition can be legitimately recalled, this was a vastly new political structure, for the representative base was completely altered and the potential power of the central government measurably increased.

The next phases of the French revolution brought fewer innovations, but they were full of drama and bloodshed. From 1792 onward the people of the cities, particularly Paris, tried to take over the government. Briefly, in fact, universal suffrage was proclaimed. There were democratic projects for universal education and some limited measures of poor relief as the economy went from bad to worse. Although never accepted by the government, small socialist movements arose demanding equality of property, the first concrete expression of what was to become a major movement. More important, the powers of the central government rose steadily as government agents were sent out to assure popular loyalty, check on economic conditions, regulate the church, and so on. Eventually a system of prefects was established to govern each local department; appointed by the state in Paris, this gave France the most centralized political system in European history, even compared to the Roman Empire, and one which has lasted to this day.

Finally, the radical phase of the Revolution brought the famous Reign of Terror. This was shortlived and killed relatively few people by modern revolutionary standards—thousands instead of the millions in Russia and China in the twentieth century—but, as in the modern cases, it was triggered by attack from abroad and within.

Foreign monarchs had never liked the revolution and were obviously distressed when the radical phase began with the decapitation of the king and queen. Catholics, conservative peasants, and others understandably battled the new regime in various parts of France. Hence the Terror, a series of revolutionary tribunals empowered to issue summary justice and capped by the awesome guillotine, a device intended to deliver a more merciful death than hanging but which came to symbolize the association of revolution and blood. All sorts of people were killed, not just dissident priests and aristocrats; rich merchants provided the highest percentage, a sign of new class tensions within the cities. At the time and long after, until there were bloodier revolutions, the Terror stood, for conservatives throughout Europe, as a sign of the evil of revolution and mob passions.

Napoleon and Empire

The Terror ended in 1794, and was followed by a confused, weak government which in turn yielded to Napoleon Bonaparte, an upstart general from Corsica. Napoleon completed the centralization of the French government, adding one important new ingredient: an elaborate system of higher education designed to train loyal and efficient bureaucrats. With some elements having been launched earlier, France had training schools for state engineers, mining inspectors, teachers, as well as the more general run of judicial and financial officials. Parliament existed under Napoleon, but it had rubber stamp powers, and Napoleon has been judged by some the apotheosis of the absolute monarch. With an uneasy truce with the church, which left the state firmly in command of Catholic affairs in France, there was little internal opposition and no structural barriers to central state operations. Napoleon even outlined a secret police to root out internal enemies. Whether one views this as the last absolute monarchy or, as seems more probable, the first modern dictatorship is a debatable point. For Napoleon undertook some new maneuvers too which showed how politics had changed from the days of Louis XIV. Not only were his central controls and police powers immeasurably greater, but he also directly appealed to public opinion by issuing bulletins about his success in war or the economic benefits the government was arranging. He held plebiscites on his various constitutions in which all adult males were invited to vote yes. They could vote no, of course, but the beauty of this kind of plebiscite is that in voting no, one is not voting for a clear alternative, which is why so many dictators have imitated it since. Napoleon himself turned up with massive support.

This state under Napoleon differed in structure from absolutism in the extent of its power and its desire for at least vague popular appeal. It differed in function less clearly. Industrialists were left free to engage in economic enterprise; the modern state was clearly out of the business of restraining economic development in the restrictive mercantilist fashion of Colbert. And Napoleon supported a few innovations, such as the planting of sugar beets. But his government was not wedded to new principles of economic growth, and his wars and tariff battles with England retarded French development in many ways. The educational function was new but reserved largely for the upper classes. Napoleon cared nothing for the lower classes and left whatever education they might receive to the church. The greatest internal innovations were in structure: new police powers (which affected intellectuals especially); far more effective taxation, with no class now exempt by privilege; and mass military recruitment. This last was not a Napoleonic invention but a logical heritage of the revolution. If all people were now equal under the law, they all owed the state duty just as the state owed them rights. So all men, not just an arbitrary handful, were liable to military service. This created armies of immense size and represented the most direct contact between government and ordinary citizen ever established. Many must have resented this innovation, and many would through the rest of modern history. But there were also many like the old peasant who blithely recalled, in 1848, getting his nose frozen off in Napoleon's Moscow campaign, with pride that he had participated in such a great venture.

Napoleon's main concept of government purpose was decidedly traditional: conquest. He wanted to be master of Europe and occasionally hankered after more distant areas such as the West Indies or Egypt. A brilliant tactician, supplementing his masses of troops with mobile artillery, he directly ruled the Low Countries and, for all intents and purposes, western Germany, the Adriatic, and northern Italy. He had indirect rule over the rest of Italy, Spain, and Poland. Ultimately he was beaten, and the balance of power principle was restored as Russia, England, Prussia, and Austria banded together to defeat him. The Congress of Vienna, 1815, carefully surrounded France with reasonably

strong states, with the big gainers being Prussia, which got territory west of the Rhine for the first time, and England, which
got virtually everybody's colonies. Poland was divided again with
Russia getting most of it. But France was not dismembered, for in
this last great balance of power treaty it was assumed that it could
play a responsible diplomatic role so long as Napoleon was kept off
the throne.

To beat Napoleon two states had imitated aspects of the
French revolutionary system. Under Michael Speransky, Russia
improved the training of its bureaucrats, gave more powers to
municipal governments, and discussed even further reforms. The
central Russian question, what to do with the mass of oppressed
and unproductive serfs, was ducked, but there was briefly some
sense of motion. Prussia returned to extensive training for its
bureaucrats, which, as in Russia, meant more universities and
secondary schools. It loosened guild controls on manufacturing and
above all relaxed, though ultimately did not abolish, the manorial
system. This created some chance for economic development even
if it did not create a modern social structure. Military reforms still
more obviously aped the French, as more people were put in the
army and training and tactics were improved. Prussia also assumed
new controls over the church, particularly as it now had many
Catholic subjects in Polish Silesia and the Rhineland. Church
lands were taken and seminaries monitored.

Napoleonic and earlier French conquests spread the principles
of the revolution still more directly to the Low Countries, northern
Italy, and the west German states. Here manorialism was abolished
and equality under the law established, religious toleration was
enacted, and guilds destroyed—and even after Napoleon's defeat
most of these reforms stuck. This meant, as in France, new opportunity for economic development, for traditional barriers were
gone. It could mean, as we have indicated, new pressures on the
common people unaccustomed to direct exposure to commercial
practices and government agents. It certainly meant a new kind of
government, definitively dropping some functions, such as
maintenance of religious orthodoxy or protection of traditional
social hierarchy or economic practices. It involved at least tentative
groping toward new functions, as in education, new military
recruitment, and encouragement to economic growth. This last
developed most hesitantly, partly because governments were afraid
of the new middle class and were still dominated by agricultural

interests. But within a decade or two states like Prussia and Belgium were actively building or backing railroad development (which had military as well as economic implications), bringing in sample factories and equipment from England and encouraging more scientific farming through use of fertilizers developed by scientists at the state universities.

Reaction and Revolution

We have to regard the period 1815–1848 as one in which governments, Napoleon having been defeated, experimented only gingerly with new forms and functions. There were more parliaments elected by the propertied classes and not on the order of the medieval estates. This was true in France and several west German states such as Baden. But the elections were typically manipulated and, overall, parliaments had little power. This was a period of repression and retrenchment, even in Britain, as governments sought to avoid change amid an uncertain atmosphere. Police spies arrested dissidents, armies put down popular revolts—Britain, despite her parliamentary tradition, was a leader here for about twenty years after 1800. But there were no real innovations in repressive methods, which is why secret societies and radical propaganda gained ground.

The period 1815–1848 can be known as the age of conservatism or the age of revolution. Both terms fit, for immobile policies begat revolution which in turn begat an effort to hold the status quo. Conservatism meant defense of religion—even in France, where toleration was maintained, a law was passed levying a death penalty for sacrilege. It meant censorship of the press, firing of university professors who spoke out for change, laws banning assemblage of more than six people without police permission. This was a newly self-conscious defensive effort, but it did not lead to a new style of government. This was not a period, frankly, where much happened from the official side of things.

But there was steady pressure from below. Businessmen allied with workers in seeking the vote in England. In 1832, the Reform Bill enfranchised most of the middle class, via loosened property qualifications. The people running the government changed little—they were still mainly landed aristocrats. But they became increasingly middle-class in orientation. Over the next two decades they made things tougher on paupers, placing the poor in dreadful workhouses (putting into effect the middle-class belief that the poor had only themselves to blame). They passed several laws regulating the work of women and children in factories (for the middle class believed special protection was due here). They did a bit to promote education (religious disputes hampered England in this area, as it was difficult to agree on whether public funds should go to Anglicans or Dissenters and in what proportion). They legalized Catholicism, soon making it possible for people of all religions, or even atheists, to attend universities, serve in government, and enjoy full equality. They reduced aristocratic power by eliminating special tariff protection on grains. They began to liberalize traditional legal restrictions on women, allowing them to own their own property even if married, later making grounds for divorce more equal between the sexes. Finally, perhaps most important in the short run, they turned city governments over to those who owned property, i.e. the middle class, taking power away from a random collection of aristocrats, church fiefs, and the like. Middle-class urban governments were even more active than the national state, building new parks, beginning to regulate housing and sanitary conditions, promoting education. After 1850, the national government itself encouraged, then required, local governments to tear down the worst slum housing and provide for sanitary inspections of markets. In sum, even without dramatically new personnel the British government became middle-class and in the process developed a decisive new function: some basic responsibility for public welfare.

All this was done without lower-class participation and some measures, like the new treatment of the poor, were extremely harsh. Not surprisingly, protest movements developed in response—most notably the Chartists, an organized mass political movement that on three occasions obtained millions of signatures on petitions asking for universal suffrage (the last in 1848). But with the middle class represented in government and with state functions changing to its liking, there was no chance of revolution. Even the repressive period passed quickly, and while England developed a new police force, it was directed against crime, not collective violence. The lesson seemed to be that parliamentary government was tops, once it was modified to become representative of a large minority of the population. It could most easily adapt to the new things governments had to do and, perhaps most important, give people a sense that they were controlling their own lives. When the vote was extended to urban workers, in 1867, this seemed logical, and no one objected strenuously.

A number of countries developed similar governments by up-dating parliamentary traditions and gradually extending the vote. Scandinavian countries did this, and they even granted women the vote before 1914, while the English and Americans proved a bit hesitant in this area. The American revolution, less a revolution than a chase-the-British-out war, set up an operative representative system. There were hints of genuine revolution, class vs. class, but the new middle-class ruling group won out and society was changed little. Popular agitation in the 1830s, caused by new economic pressures, did not lead to new institutions so much as it did to new government attention to the needs of the people against the dominant banking and merchant class. The results were meager, partly because American parliamentary democracy was so progressive compared to its other western counterparts. A dominant, conservative central bank was attacked, but little else was done and the burning issue, slavery, was long officially ignored. American institutions, so advanced politically in 1800, were becoming more like a standard model by 1850. Holland needed no revolution to modernize the parliamentary system. Belgium had a classic revolt in 1830. Having been put under Dutch rule by the Congress of Vienna, the Belgians essentially fought an American-type rebellion. There were hints of popular discontent, but the main job was to get the Dutch out, and almost everyone could cooperate in that, from radical artisan to Catholic priest. The result was an extremely liberal government, perhaps the classic model for the period. This involved: (1) extensive suffrage based on property qualifications but far broader than that of France and approximating that of England; (2) great interest in education, and an overall secularization which led to tension which the Catholic church but not outright warfare for a while; (3) desire for economic development, as in the active support of a railroad network; (4) rigorous suppression of lower-class unrest, including banning of unions; (5) a constitution giving legal equality, an elected parliament to limit the new king, and national freedom for whatever that was worth for a country tragically too small to defend herself.

Nature of Liberalism

These are all cases of evolution without, or nearly without, revolution. The result was substantially middle-class rule, even if aristocrats participated heavily, and more important, substantially liberal rule. Aristocrats could continue to govern because they behaved in a liberal manner. Liberalism is tough to define, and there are many variations in its implementation. And this is classic liberalism, the mid-nineteenth century type, not the later definition of the term. Outside the United States, for example, liberalism was usually non-democratic, until 1848 or after. Only the propertied and the well-educated were qualified to vote, though at some later time the masses, as fundamentally rational human beings (the Enlightenment lived on) might also qualify. In England and Norway liberals were particularly suspicious of government, believing that private individuals could run their affairs best by themselves. These were the only two countries where there was any per capita reduction in government expenses. English liberals, for example, wanted to get rid of colonial holdings, because they repressed local freedom and cost money. And there was, as we have seen, a strong liberal impulse to get government out of: religion, replacing function with toleration; guilds and economic restrictions; police repression of speech, press, and teaching. It is generally true that liberals wanted definite restrictions on government.

Liberals also wanted new things, and even in England city governments run by middle-class liberals showed this trend. Governments should educate. They should improve physical surroundings with parks and housing programs. Nothing earthshaking perhaps, nothing to overturn the new social hierarchy, but a real government welfare function and, with education, a mind-orienting function as well.

Here, new police forces were used as well, not just against crime but against popular recreations the middle class found revolting. Gradually, traditional entertainments such as cockfighting and bear-baiting were limited, and there were beginnings of campaigns against excessive lower-class drinking. (Ironically, by the later nineteenth century dangerous sports replaced the older entertainments; in the modern world it is more popular to see humans knock each other about than animals.) With police action, then, as well as education, government was to monitor and improve the masses.

On the continent, there was, in addition, encouragement to economic development, which governments had been flirting with for some centuries. Liberals on the continent wanted tariff protection, transportation facilities ranging from canals to railroads, and subsidies to banks and new industries. Most liberals respected the state as well as private initiative and assumed that both could combine for social progress. There is no question that there was tension within the liberal mind, and there still is, as to when the state should act, and when a problem is the responsibility of the individual. But theorists worried about the combination far more than practical politicians.

Another batch of states sought the liberal type of government but could not achieve it without revolution. France is a classic case, becoming something of a specialist in revolution (four, counting the Commune of 1871) but here revolution did produce a liberal state. Shading off from this, with but one real revolution, was Germany, where liberalism never quite made it. Serious revolution occurred in states where the social challenge was rarely met by adequate political change. Governments that at first seemed no more conservative than those of the West, after the Napoleonic threat, turned out to be outside the western tradition even if actively in its diplomatic orbit. At the same time, differences in social class were much sharper, above all because there was such a small modernizing middle class element.

France actually stood in between the two extremes. Her frequent revolutions—1789, 1830, 1848, 1871—should not be too deceptive, because they did not always indicate wide disagreement about what the political system should be. In 1830, for example, the monarch Charles X tried to do away with the new parliamentary system by changing the voting base of parliament and limiting its rights, while curtailing freedom of the press and supporting more and more Catholic influence in government. For all its troubles, France really stood in the liberal mold of state systems. It simply took a periodic reminder to return to the mold.

But France also had the revolutionary itch. So did several Italian states in 1830, and Italy more generally in 1848. So did Spain in 1820. So did Germany, Hungary, Bohemia and Austria in 1848. So did most Latin American states that freed themselves from Spain by revolutionary war in the early nineteenth century.

Nature of the Revolutionary Wave

For all the inevitable variety of the revolutions, there are three basic elements to capture. First, they occurred in states with an absolutist tradition that were unwilling to relax in favor of new demands for intellectual and economic freedom. In other words, they found it hard to accommodate even a moderate modernizing middle class. We think of Prussia's government as a great supporter of industrialization, but actually it tried to orient banking policies away from change until after 1848; it was the initiative of private entrepreneurs that got Prussian industrialization started. So, even in Prussia, the new middle class had an ax to grind. Second, the revolutionary states retained a powerful aristocracy, usually linked to an established church (Catholic or Lutheran). This was even true in France, where aristocrats recovered many of their lands and dominated the government, particularly before the revolution of 1830 but even to an extent thereafter. Absolutist traditions and aristocratic rule simply did not blend with the interests of the new middle class. Finally, and paradoxically, these were all countries with a strong artisan and peasant tradition which would prompt people to join revolution to protest change. They might briefly think they shared interests with middle-class liberals, but soon a clash was inevitable. And so most revolutions failed, in the short run, though certain revolutionary elements made some gains.

Germany in 1848 is really the crucial paradigm, for there is no need to go through all the revolutions one by one. Where there was a foreign enemy to drive out, as with Belgium against the Dutch in 1830, Italy against the Austrians in 1848, Hungary against the Austrians, Bolivians against the Spaniards, revolutions tended to last longer but had shallower internal roots. And, except for Belgium and the Latin American case, they were put down by force. Even in Latin America independence resulted in many authoritarian governments and scant outright social change. They made little difference to the ordinary peasant or slave (slavery was abolished in Brazil, for example, only in the 1880s). France, though far more advanced economically, and without the problem of slavery, offered a similar case of revolution without many results. In 1830, it dislodged a monarch and roughly doubled its voting population to 250,000 adults, still judged by property qualification, but the regime soon became increasingly repressive not only against lower class threats but against dissident intellectuals. By the 1840s, French elections were again rigged; parliament was a rubber stamp filled with civil servants—which is why there was another revolution which finally established universal suffrage if not much else.

Following the French revolution of 1848 various German states became agitated, and there was outright revolt among the common people in cities like Berlin, with barricades set up and the usual paraphanalia established. Everywhere the monarchs backed down. They appointed liberal ministries and talked about national unity, while the revolutionaries set up the Frankfurt parliament to establish the basis for German unification. Middle-class liberals and radicals met in all the German states to set up constitutional governments and bills of rights. Peasants agitated or even rebelled to gain freedom from remaining manorial restrictions. Artisans provided the urban muscle for the revolution, staffing the initial revolts and rioting periodically thereafter to gain social justice. All of this sounds very much like France in 1789, and in many ways the issues and scenario were the same. But the revolution was over by 1849, as were all the revolutions of 1848, and the reasons are not too hard to fathom.

The governments of 1848 were stronger than the weak French monarchy of 1789; they might bend, but they would not break. The middle class revolutionaries were more timid, because they had history—the recollection of the Terror—to show them what revolutionary excess could do. Except where there was foreign rule to be fought, they made no serious efforts to set up their own military force, which left them at the mercy of government troops. As liberals, they preferred evolution and persuasion to force anyway, for rational men should not have to resort to violence. And a government such as Prussia's had introduced sufficient reforms—better education, some support for railroads—so that even the forward-looking middle class was not sure it wanted to go all out in attack. This was not, then, the same situation as 1789 in France, and we need not blame middle class liberal timidity as the sole reason for revolutionary failure. Furthermore, hosts of traditional property-owners did not want revolution at all. They were all for customary social hierarchy. What bothered them were innovations like the new machines, and obviously this made the liberal businessmen and other progressives running the revolution their enemies, not the old order.

The revolutionaries also did not make fruitful contact with the peasants. Property-conscious, they said that abolition of manorialism was fine if the peasants paid the landlords redemption fees for the rights they got. The Prussian monarchy, aware that reforms were needed, offered just as good a deal, and as a result peasants not only dropped out of the revolution but became a durably conservative force in German politics. But the crucial split was between the new middle class liberals and the artisans. The former wanted a society moving forward, with individual freedom to innovate, with industrial advance. The artisans had risen to recapture the old society, to get the guilds back and do away with machines, though they asked for new voting and educational rights as well. There could be no meeting of the minds here, and within a year middle class revolutionaries were calling on Prussian troops to put down artisan riots.

The age of revolution was over by 1849. There has literally been no revolution in the centers of western civilization since that time, save in two brief cases (Paris, 1871; Germany, 1918) as aftermaths of defeat in war. Middle class liberals decided that revolution was too dangerous to their propertied interests. Artisans, a fading group, gave up on revolution or decided they could not go it alone; they turned to other forms of protest. Peasants, with manorialism abolished from Germany and Austria-Hungary and other places in the West, had or thought they had what they wanted. For all the lower classes, better food supplies and transportation ended general famines which had preceded all the major revolutions.

The Forces of Revolution

Two major factors fueled the extraordinary revolutionary wave of the first half of the nineteenth century. First was an exacerbation of traditional popular protest. Second was an ideological ferment, affecting primarily important elements of the middle class. Both factors require assessment. They help explain why most revolutions failed. But some ingredients continued to have a life of their own; nationalism is an obvious case in point. And many put new pressure on governments, for if the revolutions were put down states learned to make new accommodations; by 1870 in fact one could argue that most revolutionary goals had been substantially fulfilled.

Before each major revolution an economic crisis occurred, featuring the dreary combination of bad harvest and rising food prices plus growing unemployment in the cities. Here was a classic trigger for popular unrest. Common people frequently protested hardship outside a revolutionary context, through strikes and riots. And more was involved than material suffering. There was a basic dissatisfaction against new commercial practices, which distorted the goals of the artisan and peasant economy. In good times, individuals might adjust to, even profit by, the new market opportunities, but when times were bad it was tempting to reassert the older values.

Artisans were the key protesters, but they were joined by domestic workers eager to preserve their jobs and middle-level peasants who evoked the village tradition of cooperation and mutual protection. All these groups periodically rioted against high bread or grain prices or new taxes, in the tradition established since the late Middle Ages. They expected fair treatment. They had enough political awareness to demand that the state grant them what they needed to live—a principle that has not died, and is to some extent embodied in the welfare state which does not create equality but minimum standards of living. Again, throughout the industrial revolution, we deal with continuums as well as disruption. Artisans, as we have seen, wanted their guilds back or something comparable to replace them. Peasants wanted the old village economy. They were rising against the base of the new economic order. This was the spur to almost all the major revolutions, which the common people incited by rioting, even though political direction was invariably taken out of their hands by the new middle class.

A more concrete example can be examined. A classic concomitant of early industrialization was Luddism, the direct destruction of machines. The term comes from early nineteenth-century Britain, where machine-breakers claimed leadership from a mythical figure, Ned Ludd. The Luddites wanted the old economy back with equality among workers and protection of established skills. Most of the population, even in Britain, undoubtedly agreed; middle class judges, for example, were notoriously lenient in their verdicts on the rioters. Old-fashioned property-holders, just as most peasants and journeymen, resented the new society. So undoubtedly did the masses of the very poor. The result was a century of massive local rioting, rising rates of individual crimes, and, at the extreme, revolution.

Why didn't the resisters win? First, although many people shared their impulses, they were divided in their own minds. The artisan might revolt when economic conditions were bad but faithfully attend night school when times were good in order to become a better-paid weaver or maybe a foreman or an accountant. Here we return to the western popular culture which did not preclude change. Second, the resisters were divided. Small-town judges, for example, might resent industrialization as distorting proper human relationships, above all in the middle level of society, but they would never resort to violence. Journeymen, with a very similar picture of society, might revolt. Third, even though they, too, were divided, the innovating middle class and the governments had in common a desire for order. The first group wanted change but not social disruption, and governments always want order. This was why revolutions, after the great French effort, usually led to a new combination of middle class and established order, each supporting the other. This was why, in countries with a parliamentary tradition that could be open to new, middle class voters—Britain is the classic example—revolution was not needed at all. Fourth, most people are not basically disruptive. Parisian artisans in June of 1848, staged a bloody, three-day riot to defend government support for their unemployed. It was, of course, brutally suppressed. At best three percent of all Parisian artisans participated on the barricades. The gesture was heroic and long remembered. But the main point is that most people found sufficient advantages in the new ways of doing things, or were so traditionally apathetic and deferential, that no challenge to modernity would work. After 1848, with the exception of some intellectuals in the Romantic vein, the most obvious challenges to the industrial-commercial revolution ceased. We have discussed the reasons for the end of revolution. More broadly, a greater number of people increased their interest in material gains, enjoying not only better food and clothing but possibly tobacco or new school books for the children. Artisans got used to new ways of working which were not always totally disruptive of tradition. In 1977, a carpenter still works wood with his hands; a carpenter of 1857 would recognize him. Peasants, as we have seen, concentrated on their interest in land and their own development of rural capitalism; the owners were contented and, for a long time, the laborers were too weak to speak.

But modernization was not home free. Protest would recur. Aspects of socialism were mounted by artisans or others to attack new business forms and methods of work. Fascism was even more obviously a direct attack on modernity. But the revolutionary mood was over. Even Nazi Germany, which produced a massive lament against modern ways of doing things, does not distort this picture, for the Nazis continued the development of more productive agriculture and big business despite promises to return to the past. Yet the anti-modern current remains. Most of us have at least a streak of it in us. When we resent billboards defiling the highways with commercialism, or resent highways as an inefficient, wasteful means of transportation, we are protesting aspects of the development of modern, industrial society.

The point here is that while most protest has become modern, working for new goals, a streak of the old temptation to look backward to some ill-defined "good old days," still lingers. It can affect political behavior and even cause violence. But it was 1848 that capped the heroic efforts of the older lower classes to regain the past. Failure in these revolutions, new chances for adaptation, and constructive government measures yet to be discussed all played a role in ending a long tradition of western popular protests, though similar motifs might crop up in other areas involved in the first stresses of industrialization even today. Let us stress further that we are talking of the end of a certain kind of protest even in the west, not of protest itself. The two decades after 1848 were, in fact, rather peaceful internally, but then new strands of agitation emerged, as workers and others learned both new methods and new goals.

Ideological Attack

Just as popular unrest built up before each major revolution through 1848, so there was an ideological ferment. Four main ideologies were involved, though two were particularly important. More than one might be held by a given individual.

Liberalism has already been defined. Liberals were not eager revolutionaries. They preferred gradual change and education. But once a revolution was started they were typically drawn to participate, though their timidity about using violence helps explain why so many revolutions ended quickly. But in the early going, liberals sought their constitutions, parliaments, and civil rights; they pulled their horns in only when they saw that other groups wanted more.

Branching off from liberalism was radicalism. Radicals wanted all the things liberals wanted but they also sought universal suffrage and some social reforms, often vaguely defined, to make life better for the common people. Not all radicals were revolutionaries; in England they worked mainly through the government once the vote was extended in 1832, though previously they had been prominent in guiding street agitation. But revolution came fairly easily to the radical mentality, and a radical faction cropped up in every major outburst, taking an important leadership role but also scaring the liberals.

Scarier still, of course, were the socialists. Most socialism prior to 1848 is called "utopian" because it envisaged nonviolent methods and really did not want to use the state to accomplish its purposes. Socialists wanted equality of property, often equality between the sexes. They hoped for small producing communities where work would be evenly divided. Their optimism was boundless, even after countless communities failed. And their goals could be picked up by others who were interested in more direct methods, including revolution. A socialist leader played a prominent role in the French revolution of 1848, when socialist slogans were shouted by many artisans in Paris. In turn, 1848 helped toughen socialism up, a process already underway, lending credence to the hard-nosed doctrines of Karl Marx which insisted that revolutionary seizure of the state was vital.

Finally there was the new nationalist ideology. Hinted at in the eighteenth century, by so-called cultural nationalists who preached, contrary to Enlightenment internationalism, that each country had its distinctive character and heritage, nationalism took political form in the nineteenth century. The dominant current was liberal nationalism. Nationalists in Italy and Germany sought political unification as well as cultural distinctiveness for their countries. But they also agreed with liberal, and sometimes radical, goals; and they argued that nationalism in one country should be harmonious with nationalism elsewhere. Countries were different but no one country was superior. This was a theory that proved hard to maintain, but it was asserted. Nationalists could be ardent revolutionaries, and as we have seen fights for national unity or independence often proved more tenacious than fights for internal justice alone.

Who picked up these ideologies? Utopian socialism had some appeal to articulate artisans, for the community of production corresponded to guild ideas; but it was not yet a major force. Liberalism, of course, was solidly middle class, though artisans might seek parliaments, extension of education and the like. The same applied to radicalism, but whereas liberalism might attract businessmen as well as forward-looking professionals, most radicals were students, lawyers—in other words, intellectuals and professional people alone.

Finally, nationalism can easily seem an overriding force in

the nineteenth century. In fact, in this period it attracted only mild support, and virtually none below the middle class. It offered nothing to the common people; many, attached to regional loyalties, were offended by nationalism. Major local riots had to be put down, for example, when Italy was unified in 1860. Businessmen might favor nationalism as providing broader markets. But again, professional people, particularly students, carried the banner. Nationalism gave them a sense of worth, an alternative to loyalty to king or church. Many professionals were a bit worried about their future; it was increasingly hard to get state jobs in countries like Prussia, for example. What better doctrine than nationalism to express discontent in a noble cause and to urge a new, unified state that would undoubtedly supply new employment?

Ideological ferment was vital. We must quickly turn to the fundamental intellectual currents which produced all these new -isms. But in terms of revolutionary action the new ideologies had certain drawbacks.

1. Two, at least, were not primarily revolutionary. Liberals were gun-shy, most socialists starry-eyed.

2. Many of the ideologies, while drawing fervent support, did not draw massive support.

3. Most important, the ideologies could run into each other, almost nullify each other. We have mentioned that the more advanced *-isms* could drive liberals back toward the established order. What of a radical-nationalist? In the revolutions of 1848 many found that they had to choose between primary goals. They could fight for nationalism *or* radicalism, but not at the same time. Most chose nationalism, which weakened any possible popular base. And in choosing nationalism, they further found it difficult to maintain the fiction of equality of all peoples. German nationalists shunned the demands of the Slavs, for example; for Slavs should keep quiet and accept German rule. Revolutionaries in Vienna cheered when they learned that Prague, the center of Slavic nationalism, had been taken by government troops. As with socialism, 1848 thus served as an ideological turning point. It began to drive a wedge between liberal and nationalist sentiments and it turned nationalists toward an aggressive stance, my country first.

For if the confusing *-isms* contribute to an explanation of why the revolutions failed, all of them survived. Some would gain new adherents; all would change. All would put ongoing pressure on existing governments, though in the case of socialism this largely awaited the period after 1870. We must seek the roots and the basic implications of the mid-century outpouring of political doctrines in the broader intellectual currents of the early industrial revolution.

Intellectual Currents

Intellectuals in the Enlightenment tradition had little trouble accepting the industrial revolution, for this represented progress and progress was their most important product. But one could accept the revolution and not accept its present conditions. A series of stances, all derived from the Enlightenment belief in man's rationality, in progress, and in science, developed in the first half of the nineteenth century. They, or derivatives from them, represent the political theories we still live with, for there have been no fundamental innovations since.

It was the Enlightenment heritage, confronting the new social conditions of industrialization, that made this the age of the *-ism*. Liberals believed man could be perfected; hence the concern for education. They enthusiastically hailed industrial progress under capitalism. They welcomed scientific progress and were generally hostile to religion as representing superstition. Radicals had even more faith in man's rationality, which is why they urged the vote here and now. Some were even heard, in the 1820s and later, to suggest that women were equals as well, and deserved the same rights as men. There was feminist agitation, particularly in Paris and Berlin, in 1848, and powerful tracts, written mainly by men such as the liberal-turned-radical, John Stuart Mill, picked up the cause of women's suffrage. The utopian socialists obviously shared Enlightenment beliefs that if the environment were properly organized people would behave rationally and progress would be inevitable.

Far more important, however, was the socialism being worked out by Karl Marx from the late 1840s onward. Marx believed that history was marked by class struggle, an inevitable dialectic. Middle class wrested power from aristocracy and then faced the proletariat, the propertyless workers, in the next historical bout. Capitalism would create ever larger industrial units, driving more and more small property owners into the proletariat. Revolution was inevitable. The proletariat would win, take over the state, briefly use it as a dictatorship to rid society of all remnants of bourgeois culture, and then the state would wither away. In a somewhat fuzzy view of future society, Marx suggested economic equality, no private ownership, self-regulation, absence of classes, and the possibility of unlimited self-improvement of men and women as individuals. Marx is not a simple Enlightenment figure because his view of history held people to inevitable forces beyond their control. They could not act freely or rationally until the final stage. But Marx's final society depended on human rationality. His belief in progress was obvious. He urged material and scientific advance—on the latter point he tried to dedicate the first volume of *Das Kapital* to Darwin, out of admiration for the discovery of evolutionary theory; Darwin, a conservative soul outside of science, politely declined. Marx has been called the last Enlightenment thinker, and from the standpoint of political theory this is perhaps true.

For with liberalism, radicalism, and Marxism, the West had an arsenal of rationalistic political theories from which to draw. Intellectuals, then, were also meeting the challenge of the new society though they had to split into warring camps to do it. We do not yet know if the common intellectual heritage will overcome the vital divisions in the principles derived from it. Americans tend to think that the liberal tradition must war with the socialist. But in fact, in European history, liberal and socialist movements have often cooperated precisely because of the recognition that enough is shared—the belief in human reason, in scientific progress—so that apparent enemies can jointly seek common goals.

The Enlightenment tradition was obviously carried on in science. There was progress on every front, and science also increasingly approximated Francis Bacon's dream of serving the needs of ordinary men. German chemists like Liebig developed artificial fertilizers. Medical advances, though haltingly applied, brought improvements in prenatal care. Pasteur's germ theory was yet to come, but more and more doctors pushed public health measures such as unpolluted water and inspection of markets against rotted food. Work on electricity and magnetism, research in geology, increasing interest in psychology—science was advancing on every front. The great discovery was, of course, that of Darwin, who held that all living creatures had evolved into their present form through their ability to adapt in a struggle for survival, and that evolution via survival of the fittest was bound to continue. Darwin's approach combined observation and deduction, the tried and true scientific method. It suggested progress, albeit through a rather bloody and random procedure. On the whole, it fit the

Enlightenment mold, and popularizers of Darwin, like those of Newton, used him initially in this vein. Through competition and exercise of individual talent, the stronger humans would prevail and both man and society would steadily advance.

Romanticism

In this same period, however, a major challenge to the Enlightenment tradition arose in the movement called Romanticism. We should not exaggerate the clash. Romantics could be liberals or socialists. They typically believed in individualism. Many Romantics were not philosophers at all, but painters and poets. They properly resented the Enlightenment's disinterest in the arts, and they set about consciously to create new styles. Playwrights scorned Aristotle's rules and used non-classical themes. Artists painted in more vivid colors and a few, like Turner in England, experimented with non-representative, evocative painting. This was not the sort of thing the *philosophes* had been interested in, but in a way it carried their sense of rebellion and desire for innovation into a new area. Victor Hugo, a liberal as well as a Romantic in literature, made the connection directly in 1829: an attack on artistic conservatives, the defenders of the old classical standards, was an attack on political conservatives; both constituted a blow for liberty.

We must be careful not to turn Romanticism into a political movement of any definite stripe, however. Above all, the Romantics were artists. Poets and novelists—and the novel was essentially the product of Romanticism—worked with new forms and themes. They stressed sentiment, often appealing to the reader's desire for excitement or even for a good cry. They liked heroes, action, and swooning maidens. In marked contrast to the Enlightenment they drew on the Middle Ages for many scenarios. Musicians, beginning tentatively with Beethoven but more clearly with composers like Hector Berlioz, broke the classical canons of music, introducing new instruments and new chords. Romanticism encouraged the study of history, because of its fascination with the past. It gave rise to collection of folklore, for the outpouring of popular emotion should not be lost.

The artistic impulse of Romanticism can be seen as headed on a collision course with the crass materialism of industrialization. Actually, Romantic artists were often quite popular; if there was to be clash, it would come later and would never be complete. Romantic composers, for example, might become astute businessmen, raising the standards of performance for a growing audience of newly-wealthy manufacturers. The appeal of tear-jerking novels, if not the finest product of Romanticism, was immense, a sort of literary soap opera that has genuine links with the modern product. There were those who condemned the greed and coarseness of the modern world, and their number would increase, but Romanticism *as art* helped develop a new clientele for a host of literary and musical expressions. And Romanticism had its most enduring influence on the arts. If briefly eclipsed after 1848, save in music, the Romantic impulse to defy artistic standards, to innovate, would emerge even more elaborately in the late nineteenth century.

Yet, while stressing art and diversity, important Romantic philosophers formed part of the movement before 1848, particularly in Germany, and they faced the Enlightenment head on. Man to them was not rational. He needed faith and religion; he needed strong government and an aristocracy. Another political -*ism*, conservatism, clearly resulted from this approach. Science was irrelevant as a source of truth. One should develop, along with faith, an aesthetic sense. Progress was nonsense, at least in the Enlightenment interpretation of it. Look at the ugliness of the new factories, the exploitation of people in them, the horror of the modern world. Here again the Middle Ages were far preferable. Materialism, of course, was an outrage; man should not live for bread alone.

This attack on the Enlightenment turned into a permanent tension in the modern western intellectual world. Look at what a Romantic philosopher could do with Darwinism (if he did not reject it on grounds that it contradicted religious truth about man's creation). Man, descended from the apes, retained primal instincts; he was not rational in essence. Change resulted from struggle, even war. This might be good, for Romantics liked action and the notion of classes or races fighting for survival of the fittest meshed with this tradition, but this was hardly an Enlightenment view of progress.

All of this complicates the judgment of the final intellectual -*ism* produced in the period, nationalism. Romantics supported nationalism. They liked to refer to a people's cultural heritage, its folklore. Some saw the nation as an entity greater than its individual components, a sort of mystical vision no rationalist could share. And the Enlightenment tradition, internationalist in its belief in the essential similarity of all men, was clearly hostile to any selfish nationalist approach. On balance, nationalism was an anti-Enlightenment product and, as a political movement it has warred with the rationalist impulses such as liberalism and socialism. This was a key intellectual basis for the conversion of political nationalism from a juncture with liberalism and radicalism into quite a different beast after 1848. A nationalism that would express (and exploit) man's passions, a nationalism that would concentrate on the higher good of one's own state, flowed not only from political reality but from philosophical roots.

Without question the rationalist tradition had an ongoing challenge to cope with, in politics and in the basic philosophy of man. Though Romanticism had its own intellectual origins, its popularity was due in part to industrialization. In the long run, the Romantic tradition had to be hostile to industrialization. The goals of industrial society were wrong, the result too messy in aesthetic and human terms. Here, too, was a challenge to modernity with long-range implications.

New Political Structures

After 1848, Europe seemed to settle down for about two decades. Such a high level of social, political and intellectual ferment could not be maintained. Industrial advance continued, rail networks extended, but the lines of development seemed set. Revolutions ceased and even riots declined. This was a period of calm prosperity. New union movements formed among skilled workers, but they stressed self-improvement and sedate bargaining with employers. They proved to be the link between the old craft tradition and modern trade unionism, but their potential was not yet realized. Karl Marx busily scribbled away, surrounded by a small coterie of later socialist leaders from many nations, but his scholarly work and rather testy efforts at organizing an international movement were again to bear fruit only later. As noted, Romanticism died down. Most Romantics turned away from politics, becoming more venturesome in their styles; poets, particularly, began the experiments with non-metered, non-rhyming verse that continues today; but here too their efforts were largely unnoticed.

The main events of this two-decade period were in diplomacy, not an active area in the previous half-century. The unifications of Italy and Germany had overtones of nationalism, though only a minority of people were vitally interested until after the fact. Their sponsors, Cavour and Bismarck, were not initially concerned

with unification, but rather with traditional diplomatic aggran-
dizement by fairly traditional means—alliances and limited wars.
The result overturned Europe's map, with Germany for the first
time since the early Middle Ages the leading continental power,
but the implications of this dawned slowly on a sleepy period.

Yet diplomatic maneuvering was part of broader political adjustments to the post-1848 situation. The impact of revolution and
even the new intellectual currents could not be ignored, and
governments changed in wide areas of activity, learning new ways
to preserve social peace. Right after 1848 most went back to reactionary policies, but soon they emerged with a different air. By the
mid-1860s Germany, Italy, and Austria-Hungary had parliaments.
These bodies lacked the control over the executive that western
parliaments had, but they were not powerless. They gave people a
genuine feeling of representation in the government. Furthermore,
most parliaments new and old (Italy and Austria-Hungary are the
exceptions) were based on universal suffrage or something close to it.
Here, too, there might be some cheating. Prussia, for example, let
every adult male vote but divided the population into three classes
by amount of property held, and each class had equal weight in the
vote. Nevertheless, in countries where absolutism had long held
sway, the new kind of parliament—that is, the parliament based on
individual vote and, increasingly, even universal suffrage—constituted a major change in government form. Where manorialism
had been abolished, states also had to send out central agents
to do what the landlords had done, particularly in running local
courts of justice. Centralization of power thus steadily increased.

There were changes in state functions, too. Governments now
included it as their duty to support economic (including factory)
development. This was designed both to appease the new middle
class, which it did, and to provide the economic base for modern
military power. Prussian wars with Austria and then France in the
period 1866-1871 showed how modern heavy industry, providing
rails and guns, was vital to successful warfare. Prussia was supposed to lose both wars because of her small size. In fact, she won
easily and quickly, because her industrial base was greater and her
army larger and more attuned to modern technology. The result
was the unification of Germany and a major reshuffling of Europe's
power alignments. So there were traditional as well as new reasons
for state attention to industry, but the result was a definite new
role. Governments backed investment banks and continued their

development of transportation networks. Where private initiative was inadequate, as in eastern Germany and Russia, they even built and ran many factories and mines themselves. Western countries, particularly England, did not need to get into this degree of economic activity yet, but here too there was growing attention to industrial training and economic encouragement.

More haltingly, the state took new measures to help the poor. Charitable assistance was not new, but now states passed laws regulating conditions in factories and houses. Safety measures, hours of work, and sanitary conditions were open to regular inspection. Soon—Germany leading the way in the 1880s—governments legislated social insurance to protect workers who were ill, disabled, or too old to work. The motive: keep the lower classes happy enough to prevent revolt; have a strong population, not debilitated by urban conditions, for military purposes; and perhaps make the state an instrument of public good. The result was the beginning of welfare as a state function.

Finally, governments got into the education business. This, like keeping of civil records of marriages, deaths, and the like, was too important to be left to the church, although a religious element might remain in education. The secularization of the state and the whole society thus continued, and the government opened its most important new direct contact with each citizen. Education was soon made compulsory and free. It had to be. Industry needed literate people who could read instructions, calculate—and read advertisements. Even more, states themselves, having granted the vote to the populace, had to make sure it would toe the line. So education was designed to improve technical skill levels, but above all to inculcate loyalty. And the key here was nationalism, belief in the overwhelming importance and glory of one's nation and, usually, the inferiority of others. Nationalism, preached not only in schools but by the press, and by the armies (who now, in imitation of Prussia, recruited a substantial portion of the population for a term of military service) caught on extensively. In the schools, national history was stressed, and, of course, the nation's past was put in the most favorable possible light. National literature and language were emphasized, and where there were minority languages, like Polish in Germany or Breton in France, the authorities tried to expunge them. Education did not prevent social discontent. It did not make most people ardent nationalists. But it clearly had an effect on popular loyalties, tying many actively to the state.

Here, in fact, was the clearest change in the nature of the state. Now aiding economic advance, providing some welfare measures, and educating, the state was in unprecedented contact with its citizens. The latter, who now voted and gained steadily in political consciousness, could feel part of the state. Traditional governments had not cared about active loyalty; lack of disorder was enough. The modern state demanded more.

The state, in sum, by changes in form and function, met the challenge of the first industrial era after intense revolutionary pressure and only at the era's end. It did not create a perfect society. It did not restructure traditional functions, such as military strength, so much as add to them. But, aided also by improved police forces, the state came to pass the first test of being a state: from 1848 onward, it survived. Indoctrination, repression, and positive benefits to the citizenry combined to keep it alive, and the combination, though much more sophisticated now, still works.

Statesmen and many ordinary citizens, particularly of course in the middle class, could thus look at the Europe of 1870 with great satisfaction, and this mood of self-congratulation substantially continued until shattered by World War I. The scourge of the nineteenth century, revolution, was under control. Protest was manageable because most people, even criminals (and crime rates were themselves stabilizing) were working for gains within the system, even when they engaged in agitation. They wanted more out of it, not to replace it. And many did not even need to protest to gain not only greater material prosperity but also a sense of opportunity and individual self-expression. There had been wars, of course, as the Italians with French help drove the Austrians out of Italy around 1860 and then took over Rome in 1870, and during the process of German unification. But they were brief and not too painful. Even France, the clearest diplomatic loser, took her diminished stature with fairly good grace, ignoring the minority who cried for revenge and militarism. Advances in knowledge and a new range of choice among the arts were undeniable, even if sometimes a bit contradictory. The parade of progress seemed endless.

Formal Culture

This is frankly a tough area to deal with, because so many Enlightenment assumptions have been accepted that areas of intellectual activity have withered. Political thought is a case in point; here was an area of concern to intellectuals from the Geeks onward. Yet we have not had a full presentation of political theory since Marx. Socialists and Communists have embellished Marxism. Lenin's main contribution was to hold that Communist revolution could occur anywhere in the world, as in Russia, even where industrialization was not advanced, because foreign capitalists had spread their net everywhere. He was right, in fact, although one may quarrel with his theory, but this was hardly a new overall political formula. Most of the rationalist tradition in social thought has been broken down into separate university departments—in sociology, economics, and so on—where huge advances have been made in theory and data collection, but no overarching view of society has been produced.

The intellectual of the earlier period became an anachronism. We may view this as a misfortune, but the fact is clear. In agricultural societies most intellectuals were priests; the few exceptions were those patronized by aristocrats. Then for a brief period, in the eighteenth and early nineteenth centuries, intellectuals captured political interest and seemed to be heading toward a leadership role in society. But they could not sustain the interest. In a democratic society, politicians may use intellectuals and their ideas, but they will not be run by them. The intellectual who accepts the social order, including its ideological underpinnings, has gone back to the university, like his medieval counterpart. There he earns his bread and can do all sorts of interesting things.

The two great minds of the twentieth century jostle these assumptions a bit, but do not dislodge them. Physics departed from its neat Newtonian base. Niels Bohr in 1913 formulated a rational theory to explain the movement of electrons, hoping they observed regular behavior, but by the 1920s it was clear that not all electrons did move in an easily predictable manner. So physicists, long the source of scientific truth, began arguing, some talking of particles, others of waves. Even earlier, Albert Einstein had called physical certainty into question, using the word "relativity" to describe time itself. Time depends on the observer; it is not an absolute. We see events now in outer space that took place millions of years ago. Natural laws that explain the universe simply are no longer acceptable. Scientists continue to use the rationalist method, but they do not expect to find the convenient Newtonian universe, where a couple of statements cover everything. Rather, physical events occur in more or less random fashion, though their overall statistical probability can be calculated.

The other great mind of the modern period, Sigmund Freud, also complicated any simple Enlightenment view, in this case not of the universe but of man. Man had an unconscious element in his mind, which might dictate acts of madness at an extreme, over which he had no deliberate control. At the same time, however, most people used the rational segment of their mind to control their major acts, and even the insane could be cured by a rational method designed to explain to them why they were troubled. Freud thus modified the conclusions of rationalistic students of individual and collective behavior. It is now easy to ridicule Locke's belief in man's being born with a clean slate, for experiences before and during birth, often traumatic, already beginning to shape the unconscious. In the end, however, Freud maintained faith in reason, for man had this capacity, could use it, could even cure serious disorders with it. Freud has had a diverse following and many dissidents from his precise theories, but most psychiatrists and more psychological theory still leave room for rational understanding and control.

A further problem exists within the intellectual community itself. E. P. Snow has written persuasively of two worlds, one artistic, one scientific, that do not know each other. This is exaggerated. Scientists, however rationalistic, have often appreciated the modern arts. Architects and even musicians, who work on new mathematical models, help bridge the gap. But if most artists are bent on portraying a mad universe—see, for example, the work of the Dadaists from the 1930s onward, where normal shapes were distorted to indicate the senselessness of ordinary sensory perception—then we may have a real problem. For, although the world of the students of man and the physical universe has become more complicated since the times of Newton or Adam Smith, science/social science remain wedded not only to a rational method of study but to the assumption that their objects will be ultimately rational. There are rules that describe natural and human behavior. Nature can be controlled to man's benefit, and man and society, despite problems, can improve through better self-understanding. Is the intellectual community dangerously divided as to what the world and man are about? The heirs of the Enlightenment dominate the universities, as theologians once did. But will they be successfully attacked from outside by thinkers who resist the rationalism and organization-mindedness of university life? To posit a major crisis would be exaggerated. In fact, the development of a new strand of artistic creativity has given the Enlightenment tradition, which was a bit dry, what it sorely lacked. Although there has been friction between the two approaches—art and science, science has admitted more uncertainties, and some areas of art put science to use.

Suggestions for Reading

National histories best cover political developments: David Thomson, *England in the Nineteenth Century, 1815-1914* (1964); Alfred Cobban, *A History of Modern France* (1966); K. S. Pinson, *Modern Germany* (1966); A. J. P. Taylor, *The Hapsburg Monarchy* (1965); D. Mack Smith, *Italy* (1959); L. Stavrianos, *The Balkans Since 1453* (1958); Lionel Kochran, The *Making of Modern Russia* (1962); H. V. Livermore, *A History of Spain* (1968). For a factual outline of diplomatic developments, René Albrecht-Carrié, *Diplomatic History of Europe since the Congress of Vienna* (1958).

For intellectual history the best survey is George Mosse, *The Culture of Western Europe* (1962). See also: C. Gide and G. Rist, *History of Economic Doctrines from the Physiocrats to the Present Day* (1948); J. Jeans, *The Growth of Physical Science* (1948); Charles Singer, *A Short History of Scientific Ideas to 1900* (1959); K. C. Greene, *The Death of Adam: Evolution and Its Impact on Western Thought* (1959); Jacques Barzum, *Classic, Romantic and Modern* (1961); E. H. Gombrich, *The Story of Art* (1956).

On economic and demographic development, David Landes, *The Unbound Prometheus: Technological Change and Industrial Development in Western Europe* (1969); E. A. Wrigley, *Population and History* (1969); Adna Weber, *The Growth of Cities* (1963); Phyllis Deane, *The First Industrial Revolution* (1967).

Social history is covered in Peter N. Stearns, *European Society in Upheaval* (1975); another interpretive approach is Barrington Moore, *The Social Origins of Dictatorship and Democracy* (1966). For special topics in social history, E. P. Thompson, *The Making of the English Working Class* (1964); Peter Stearns and Daniel Walkowitz, eds., *Workers in the Industrial Revolution* (1974); Michael Anderson, *Family Structure in Nineteenth Century Lancashire* (1972); and Patricia Branca, *Silent Sisterhood: The Victorian Woman in the Family* (1975). On the nature of early industrial protest, see George Rudé, *The Crowd in History* (1964). For the history of women, see Patricia Branca and Peter Stearns, *Women in Nineteenth Century Europe* (1975).

The revolutionary era is treated by R. R. Palmer, *The Age of the Democratic Revolution, 1780-1848* (1959-64) and E. J. Hobsbawm, *The Age of Revolution* (1969). The best specific study of the French revolution is Georges Lefebvre, *The French Revolution* (1961-64); see also Alfred Cobban, *Social Interpretation of the French Revolution* (1964). On 1848, Peter N. Stearns, *1848: The Tide of Revolution in Europe* (1974).

German unification is covered in T. S. Hamerow, *The Social Foundation of German Unification, 1858-1871* (1969). Nationalism as a phenomenon is examined in Hans Kohn, *The Idea of Nationalism* (1961).

Political Structure

MOST POLITICIANS FELT INCREASINGLY uncomfortable as they approached 1900. They had adapted to the beginnings of a new kind of state but could not carry their initiative through to a logical conclusion. They were still wedded to a traditional set of governmental functions, including expansionary war, that some new trends, notably nationalism, actually seemed to support. But certain key political traditions were given away.

Stage I: 1870–1914

English liberalism had shot its bolt. Its goals were not irrelevant, but they had been achieved. England had education, a free press, and religious toleration. Liberals on the Continent had been less fully successful, but they had won parliaments, religious toleration, and at least partial freedom of press and speech. What were they to do now? They could stay liberal, which meant they would lose popular support because they offered nothing new. This is essentially what happened in Germany and Austria, where the liberal parties faded. French liberals did better, distracting the public by fighting old battles against the church; state support for the church was finally withdrawn in 1904. Or politicians could abandon liberalism in its classic sense and turn to moderate social reforms, as occurred in England. Here, liberals passed graduated income taxes, unemployment insurance (in 1911, the first such measure ever legislated on a national basis), and so on. But why

263

vote for liberals for such measures when socialists promised more? So even in England the liberals by 1919 were becoming a small third party.

The English pattern is not atypical for western states from 1900 to 1920. A spate of new reforms were introduced under liberal auspices. Radical liberals in France introduced new regulations into the factories and developed some social insurance measures. Progressives in the United States, particularly in industrial areas like Massachusetts, put through similar acts; and even on a federal level there was some action as the government introduced some regulation over railroads and other big business. But with limited social legislation plus the completion of the liberal program—from universal education to parliaments to civil rights—it was not clear what to do next. This meant that the ordinary voter was increasingly tempted to vote for a party that didn't even pretend to want further change—the conservative impulse, whether clad in British Toryism or French moderate Republicanism or the American GOP (which had a progressive background but by the 1910s was turning toward the status quo). Or the ordinary voter was tempted to go for something really new—socialism.

Socialist parties bloomed in Germany, France, Austria, almost everywhere in the 1890s. They were mainly Marxist in inspiration and therefore professed to be revolutionary, and they did want a radically new society. But they never tried to start revolutions. They in fact pioneered in calm, democratic politics. They had mass membership, good local organization, careful electioneering. And they appealed to the concerns not only of workers but many peasants and middle-class people who wanted further reform—more democracy, better allocation of wealth, attack on the big business tycoons. As they gained votes, most socialist politicians became ever tamer. A movement arose called revisionism, which held that Marx was wrong; the workers were not getting poorer, the property owners were growing in numbers, revolution was neither possible nor necessary. Most parties rejected this in theory but adopted it in practice, and most of them have hewed to this practice ever since. The socialists worked with liberals and radicals to defend basic freedoms. They cooperated on moderate welfare measures, hoping of course for more in the future. British socialism was a bit slower to develop—the Labour party became a significant force only after 1906. In America socialists were a smaller minority, though an important third party until after World War I. American prosperity, divisions among immigrant workers, and prior political commitment of native-born workers to one of the two major parties differentiated American labor, even though it was active—sometimes radical—in strikes and the trade unions. America was to prove distinctive in lack of, even hatred of, socialism. But despite national variations, a common western pattern could be seen. Through socialism, unions, and possession of the vote, workers were putting new pressure on governments to deal with social problems, and they found support from some middle-class politicians. At the same time, the measures taken did not meet many needs and demands; a social question remained for the future, a question of how to treat the lower classes more equitably or, to put it crassly, to make them more contented. For many decades governments were tempted to react to the "social question" by trying to distract new voters through diplomatic and military initiatives abroad.

The New Empire

The real action before World War I was conducted by conservative politicians, who bent the basic purpose of the western state to imperialism. Europe after 1870 gobbled up Africa. France, England, and to a lesser extent Belgium, Italy and Germany held virtually the entire continent by 1911. Europe and America took over the islands of the Pacific and dominated the key areas of China (on ninety-nine-year leases; but the landlord was not the controlling factor). The Middle East remained tacitly independent, but Britain and Russia struggled for spheres of influence in Persia and Afghanistan. Without formal rule, the United States gained economic control over many enterprises in Latin America.

This, then, was a thirty-year-plus period of imperialism, in which the west virtually took over the world. Of course, there was precedent in earlier colonialism, but for the most part colonialism in populous regions, like West Africa, had involved setting up trading stations and controlling trading bases. The new imperialism involved not only new areas but a more total economic penetration and complete government control.

All sorts of factors entered into this extraordinary movement. Christian missionaries, unhappy with increasingly secular society at home, poured out toward the natives. Often government would follow. A mistreated missionary could bring the state in to rule a whole area; this happened as part of France's takeover of Indochina.

Aristocrats in Europe were itchy. They were no longer Europe's leaders, for where money talked big business ruled. But if they could devise new functions as spearheads of the West conquering the world—bringing it civilization, Christianity, the end to slave trade, and a new taste for pink gin—they could feel happier; and of course, from a practical standpoint, there were jobs to be had in empire. Somebody had to rule the savages.

A more popular explanation stresses the role of anxious capitalists, worried that they could not make profits in a world of growing international competition, with one state after another becoming industrialized. So empire was needed to assure markets for goods, guarantee supplies of raw materials, and perhaps provide outlet for excess investment capital. It has been shown that almost all these arguments were incorrect. Capitalist nations traded mainly with each other and invested mainly in each other's industries. A few sources of raw materials were important, and individual entrepreneurs could make a bundle by exploiting native labor. But what actually happened—the fact that new colonies cost more than they paid—and what was believed were two different things. Unquestionably, capitalists and other elements of the general public who were worried about economic growth backed empires because they thought they would bring in new money, along with the glory that would enhance the nation's prestige and excite clerks or workers whose lives were dull and who welcomed the news that the nation's army had just conquered and civilized another "inferior" people.

Yet with all these elements entering in, the fundamental basis for the new imperialism goes back to the nature of the western state. Without radical reform through socialism, there was nothing new to do. The hand of tradition was strong, and that meant war and expansion. Enough people seemed to like imperialism to keep conservatives in power, when in a new age of democratic suffrage it was difficult to offer much else to the people without jeopardizing the social structure. And, with all this as background, the clincher was the new balance of power in Europe and, to an extent, the rise of America and Japan as world forces.

In Europe there were obviously two kinds of states/societies. They should have stayed away from each other, even though they shared a continent, but they did not. One society included Britain, France, and Germany for the most part—the familiar western lineup. The United States would fit as well. Here there were great internal tensions but a flexible governmental system that could handle them. Witness the taming of socialism into responsible parliamentary groups in all these countries.

The second group includes Russia, Austria, and, to a great extent, Italy. They were countries without universal suffrage, at least until right before World War I. They were just beginning to industrialize, and internal social tensions were immense. All faced periodic riots. Austria had a special problem with ethnic minorities. She had resolved the worst dilemma—what to do with the Hungarians—by splitting internal government in 1867; Hungarians could now control their internal affairs. But in both halves of the Empire, minority Slavic groups still had no voice and their strivings for self-expression were brutally repressed. Russia and Italy faced major risings by workers and peasants; a 1905 revolution in Russia forced a few concessions but still the tension continued. These were weak countries, eager to use diplomacy to distract from internal problems.

Add to this strange equation, finally, the balance of power. Germany was Europe's most powerful state, industrialized, united. However, it suffered from an inferiority complex—it lacked England's empire as an emblem of greatness—and a fear that France would somehow manage to recover from her 1870–71 defeat and undo German unity. After all, Germany had been a European patsy because of disunity for centuries, and concern for preservation of the new achievement was not surprising. Now that Italy was united, too, most of the traditionally weak areas of Europe were gone. So, initially, European states turned their customary militarism to new areas. France led the parade, getting empires in Africa and Southeast Asia. This actually helped compensate for the embarrassing defeat at Prussia's hands, for conquering somebody was better than nothing. But once France started, everyone had to chime in for prestige and to protect established holdings. Britain expanded in Africa to block France and Germany; Italy tried with limited success to get an empire to prove she was in the big league; and so it went.

The point is that the western states, having begun to adapt to industrialization, failed to follow through. They turned to imperial gains instead. The international effects were colossal. Africans and Asians gained new contact with western technology and political ideas, which could serve as the basis for modernization even if the Europeans had to be kicked out first.

In Europe, however, imperialism was a false start in the next stage of political modernization. The world was soon carved up. By 1900, one great power ran into another in Africa or Asia. The impulse for muscle-display persisted, however, and attention returned to Europe and to the genuine difference between the two sets of European states.

Here is a final irony. Alliance systems developed that linked modern with unmodern states, and, given the desire for diplomatic strength, the modern tended to bow to the unmodern. Germany, Austria, and Italy formed the Triple Alliance (Italy was an uncertain partner). By 1906 Russia, Britain, and France formed the Triple Entente. The interests of the two alliance systems converged on the Balkans, the one pocket of power left in Europe where small states predominated. Yet only Russia and Austria had pressing interests there: Russia because she badly needed diplomatic success after internal revolt had shaken tsardom, and because she could claim that most Balkan peoples were brother Slavs; Austria because Slavic pressure was an internal nuisance and, here too, because any diplomatic gain might distract from internal tension. So the two powers jockeyed, encouraging little Balkan wars. Finally, in 1914, a Slav shot the Archduke of Austria. Austria declared war on the most important Balkan state, Serbia; Russia declared war on Austria. The fatal dance began. Because they had tied themselves to weak powers, because in the larger sense they were wedded to diplomatic and military conquests, Germany, France and, a bit more reluctantly, Britain, went along. They all went to war.

World War I

World War I was a bloody, horrible war, worse for some of the Entente states who "won" than for some of the losers. The war greatly increased the power of the central states who now ran propaganda machines, often untruthful. Many Germans did not even know they were losing the war after 1917 until the end had come. The British were told in 1914 that Germans were killing Belgian babies or cutting off their heads—another lie. Governments drafted soldiers; they drafted workers for factories; they rationed goods. Here was more than a clue as to what the modern state could become. The power of parliaments inevitably decreased as the war went on, for efficient orders from the top, that is, from the executive branch, seemed vital in the name of victory. In

Germany, a pair of generals pretty well took over the state directly.

Ironically, Europeans went to war rather gaily. Some were spurred by nationalism, others by a taste for excitement. Socialist parties, long opponents of war, almost uniformly backed this effort. Some historians have seen in all this a drive to replace modern rationalism and materialism with an atavistic lust for blood. Perhaps so. But the initial attitude was based on two beliefs: first, that one's country was defending itself against attack and second, that the war would be short if glorious. It was neither, and when the blood began to flow people at home as at the front began to sicken of the monster that war had become.

France thrust briefly into Germany in the late summer, but on the western front the German conquest of Belgium and advance through northern France was the big news. Soon northern France was pockmarked with trenches, from which little advance was possible. Occasional offensive efforts, through 1917, cost tens of thousands of lives a day, with a gain of perhaps a few yards—and the necessity of digging a new set of trenches. Artillery bombardments harrassed the trench fighters. In 1916, stalemate had turned into nightmare. The Germans lost 850,000 men along the western front in that year, the French 700,000, the British 410,000.

The eastern front was more fluid. Germany successfully fought back a Russian invasion but had to help out Austria-Hungary, which the Russians could handle. Austria-Hungary bloodily crushed Serbia but fought another stalemate war against Italy, which entered the fray on the allies' side in 1915, hoping for major territorial gains. There was fighting also in the Balkans, where most states aligned with one side or another, and in Turkey, which allied itself with Germany. Japan joined the allies and happily seized German holdings in the Far East. The United States, goaded by German submarine attacks on shipping, entered the war in 1917 and provided fresh if poorly-trained canon fodder for the western front.

Germany managed to penetrate huge sections of Russia, which helped trigger revolution (which the Germans abetted by sending the arch-agitator, Lenin, by train from Switzerland into Russia). When the Communists took over the new government late in 1917, they signed a peace pact with Germany. The focus was now on the west. Here, however, a German offensive failed, and the allies routed their opponents in August, 1918. Austria was also pressed, and riots by minority nationalities forced her to her knees; the Empire sued for peace in November. Riots in German cities forced the Emperor there to abdicate, and the new government agreed to unconditional surrender on November 11.

Yet the war was not over. With over 10 million people directly killed, virtually every family in Europe had at least one death to mourn. Young men, including potential leaders of a new generation who had been in the forefront of the futile efforts to charge out of the trenches, were gone, a bleak prospect for Europe's vitality for the future. Destruction of property and distortion of Europe's economic position could also haunt the continent for two decades. Foreign trade and capital were lost, and Europe became a debtor continent. Excessive wartime spending made inflation inevitable; from Europe's new economic weakness depression was probably inevitable as well.

The war created a cult of violence, preached earlier by some intellectuals, that would mar the next two decades. Former soldiers, bewildered by civilian life and the complacency of those who had stayed on the home front, were ripe for action, be it rebellion, political assassination, or simply brave marches which recalled old comraderie.

But the war, more subtly and without initial impact, created the first modern movement of revulsion against violence. Some of this was expressed in the bright hopes for the new League of Nations. From America, little touched by the war save as a means of making money so others could kill themselves, President Wilson proclaimed the war a battle to end all wars. Pacifist groups, backed by socialists, university students, and many women's organizations, sprang up widely. Strongest in western countries, they have been accused of delaying preparation for an inevitable second war with Germany. Perhaps so. But they may be given credit for launching a sentiment that has wider currency after the experience of this second catastrophe, possibly even modifying the strain of belligerence we have noted in western (and one might add, Japanese) culture.

The Settlement

The way the pieces were picked up after the war did not help Europe's mood. The Versailles treaty and other treaties applying to most of the northern hemisphere satisfied almost no one. France was bent on revenge against Germany and assurance that Germany would be weakened, unable to attack a third time. Groups in

EUROPE 1871-1914

eastern Europe were busily carving out new national states from the rotted hulk of the Hapsburg monarchy. Russia, not represented because the communist regime was an official pariah, had nevertheless to be dealt with. Italy simply wanted land anywhere. The United States briefly wanted Ideals, involving national self-determination but also, somewhat contradictorily, a new world order of harmony; but then the American turtle crawled back into its shell, refusing even to join the League of Nations which it had largely created.

Overall, the peace settlement reflected the desire to punish, in contrast to the settlement of 1815 which had tried to reconstruct a viable diplomatic balance. The rash of new, small countries recognized in eastern Europe—Poland, Czechoslovakia, states in the Baltic and Balkan regions—were individually so weak that they hampered Europe economically and created an obvious temptation to Russia and Germany, the big power on either side of them, after the latter had a bit of time to recover. The small states also bickered among each other, which made matters worse. France got Alsace-Lorraine back and Germany was pledged to disarm all territory west of the Ruhr; she also was forced to pay huge reparations, the dubious assumption being that she alone was responsible for the war. This did not give France enough protection, and obviously it made the Germans unhappy. Italy got almost no territory; just enough, in the Austrian Alps, to make Austria unhappy too. There simply was no way to reconcile all the nationalist demands, so the whole principle was an unsound basis for settlement.

Finally, Europe's imperial structure was shaken by World War I. Through the newly-created League of Nations, France and England took over Syria, Lebanon, and other territories of the now-defunct Ottoman Empire. They were supposed to take over Turkey as well, but a new, modernizing leadership under Kemal Attaturk fought successfully for his nation's independence. On paper, Europe (plus Japan and the United States) ruled more of the world than ever. In fact, huge looses in the war—in the French case, almost a tenth of the population was killed—and economic waste, as money was poured into armaments soon to be destroyed, made Europe a weaker continent. There was the chance now in India and elsewhere for significant nationalist movements to arise, demanding independence. Although this was not gained in the case of India until 1947, Britain was forced much earlier to promise concessions.

Stage II: Since 1914

So the post-World War I history of Europe is in part a history of loss of empire only recently acquired. But before this trend became fully clear, the continent had to undergo another shattering World War and had to deal with the immense ramifications of the First World War more generally. Shattered morale was perhaps as important as shattered diplomacy and economies. Many people believed that western civilization had come to an end, and belief can be self-fulfilling. The next two decades were a time of immense chaos. But ironically, amid this chaos, three durable kinds of states developed. They were diverse and some may seem repellent, but they were proof that Europe had not lost all creativity. State One was totalitarianism. State Two was the welfare state. State Three was the authoritarian state. We must deal with the conditions of the rise of each, but first let us venture a definition of key types.

The authoritarian state, most common in economically backward countries like Spain (or in those of the Third World) has some totalitarian trappings. But its controls are limited and it is basically committed to the social status quo. Though Third World regimes particularly may attempt economic development, European authoritarianism long shied away even from this, lest landlord and Church power be disturbed. This is in many ways, like the government of Napoleon I, an updated absolute monarchy, with or without a legitimate monarch to sanction it. It offers less that is new than the other two forms, but remains pervasive.

The totalitarian state, strictly speaking, is a state that has no competing political units within it. It runs everything—business, unions, family, and education. It tolerates no competitors and demands active loyalty, not just passive obedience, from its citizens. It controls the press and uses brutal police tactics to prevent any dissidence. In fact, one can take this a bit too far, for what looks effective in a definition on paper does not always mesh with the facts. Nazi Germany, for example, has to be called totalitarian, but the state ran the economy in a sloppy fashion, letting profiteers distort production efficiency, and was really effective only at one thing: police repression, via the Gestapo. It prevented internal challenge but did not, for example, do as well in war as it could have, even granting that it was outnumbered and doomed to ultimate defeat. Russia more effectively is totalitarian. It has had more time to develop the relevant structures. But eastern European states created under Russian control after World War II do not fit the pattern so clearly. At various periods Hungary, Czechoslovakia, and Poland have allowed considerable freedom of expression. Outside the direct Russian orbit, Yugoslavia, though essentially a one-party government ready to arrest any significant dissident, has developed democratic workers' councils in factories, with a voice as to what the factory should invest in as well as the conditions of labor, that many western states seek to copy. We must beware of tossing terms around too loosely. We must certainly beware of assuming that one system works uniformly better than the other, even in terms of ordinary popular happiness. In fact, we may conclude that many goals are shared. It is clear that the governments we would call totalitarian since the late 1940s are in the eastern zone of Europe. This does not mean they are bad or ineffective. But it calls attention to the fact that the welfare state is the more typical product of western civilization, and may, at this point at least, fit social needs and culture only in this zone.

The welfare state defines its primary functions, along with provision of justice and preservation of internal order, as the encouragement of economic growth and full employment and the provision of welfare measures against key problems of all citizens, particularly the poor but not excluding the better-off. The general welfare category has normally included: state medical care or medical insurance systems so that no ill person need miss professional attention on financial grounds; expanded educational systems, granting more scholarships and more places at the university level; aid to large families (most western European countries now having a slow rate of population growth), which can add immensely to the income of a poor worker with four or five children; efforts to reduce class conflict by enforcing bargaining procedures, or even imposing new governing boards in industry, so that workers have a say along with owners. (Key industries, such as mines, have in fact been nationalized outright.) There is no overall pattern here; one state stresses one point, another stresses another. But the purpose, long hinted at in western society, is the use of government to benefit people, at least to provide minimal standards which assure the possibility of life. Totalitarian states fulfill many of the same purposes. The welfare states differ in that they intend these goals without total state control, with much private initiative. Their governmental structure retains elections with choice among candidates and parties, parliaments with some real power to restrain executive orders and bureaucratic controls.

These are models. They will be discussed again, particularly to point out that while the welfare state works it should not be overrated. The United States, in fact, has got along without a full welfare state at all, tolerating more unemployment and worse average health levels than the west European nations. But before elaborating on the models, an obvious chronological note. Totalitarianism developed from the government controls of World War I, and Lenin, when in power in Russia, deliberately copied measures taken by the German military command. But even he could not make this stick, and it was not until the late 1920s in Russia that a genuine totalitarian regime developed. The welfare state first arose in Scandinavia in the early 1930s, but its major extension occurred after World War II. To grasp all the major types of regimes, we must briefly outline a period of troubles, whose severity alone forced such radical alterations in government form.

The Interwar Period

MIDDLE CLASS PEOPLE OF western Europe, including many intellectuals, felt that the world had come to an end by 1918. Europe's position in the world was less strong. Death had literally affected almost every family in the nations involved, bringing raw statistics of casualties to the more real level of personal mourning. And the war simply should not have happened. This was a civilized, or had been a civilized world, yet it got itself locked in trenches and faced technological nightmares of destruction: tanks, poison gas, submarines and aerial bombing.

Europe's economy was shaky. As a new debtor continent, it owed money particularly to the United States. It had lost export markets to the United States and Japan. Above all, it was doomed to endure severe inflation. Governments, not wanting to disturb the social order, had rarely increased taxes. They had kept prices down by wartime controls, even though by 1917 prices were creeping up by fifty percent a year or more. But once the war was over inflation was inevitable. This in turn hit the middle class, labor unions, and ultimately even peasants. Anyone with savings, and many without, had to be affected when a person needed to take a huge basket of money simply to buy shoes, as was true in Germany in 1923—and hope that the price would not go up if one had to wait in line. Although, governments did manage to relieve inflation during the 1920s by massive devaluation of currency, this did not restore the property or confidence that had been lost. More fundamentally, the European economy, once it recovered from wartime destruction, was faced with overproduction. Technology continued to advance, affecting even office work with typewriters and business machines. Businesses became larger and better organized. But purchasing power did not keep pace. Peasants' incomes were low. Areas like eastern Europe which were primarily agricultural suffered keenly from this, for their western markets were not growing as fast as their own production and that of their competitors. More directly, foods from the Americas, Australia and elsewhere, more efficiently and extensively produced, kept the earnings of European farmers, east and west, at low level. This in turn meant little ability to purchase manufactured goods. Workers' wages improved in the cities but their ability to purchase the many new products was limited. The income of old middle class property owners was hit, sometimes wiped out, by inflation which made savings worthless.

Economic disaster ended in the great depression of the late 1920s and onward, in which up to a third of all workers (clerks as well as factory hands) were unemployed. The depression revealed immense structural weakness in the western economies. Tariff barriers made trade difficult. Unwise speculative investments, after creating a brief aura of prosperity, collapsed. The key problem was that production exceeded purchasing power in a class-ridden society. Peasants and workers, plus many impoverished clerks and shop keepers, simply did not make enough money to buy all the products available. And exports could not compensate, for the price of raw materials was low and underdeveloped countries, including those of eastern Europe, were themselves locked in depression, unable to purchase new manufactured products. So unemployment soared, and many workers endured years of joblessness; this was not a material fact alone, though suffering was immense, for morale could be shattered by a sense of worthlessness. Inevitably the depression had immense political repercussions.

Finally, although the 1920s saw no European wars, the diplomatic atmosphere was new and disquieting. Most of the tiny states in eastern Europe gave few signs of solidity. Germany behaved peaceably but made it clear that the Versailles settlement was not satisfactory. France was edgy, but after a brief display of muscle in occupying the Rhineland in 1923, retreated to a defensive stance. Here, then, was the confused atmosphere in which new regimes were born.

The Russian Revolution

Most dramatic was the rise of totalitarianism, which sprang up first in Russia. Russia suffered horribly in the war. Inept government under a stupid but stubborn tsar, Nicholas II, added to the inherrent weakness of a largely non-industrial economy. To bitter defeats in the field was added economic privation at home. Faced with massive unrest even before the war, the regime could not endure. During 1916 strikes and bread riots increased, for prices had risen almost 700 per cent. In March 1917, strikes broke out in the capitol and gradually assumed revolutionary proportions, as troops joined the strikers and gave them weapons. A council, called a soviet, was formed and took control of the city, arresting the government ministers.

Initially the government was headed by liberals, bent on constitutional rule and continuation of the war. But the revolution was most explicitly directed against the impact of the war; yet the new government vowed to fight on—here was a crucial blunder. Workers kept control of the major cities, and in November (October, by the Russian calendar) the liberal government was swept away in turn. The Bolshevik party, headed by Lenin (real name: Vladimir Ilyich Ulyanov), took charge. Only a minority even of the workers were Bolsheviks. Other Marxist and social revolutionary groups were strong rivals. But Lenin was no ordinary Marxist radical. He added to Marxist theory but also preached the importance of tightly-knit, small revolutionary cadres—the majority could be won over later. So he simply out-organized his opponents, and soon liquidated their groups.

One-party, one-leader government was not set up easily. Russia faced years of bitter and bloody civil war. Lenin, though bent on total state control, had to make temporary concessions, allowing peasants to farm their own plots and small businessmen to operate. But the outlines of the new state were quickly clear. The Duma, the Russian parliament, became a rubber stamp. New trade unions, often attracted to Bolshevik communism anyway, were taken over. Major business was nationalized. Lenin briefly had to bow to older motives by allowing peasants and small businessmen some leeway, for there was bitter internal opposition to the regime. Foreign states from Japan to America felt threatened by the revolutionary government which blatantly talked of subverting the whole capitalist order, though outside intervention was not too serious because of the exhaustion of most countries after the war.

Internal and foreign opposition are standard ingredients in any major revolution and they tend to produce more authoritarian controls in response (as in the radical phase of the French Revolution). What was distinctive here was a regime wedded to dictatorship as a matter of principle to get rid of all remnants of the past. The result was totalitarianism. If Lenin briefly relaxed, out of the sheer necessity to assure food supplies from peasants who wanted to run their own farms, his successor, Stalin, resumed the quest for total state control in the later 1920s. The state set all economic goals. Private property in land was seized from the peasants, and many of the wealthier peasants were killed or deported to Siberia. Members of the Communist party supervised every factory, almost every street corner, either privately or as members of the pervasive new secret police. Elaborate propaganda proclaimed the virtues of the new regime and urged devotion to it through hard work—Russia was still trying to gain the status of a major industrial power—and even by reporting on relatives who might be suspected of reactionary thoughts.

So here was the first example of the new totalitarian regime. Russia was elaborating her long tradition of absolutist rule which had never allowed even serious pretense of parliament. Her regime might be effective; it might turn out to be dominant whether desirable or not; it was in many ways predictable. Add to the Russian political tradition the example of wartime controls, made possible through new technology such as the radio. Add the urgently felt need to industrialize fast, to catch up with the West—but through state and not private auspices as these had proved inadequate given Russia's lack of capitalist tradition. The inevitable tendency—as in France under Napoleon—for revolution to turn toward dictatorial controls to settle the disputes which revolution caused in the first place. Mix it all together, and Russia's regime is not surprising. But it was new—the first totalitarian regime and the only one that has lasted for much more than a generation.

Nazi Totalitarianism

Germany presents a more surprising case, for here was Nazi totalitarianism in a country industrialized and sufficiently in the western political tradition to have decades of parliamentary experience. Yet here arose the only clear western case of a totalitarian regime. It did not last very long, 1933 to 1945. Yet though there was serious internal opposition, the only thing that overturned this regime was defeat in war. Then, ironically, the older traditions—liberalism, socialism—picked up again, save where the Russians prevented their outcropping. After a nightmare the Germans seemed to wake up again.

Hitler came to power in 1933. His ideology was vastly different from that of Lenin. Indeed the Nazis had little fixed ideology, preferring to speak to whatever group they encountered in terms that would be appealing. The regime that preceded Hitler, the Weimar Republic, was genuinely parliamentarian and had the difficult legacy of wartime defeat, for the groups that had really lost the war, the generals, carefully forced this new government to be responsible for carrying through peace negotiations. It resulted from a mini-revolution, led by socialists who kicked out the Emperor and set up a genuinely democratic republic. But the moderate socialists did not tamper with society; perhaps they could not, without bitter civil war. They thus left landlords, the army and big business alone, and brutally repressed real revolutionaries. Further, the Weimar regime had to contend with inflation, then the depression. It was bitterly divided internally. Some political parties disapproved of the regime itself, from monarchist-nationalists on the right to communists on the left. But so long as there was adequate prosperity, the regime seemed to be catching on; it even helped Germany regain some diplomatic prestige. But everything fell apart with the depression. And this is where the Nazis moved in. A small, but noisy party before, it now would capture, at its peak, over forty percent of the total German vote.

Hitler offered workers jobs. He offered artisans a return to a guild economy. He appealed to the peasants, talking about the virtues of small-farm life. He told shopkeepers that big stores were evil (and Jewish) and again implied a return to a simpler commercial life. He even won disproportionate support from women by talking of home and family. Traditionalism was the source of his vote, from people who wanted a return to the past for a solution to immediate economic problems. There is no question that Hitler showed that Germany, though an advanced industrial nation, had not developed the widespread modern mentality that could accept what was actually going on. Hence some people working in department stores—the new, classy and efficent units of consumption—voted with Hitler that these should be abolished. And of course Hitler had a key scapegoat: the Jews. Jews caused big business. They caused big labor which was gaining more than the workers deserved. They should be "handled," though this presumably meant just put in their place; even Hitler did not think of mass extermination until the late 1930s, by which time there was no one to control him. Naturally, Hitler attacked Germany's military and diplomatic weakness; he talked directly of undoing the Versailles treaty and vaguely of war and conquest, appealing to those with a taste for action. Hitler stood also for anti-communism. Class warfare divided the nation and had to be taken in hand (the fact that the depression drove the Communist vote up aided him here, while proving that Germans were not united in a drive toward fascism). But Hitler did not come to power via revolution. Having tried a farcical revolt in 1923, the Beer Hall Putsch, he had correctly learned that one cannot directly revolt against a modern state. He also never received a popular majority in a free election, and though at his peak he won over forty percent of the vote the part was declining when he came to power. Given massive backing and the use of violent shock troops to disrupt the political process, the key to seizure of power was in fact rather prosaic corruption and wheeling-dealing. By 1932 Hitler was making deals with businessmen, promising them that his attacks on banks and department stores were just gimmicks and that he would leave them alone to make their profits and with the army, for generals serving in political office proved vital to get him in power. He was legally appointed chancellor by an aging general and with the support of all political parties save the socialists (who alone defended the real democratic tradition); the Communists had already been outlawed. Then he proceeded to set up this second version of totalitarianism.

Does all this adequately explain Hitler's rise? Defeat alone did not undo Germany; democracy worked reasonably well in the 1920s. Anti-semitism, though present, was not particularly virulent. It took massive economic collapse to propel the Nazis forward, for collapse brought out yearnings for the past and fears of the radical left that Hitler readily exploited, along with intense material suffering. But was there something deeper in German character, an authoritarian instinct that yearned for strong leadership as an expression of a mystic German soul, that Hitler brought out? Historians have penned volume after volume on the subject; it is fascinating, particularly in relating Germany to the broader stream of western history. But the factor does not have to be invoked to explain Hitler's rise. What is clear is that once in power, like Lenin and Stalin in Russia, Hitler quickly made opposition impossible. This does not mean he won all Germans over, as the restoration of democracy after World War II suggests. But apathy and repression worked wonders until Hitler destroyed his own edifice by war.

All competing unions and parties were banned, many of their leaders (initially mainly ethnic Germans and not Jews) sent to concentration camps. State governments were abolished and replaced by new units ruled by Nazi officials. Churches were attacked, though here Hitler never succeeded fully in taking over some of the Protestant groups, not to mention the Catholics. Nazi youth groups replaced church organizations, and obviously the schools taught the Nazi version of loyalty to the leader, the Führer, and the racially-pure Fatherland; the few teachers who dissented were fired. Workers were provided with state unions, and while the government did restore full employment, it lowered the average standard of living. Programs of recreation-cum-propaganda were supposed to distract from material problems, but there is no reason to believe that many workers became ardent Nazis; they, like many others, simply went along for want of alternative.

Hitler's intent can be summed up in two ways, both under the rubric of preparing for war. One: *Gleichschaltung,* leveling everything under the state, and the state under the party and the Führer; here was where the Leader had partial success. Two: to make new men, athletic and militaristic rather than rational; to this his educational program was geared, downplaying intellectual subjects. But success here, though undeniable among some docile, action hungry youth, was limited at best.

Hitler's promises of bringing back the old society were pretty well ignored. Guilds were restored for show; peasant dresses were encouraged. The Nazis, bent on war, continued Germany's industrial development, which meant bigger business and bigger agricultural units. Some controls were even placed on businessmen in this venture, through allocation of capital and goods, but the Nazi version of totalitarianism did not involve total economic control here. Indeed, the Nazi state left a lot of people moderately free to act as they pleased, so long as they caused no political trouble. We now know that Nazi economic guidance was quite inefficient. But what the Nazis did do was create an overwhelming police force. This, even more than constant emotional propaganda and huge rallies, kept the people in line—until, of course, war came. This followed from Hitler's desire for conquest and action as man's purpose in life and Germany's obligation as a great nation. When this was lost all was over.

World War II, Hitler's product, allowed Russia to extend control over small eastern European states and the eastern section of Germany itself, where totalitarian regimes were established. Some of these ultimately proved a bit looser than their Russian progenitor, allowing a bit more intellectual freedom, even satire. Poland did not even try very hard to collectivize agriculture because of peasant resistance. But before we can interpret these regimes, we must turn to the authoritarian political form, which borrows from totalitarianism, but is not totalitarian.

States in Southern Europe and the Eastern Fringe

The first authoritarian regime of the new sort was Mussolini's Italy, which arose right after World War I. Italy had been officially a winner in the war but had not received much territory after taking terrible losses in battle. This plus social tensions, including massive strikes, induced segments of the middle class and, above all, the army and the government to bring to power the leader of the new Fascist party, Benito Mussolini. Mussolini was a low-key figure for a while of necessity, for his popular strength was not great, but gradually he, like the totalitarians, eliminated rival unions and parties and set up a leadership state. Party officials, political police, massive rallies, and propaganda—the whole apparatus seemed installed. And here, too, though there was resistance, the regime stayed in power until wartime defeat brought it down—from 1923 to 1943, a better record than Hitler's. Mussolini tried to encourage Italian industrialization. Once Hitler came to power, Mussolini engaged in one war after another, to show the action potential of Italian fascism. He conquered Ethiopia, but had more trouble with Albania and Greece. He even adopted anti-Semitism, again to imitate Hitler (whose power and personality overawed him), even though there were few Jews in Italy and racism had never been part of the Fascist program.

But for all these similarities, this was not a totalitarian state. Mussolini could prevent political resistance of major proportions, but Italy had never been a democratic country, so this was no total change. He quibbled with the church but could not risk attacking it. He did not impose even mild controls on landlords and big businessmen. This was a regime of a new sort, illegitimate in the sense that the monarch became a mere figurehead; militaristic; possessed of abundant police. But it was a regime designed to protect the established order, not to overturn it in the name of a new kind of state, a new society, a new kind of man. Hitler failed massively to create his new man of action—blond, athletic, and war-like—or his new woman, back in the home rearing children who would be soldiers. But if he had had more patience, he might have brought it off through constant propaganda and the new education system. Fortunately, he was not given the time. Mussolini, lacking the economic base and the will to be really totalitarian, did not really try.

Authoritarian regimes developed during the interwar period in most of the eastern European states created after World War I. A country such as Poland simply was not ready for parliamentary democracy. Give peasants the vote, and they would want land reform which the landlords could not stomach; so the latter backed an authoritarian ruler. There were Fascist trappings—fake elections; the famous plebiscites where people voted for candidates with no one else to choose; parades; police; and propaganda. But, less industrialized than Italy, these countries were still further from totalitarianism. They protected the established upper class (both landlords and merchants), the church, and the traditional army. The same was true in Portugal and, after a bloody civil war, in Franco's Spain. Indeed, in Spain and Portugal the regimes have just been displaced with incalculable results.

The difference between authoritarianism and totalitarianism, both products of the 1920s and 1930s, is social intent. Even the Nazis, though hazy on ideology, wanted a new society and a new kind of person. Russia consistently struggled for precisely this. This means, in principle, total loyalty and total control. Regimes, even in Russia, do not always win. Dissident intellectuals have arisen. Peasants, though yielding to the program of collective agriculture, show something less than great enthusiasm by maintaining low productivity. But the intent of the state, its form, and its belief in its function of total control, distinguish it from anything known before. The authoritarian regimes are less new, and they take root in countries less developed economically. They create new political forms, but they resist major social change. In Europe they have almost disappeared, because they are not sufficiently modern; one cannot really resist change. But in a host of countries elsewhere they retain real validity, suppressing opposition, attacking scapegoats like former colonial rulers, pretending to change, but in fact bent on self-preservation and protection of the status quo as prime goals. The totalitarian states of the world remain very few, for this requires sufficient development actively to control and motivate the population and a desire to use the state for change.

Russia remains totalitarian. China is. Cuba probably is. Rumania may be though there is a more traditional authoritarian element. Many eastern European states have modified initial totalitarianism with a bit more responsiveness to popular interest, a sort of compromise between control from above, which remains very real, with interest from below. It is tempting to suggest patterns of westernization here. Without pretending one governmental system better than another—indeed one might contend that different societies need different systems; that Russia, say, could not have industrialized without totalitarianism—there does seem to be an obvious west-east progression in modern government form. Totalitarianism has immense virtues. It can develop new economic systems; it can provide welfare mechanisms even in poor societies; it can educate more quickly than western nations did, given the initial base of illiteracy. So we need not play cold war games about who's better than who. But totalitarianism, though a modern government form and developed from western models, ranging from the theories of Marx on proletarian dictatorship to the actual wartime powers western governments could impose—Britain's World War II controls, for example, were more thorough and efficient than those of Nazi Germany—is not a western form of government. It takes and exaggerates one strand, neglecting the other, a pattern we have traced from feudal and church controls to modern parliaments and declarations of human rights. Germany is the odd exception, though, of course, it has always teetered from eastern to western influences; but Nazi totalitarianism was the product of a very special set of circumstances and proved to have limitations even as a totalitarian form.

The Welfare Model

The welfare state has become the typical modern western government. It must be noted that the major western governments did not do well in the twenty years before World War II. This is important to our larger story, because western states emerged eager to prevent such collapse in future. Class strife, diplomatic quibbling, and political party fights prevented preparation for renewed war. They also largely prevented creative response to the depression, leaving millions in needlessly prolonged poverty. An obvious example: most governments first fired officials when the depression came, for the thing to do was balance the budget and prevent inflation to protect property owners. This was fighting the previous economic problem, not the new one, and meanwhile the ranks of the unemployed and politically disgruntled swelled.

The western governments were diplomatically weak, almost paralyzed. They could not decide whether Germany or Russia was the biggest enemy. In France, near-civil war between conservatives plus Fascists, on the one hand, and communists and some socialists on the left, made action impossible. Even a well-intentioned socialist government, in 1936, could not oppose German and Italian intervention in Spain, on France's very borders, lest the rightwing attack; and it lasted but eighteen months. Small wonder that France and Britain long stood by while Hitler gobbled up European territory, hoping that he would stop sometime.

This situation could endure only if the west was to be progressively destroyed. Depression and the new world war convinced governments like that of Britain that a new approach had to be taken. It convinced groups formed in resistance to Nazi occupation on the continent, from Christian democrats through Communists who formed the post-war government coalitions. And from this the welfare state was born.

There is no neat theory behind the welfare state, no common pattern, and, of course, there were precedents in earlier measures taken for the poor. But let us try to get at main elements as they developed in the thirty years after 1936, when constructive responses to the depression began, even if we depart a bit from strict chronological order. Point one is acceptance, if grudging, of decolonization.

Many of the colonial areas, such as India, developed strong nationalist movements by the 1930s that were already putting great pressure on the ruling regimes. These regimes were further weakened by the tremendous destruction wrought by World War II. It was difficult to afford either manpower or money to keep order against guerilla warfare, as soon developed in Indochina against the French, or even peaceful protest, like that led by Ghandi in India. Finally, new resources were demanded at home. People insisted on a better life, and this included new allocations for state funds. The British, for example, elected their first majority Labour Party government in 1945 mainly because they wanted the government responsible for building better housing. Amid all these pressures the colonial powers gave up. The British pulled out of India in 1947 after over two centuries of rule. A bit later they moved out of their African colonies. The Dutch gave up their hold on Indonesia, and Belgium later left the Congo. France yielded less readily, for as she had not performed well in World War II, her military wanted to redeem themselves by beating the rebels in the colonies. A bitter war in Indochina ended with a pull-out only in the 1950s. It was followed by a decade of bloody struggle in Algeria. But by the 1960s, Algeria too was independent and, without fighting, France's other African colonies were freed as well. In the 1970s the last colonial holdings, those of Portugal in Africa, were given freedom.

There is no question that Europe would not have abandoned her colonies without key pressure in certain areas, at least not so quickly. We need not pretend great generosity. But it is true that a decision was made quite different from that of the Roman Empire when faced with new attacks. Rome poured her resources into military defense. Europe on the whole made the opposite decision, and indeed has continued to scale down most military costs even for purely internal defense. The nations of western Europe were democracies, however imperfect. Voting was in fact extended to women in France after the war, as in England and Germany after World War I. The voters, many of them moving toward socialist or even Communist parties, insisted on a new kind of state. The leaders who had emerged in the war, many of them young, imaginative politicians who had fought in Resistance movements against Nazi occupation, also wanted no repetition of the old Europe. There could be no more collapse of morale, no more depression, no more callous treatment of the lower classes. Since it was clear that these goals were incompatible with the expense, even the morality, of dominating non-European peoples, the empires were given up.

For Europe, at least, the welfare state has involved a reduction in the importance of military and diplomatic activities. Europe's position in the world has diminished, not just because of decolonization but because of the rise of gigantic superpowers, Russia and the United States, whom no European state could rival. By 1947 Russia and the United States were locked in the Cold War, and they are still sniffling at each other. Russia took over fairly direct control of states through East Germany, though this control has not been uniform. American influence was less crass but no less effective from West Germany to the Atlantic. When America formed an alliance (the North Atlantic Treaty Organization) against the communist powers, few western European states failed to join, for they needed American aid and military protection. Russia responded by organizing the eastern nations through the Warsaw Pact. It was easy to see once-proud states now mere puppets on a string. But diminished influence does not mean no influence. Europe has resumed close ties with many former colonies, often involving tighter trading relations than before. Many countries continue to send teachers and advisers to the areas they once ruled directly. And, for their part, former colonies, eager to industrialize and improve health and educational facilities, are adopting at least certain western values and Europe has even rebounded against the. super powers. Europe's weight in the world remains considerable.

A New European Diplomacy

Yet prospects long seemed bleak. Overshadowing the disruption of anything like a traditional power balance was the atomic menace. First the United States, then, in 1951, Russia, developed this immense destructive capacity. Into the 1950s a new war seemed almost certain, and fears have not disappeared since. It is difficult to assess the psychological impact of the atomic threat. Europeans know that an atomic battle between the two superpowers could mean the literal destruction of their continent. Britain and France managed to create small striking forces and deterrents, but these have provided little new diplomatic leverage. Many Europeans suffer acute anxiety about this combination of menace and impotence.

In the West, France particularly began to thumb her nose at the United States, taking a more independent military and diplomatic stance. She had the economic power and the nationalist tradition to pull this off without losing American military protection. Eastern Europe loosened up as well. So long as Russia was not directly challenged—for this would bring decisive military intervention, as in Hungary in 1956—states could adopt more liberal policies toward intellectuals and even make independent diplomatic contacts, as in the case of Rumania.

Yet as war did not come, and the giants balanced each other

out, anxiety declined. The stable, pleasure-seeking culture that defines modern Europe leaves little room for worried thoughts of impending doom. Further, by the 1950s there was space for some diplomatic maneuvers. American tolerance and support plus the distractions of conducting the cold war all over the world, sometimes in hotter places than Europe, combined with the new openness to innovation of the western governments to produce a new diplomatic climate.

The great diplomatic experiment was the partial unification of the nation states. Beginning in the early 1950s key continental states began to cooperate in industrial decisions involving coal and steel. American encouragement was involved, but the primary motive was to prevent western fratricide and particularly to integrate a resurgent Germany into the western orbit. The contrast with the primitive approach taken toward Germany after World War I was marked, and it has been successful; the West German Republic remains among the most eager supporters of unity and traces of militarism and aggressive nationalism have largely disappeared. From this beginning, cooperation expanded, mainly in the economic sphere, until in 1957 the Common Market was created. This was designed gradually to eliminate all internal tariff barriers and create a common economic policy toward the outside world. It was to mesh policies on control of cartels and monopolies, free movement of labor within the member nations, and to harmonize welfare and currency decisions. Initially launched with six members, the organization now has nine: France, Germany, Britain, Italy, the three Low Countries, Ireland and Denmark. It has not always functioned smoothly, for its administration, though genuinely international, has mainly advisory powers, and national interests often predominate. But the Common Market has become an economic force in its own right, and it may lead, as many hope, to further integration, perhaps to political federation. After centuries of disunity, punctuated by only three brief attempts to create unity by force—those of Charlemagne, Napoleon, and Hitler—Europe might be on the way to the gradual creation of a sophisticated political structure above the nation-state level. Certainly the Common Market has at least fulfilled the primary motive of drawing former enemies, notably France and West Germany, together to prevent the recurrent wars of the previous seventy years admirably. Internal European war, a motif of western history since Charlemagne's empire collapsed, is now virtually unthinkable. Further, the Common Market neatly unites those areas in which western civilization has always been strongest, with friendly relations preserved with the next zone of western culture, such as the United States and Australia.

Important as the Common Market may become, however, it remains true that the key interest of each individual European state is now economic development and social welfare. Religion has disappeared entirely as a state function. Provision of justice and internal order of course remain vital, but a genuine reorientation of state functions has developed.

Internal Policies

European governments, beginning with the Scandinavian countries in the 1930s, have expanded social insurance to cover most conceivable material hardships, from unemployment to old age. New housing has been built. All state governments provide inexpensive medical care, which may be one reason that their health levels are better than those of the wealthier United States. Educational facilities have been increased. State-sponsored collective bargaining has reduced, though not eliminated, class tension. The percentage of budgets going into welfare programs has risen steadily, now commanding more than any other category of government activity.

The welfare state is based on a belief that society has responsibility for banishing poverty. A clear effort is made to set minimal conditions in agriculture as well as factory work, minimum income levels, and minimum health standards for the whole population. The welfare state seeks to limit class tensions and barriers to opportunity by the new educational facilities. It is also committed to promote economic growth through state planning and to prevent significant unemployment.

All of this involves new contacts between state and citizen. It involves new bureaucracies, a new sense of planning at the center, and this has led to criticism of the welfare state as a technocratic monster, making decisions on the basis of technical factors without taking human elements into account. There is more government regulation, more direct government activity as the welfare state requires participation in insurance plans, sets doctors' fees, and, of course, levies new taxes to pay for new programs. But the welfare state does not involve rigid or complete domination by the government. Great individual initiative remains. After setting minimum

standards and certain guidelines for general economic development, the welfare state intends to leave society with more opportunities for effective initiative than ever before.

The welfare state offends Europeans in the classic liberal
tradition. Its bureaucracy can be insensitive, and it certainly has
unprecedented power. At the same time the welfare state offends
socialists and Communists by doing too little, by allowing too
much inequality for example. Yet the new state draws on both
liberal and socialist tradition. It benefits both middle and working
classes.

For the middle class it offers bureaucratic jobs, more
educational access as well as material protection that helps this
group as well as workers and peasants. It also eliminates most
offensive poverty and has so far reduced class strife. In these
respects it is in a sense an ideal middle class state, which had been
hinted at since the advent of the class with early industrialization
but delayed by the class's failure to seize full power from the
traditional ruling class. And thus far at least, it has functioned.
Disorder has continued, of course, in the form of strikes. Communist parties remain strong as protest vehicles in France and
Italy. But western communist parties have essentially disavowed revolution, working to participate in the government by
democratic means. In the 1970s both the French and Italian parties
insisted that, if in power, they would not accept Russian
dominance or follow the totalitarian model. In fact the welfare state
itself has been challenged only once, and it weathered the challenge
without undue difficulty. In the late 1960s, worker agitation increased because of inflation and reduced real wages. At the same
time students grew dissatisfied with crowded universities and a
lack of voice in university affairs; here seemed a clear example of an
impersonal organization running peoples' lives. Some students
went on to a general condemnation of over-organized, materialistic
society. Riots occurred at many universities. In May 1968, revolt
broke out in France. Students threw up barricades, while workers
and clerks, in a largely separate action, went on a general strike.
But order was soon restored, and a subsequent election revealed
majority satisfaction with the existing government. Recent
reforms, including higher and more secure pay for workers and
greater student voice in university management, have defused
massive protest at least for the time.

No one can say how the welfare state will fare in future. It does rest on key political traditions of the West. It continues to combine parliamentary representation, with real choice and with central power, though with the complexity of welfare activities the balance has shifted again more toward the central executive branch. The welfare state, then, represents a logical evolution of the western political tradition. Western nations that have not fully adopted it, such as the United States, seem to be moving toward it. America's military commitments, whether necessary or not, have limited its welfare programs. So has a more individualistic political tradition, more suspicion of state power. But pressure for greater economic guidance, less tolerance of high levels of unemployment, and state action in areas such as medical care are probably mounting. Already similar to Europe in the definition of state functions, Americans may move steadily closer to the European model.

Economic Development

A mature industrial society developed in Europe from about 1870 onward. Let us try to define what this maturity means:

Most manufacturing is done in factories, and craftsmen, though still alive and flourishing, are usually working for a larger organization.

Rural residents convert to market agriculture fully and adopt urban values. They decrease steadily in number, since agricultural efficiency requires less labor and the attractions of city life grow. The people that remain on the farms are really no longer peasants at all, but farmers, eager for new technology and showing few remnants of the peasant tradition.

Organization increases. Big business develops beyond the single factory, linking industries into giant corporations. These rely for their financial base not on the funds of a single industrial pioneer, but on sales of stocks and bank finance. Organization develops in agriculture, with the formation of cooperatives to pool the resources of farmers or, in the United States, with massive commercial farms. Organization develops in labor as trade unions grow and gradually gain the right to bargain with employers over conditions.

With organization comes a new kind of businessman and new kinds of workers. The entrepreneurs, striking out on their own, become less important. Increasingly, the economy is run by a bureaucratic hierarchy. The managerial mentality that can plan carefully for the future and simultaneously run a huge personnel operation becomes predominant. This evolution is obvious in big business. It occurs in big labor, too, as the early doctrinaire enthusiast gave way to careful bargainers. Organization in labor, but particularly in business, involves new research. Invention no longer stems from the isolated genius. Trained technical staffs produce new technology and new products. Finally, bureaucracy requires massive clerical support, and a new white collar class develops.

Service functions increase at the expense of production. Production rises massively, of course, with tragic interruptions such as the depression of the 1930s. But most people now work in service occupations—as barbers, salesmen, telephone operators. A key example is teachers. Education becomes increasingly important in a mature industrial economy. Workers need more skills with more complex equipment; white collar labor obviously depends on literacy and mathematical ability. So the variety of educational offerings and the numbers of teachers swell, while society in turn becomes increasingly dependent on advances in knowledge.

Finally, property ceases to become the key criterion of social status. Rather, income, education, and position of power in an organizational hierarchy mark one's place more clearly. The middle class, the fastest growing group in the new society, most obviously switches from reliance on ownership of shop or factory to position in management. This is an immense movement away from traditional values, capping the creation of a new middle class largely free from nostalgia for the past and pioneering in new styles of leisure, new sexual activity and family roles, as well as economic functions.

These are the key changes. They did not occur overnight nor are they complete. But they add up to the full realization of the Industrial Revolution, which had only scratched the surface of society before. The revolutionary implications produced new efforts to resist innovation and return to the good old days. Direct attack was impossible; the state now had too much power to allow a classic protest of the 1848 variety. But demonstrations against department stores or unions, political movements that used anti-semitism as a means of attacking modernity—blaming Jews for everything from big banks to labor organizations—all reflected the profound uneasiness of the "little man," who wanted to run his own operation and avoid the new organizational controls. Nazism was a final, horrible example of the resistance effort.

Resistance has declined since World War II for three reasons. First, older groups have either been shoved aside or died off. Small shopkeepers still exist; they still protest, for example, against supermarket chains in countries like France. But they are vastly outnumbered by the new kinds of workers and technicians who may be dissatisfied but have no reason to go back to the old ways—which leads to reasons two and three.

Two, while organization and bureaucracy sound ominous, they do not necessarily involve the swallowing up of the individual in some giant monolith. They are far less confining than smaller units like villages or guilds used to be. Modern freedom can lead to loneliness, to a sense of alienation in a society that does not tell you your exact place the way the village used to, that gives you a host of choices about what to become or what to buy. Most people seem to be able to accept a freedom that gives them some chance to change stations in life, for while class barriers remain important, social mobility has obviously increased in the mature industrial society. And people have cushioned change by retaining family ties and developing new networks of community and friendship.

Three, particularly since World War II, the whole process of change has been greased by steady increase in the levels of prosperity. With the help of state guidance major recessions have been avoided and unemployment has been low. Workers' wages and middle-class incomes have mounted fairly steadily, in most years well exceeding price increases, and while farmers' earnings lag a bit, their conditions too have improved. European economic growth has in fact been unprecedented, reaching levels like eight percent a year in countries such as France. Correspondingly, material expectations have steadily increased. This is built on western traditions but has reached new heights as the majority of families obtained refrigerators, television, and some form of mechanized transportation—a motor scooter or, increasingly, a car. Obviously a booming economy depended on the passion for things. Life had meaning only if one could get more goodies. This was materialism, and there was status seeking involved. But there was also good sense. Hard work in a changing economy could be justified if life became easier in other respects. Housework involved less sheer physical drudgery. The car gave the family new freedom to roam. And individual choice was involved in what item to work for next. The choice might be difficult, but it was interesting to make and immensely satisfying when the goal was achieved. Particularly in a society in which, though unusually attuned to the importance of things, sheer survival had been a problem just a century before, this new form of satisfaction made sense.

The Birth of
Contemporary Society

WITH THE NEW ECONOMIC STRUCTURE and the reasons for its growing acceptance, we are dealing with genuine revolution. A small capitalist current in the West had grown into a total restructuring of the way society was organized and had become the basis for social classes. The aristocracy was gone, even the propertied merchant; the new ruling class, the managers and scientists, had replaced them. And in the process, the popular mentality had changed.

Class differences continued to mark mature industrial societies, but increasingly there was some cultural interchange. Obviously workers, with lower earnings, took less elaborate vacations than their bosses. But a general leisure ethic developed that affected all groups. Life off the job became increasingly defined. Work might still be regarded as pleasant, even on the assembly line, but it was a segment of life, not its entirety. For most Europeans, life off the job no longer involved the traditional customs. Few went to church—about five percent of the English population on a given Sunday. More went to bars, but public drinking became less common. The new passions were sports, dancing and the stage, the movie, and finally TV entertainment. This was a faddish culture, shallow in some ways, but it represented a people groping for secular enjoyment and faced with more choice, more cultural outlets than ever before.

The family represented a vital part of the new culture; here there was definite continuity with the past. More people married, often at a young age, than ever before. But the family was no longer primarily a baby-producing unit. Birth control spread steadily with artificial devices—at first diaphrams and condoms, then the pill—making intercourse possible without distorting sexual enjoyment. The children that were born were given new love and attention. Most would now survive to adulthood, given modern standards of living and medical care, so it was not a risk to lavish affection on them; and at the same time more affection helped create healthier children.

The family became less patriarchal. Children, particularly once they reached adolescence, were less dominated by the father; this was especially noticeable after World War II. Wives were also more equal partners in family decision-making, and the desire for husband-wife affection increased as the family turned its main functions away from sheer economics, from working as a producing unit, to emotional satisfaction. More wives worked outside the home, which gave them supplementary interests and also, as bread winners, a right to have a say in what was going on. Women were still not treated as equals, in the family or out, but they had steadily gained in independence.

Once the shock of novelty was over, then, the industrial revolution proved a boon to most people. There were many aspects disliked, and there was fear of further change. An individual's life might crumble if his family failed to provide needed affection, if divorce or a fight with a child threw him or her into loneliness, for the new industrial world could be cold and impersonal. The dependence on steadily increasing prosperity might prove dangerous. An individual might not make the desired gains and feel a failure. And perhaps the economy itself might be unable to keep pace with new demands, particularly as crucial raw materials, such as oil, proved limited in supply. Even before the energy crises, Europe as well as the United States faced mounting inflation, as growing demand for goods was now not matched by production increases; here was a persistent source of tension. But collectively, most elements of western society had improved, particularly in the thirty years after World War II. In the process the earlier features of western civilization were accentuated. Certainly people were more individualistic. Perhaps, through education and self-development, they were more rational. Values that had been preached by a small number of intellectuals, and were accessible only to a few elements of the upper classes, gained wider circulation on the crest of economic upheaval. The western world was far from perfect, even by its own standards. Happiness cannot be quantified. Nevertheless, in terms of western goals and the expectations generated by industrialization, there was a greater sense of satisfaction with life than ever before. All one can add is what Napoleon's mother said when he was at the peak of his power (and, of course, in her case forebodings were correct): if only it lasts.

Criticisms of the new society abounded. Many intellectuals were disappointed that workers seemed so easily contented with new cars and other material goods. Hard-nosed labor leaders had to worry when their constituents were either working overtime to pay off a car or were driving around with the family in their new toy; either way, they were less likely to come to union and party meetings. White-collar workers, on the other hand, showed signs of new anxieties. Like many factory operatives earlier, they found their jobs increasingly routinized, their supervisors impersonal. And at the top of society, the new governing elite, while far more attuned to the needs of a new economic structure, could be justly accused of a planning mania, a desire to blueprint areas of human life that simply could not be fit into a single mold. The scientists and managers, often called technocrats, could easily lose the common touch.

Outside the government orbit there were new tensions as well. If parent-child relationships had mellowed, generational friction was serious; the idea of a gap was not an invention of the 1960s but seemed almost endemic in industrial society. Kept in school well past their sexual maturity, which occurred at an ever-earlier age (puberty has dropped 3-4 months each generation in the twentieth century), youth might feel superior to their parents, who often lacked their educational levels, but gallingly dependent on them as well. At an extreme, rising juvenile crime and, after 1960, a new increase in illegitimacy reflected frustration, though here the American version of western society produced rates that no European country could approach.

Women had yet to find a fully acceptable role. Their legal situation improved. Those European countries which had denied them the vote, like France, granted it after World War II. In the 1960s and 1970s remaining restrictions on birth control were lightened and abortion was legalized in many countries. But women were not only paid less than men but were still concentrated

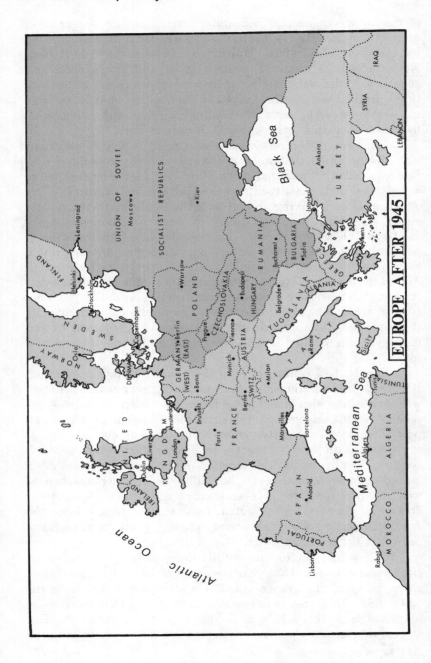

EUROPE AFTER 1945

in distinctively "female" occupations, like nursing. There was a historic switch: better-educated than ever before, more and more women' went to work outside the home after the first years of marriage and child-bearing; their percentage in the workforce rose dramatically. At the same time many women professed not to want the same career stress as men.

Not surprisingly, in a society undergoing continuous change, ambiguity pervades topics ranging from class relationships to family ties. As severe material problems eased, new difficulties surged to take their place. Rising expectations might outstrip gains. Inflation, a constant problem, was in the 1970s supplemented by the more ominous threat of energy shortage; and what would western society do, now attuned to steadily advancing prosperity, if the merry-go-round was turned off? And bread, or even oil, did not describe life. The modern western man was more dependent on emotional attachments, on love relationships with spouse or children, than ever before; what if these would sour? Yet the postwar world was good to the west, after some painful rebuilding. The last three decades have not completed the cycle of change or adjustment, but they constitute a fuller development of the possibilities for human growth inherent in industrialization.

Conclusion

Western civilization, not surprisingly, is something of a will-o'-the-wisp. We raised earlier the basic question of when it began. The answer seems to be at that point when Germanic and Christian cultures assimilated selected classical values into a threefold merger—in other words, as medieval civilization took shape. We can find western elements earlier, but not a coherent package. But this question remains open for any reader to judge. No matter where one starts, change is constant. We have stressed certain continuities, in intellectual tradition and in political tensions that distinguished the West from other areas. But one can certainly argue that the industrial revolution, albeit initially a western product, changed the whole ballgame, giving concepts like rationality or the limited state a different meaning.

Science obviously continues to boom in western society, but it is no longer the investigation of the essence of nature so much as highly compartmentalized research inquiries into specific topics, often with technical application. The work is based, still, on the assumption that the world follows rational laws, but few people inquire into the basic laws. Aquinas or Newton would have difficulty in understanding the approach, though they would be interested in some of the results. But have science and western rationality evolved, or have they changed decisively over the major stages of the past?

Louis XIV would delight in the power of the central state even in its welfare version, but he would be bewildered by the technocrats, the absence of aristocratic ceremonies, and the attention to the poorer classes. And run for office? Voluntarily withdraw from conquered lands? Inconceivable to the sun-king. Yet his innovations in bureaucracy and state functions do genuinely relate to a government he would disavow.

But this of course is, in a way, simply saying that western civilization has had a history, and history is change. The problem, continuity vs. change, is most difficult to measure with regard to the common people, men and women alike. Compared to classical civilization, common people gained a measure of freedom as it was recognized that they, like the rich, had souls. Serfdom was not slavery (though westerners showed no reluctance in enslaving non-Europeans). Women might gain new prominence. To be sure the daily grind continued for most ordinary people. But the West never developed the caste system, the extreme of segregation by which Hindu society was organized, with some people considered so inferior they were called and treated as untouchables at the bottom of the heap. Only legal and property measures have stratified western society from the Middle Ages onward, and they are slightly less rigid, slightly less exclusive of an ambitious newcomer.

If we turn from continuity to change, it seems clear that the West was distinctive, always within the general constraints of an agricultural society, in the unusual role it allowed to merchants and in the relative freedom won by the common people by the end of the Middle Ages. Both produced first gradual, then revolutionary change in the economy and in popular mentality.

So we get a complicated picture: Certain distinctive western elements may be viewed as evolutionary—changing greatly but preserving indentifiable features over time. We have suggested intellectual and political life as prime areas of consideration here, but every reader must decide what is evolution and what is a decisive break. As an example histories of the English welfare state generally begin with measures taken by Queen Elizabeth late in the sixteenth century to aid the poor. Yet these were designed to tie the poor down as much as to let them survive. Maybe the modern welfare state has the same Machiavellian motives in mind, to use modest welfare aid to lull the poor into passivity. But one must admit that at least the scale of aid has vastly changed. Is this evolution of state function, or revolution at some point? As to the common people themselves, no question but that we have had revolution, even though formal attempts at popular protest more often failed than not. The industrial revolution, though in part the product of initiatives by ordinary artisans or domestic workers, changed the position of the masses in society dramatically. Peasant culture has virtually disappeared, with a rich mixture of popular values taking its place. The masses do not rule even though they have the vote. They are exploited, in the sense that their labor produces excess money for a rich minority. But they influence cultural outlets, from TV to primary education. They cannot be ignored by governments even when they are not in full, violent protest. They may still be mistreated, but their mistreatment occurs at a much different, more subtle or moderate level than ever before.

This leads to three final questions: Where are we heading? Where is western civilization now? How do we judge its qualities? As a final perverseness, we will take these up in reverse order.

We have implied a certain progressiveness to western civilization as governments become more stable, societies more secular, and the lot of ordinary people more varied and interesting. One can quarrel with these or any other judgments. The welfare state, for example, can be seen as a horrible cramping of individual initiative to the profit of slobbering masses. I think such a view is nonsense. But anyone has the right to disagree, with one proviso. There is a tendency not just to say the present is bad, which is perfectly possible, but that it is worse than the past. Now this latter is also possible, but when one takes this approach, one must realize that one is talking about history. We constantly are tempted to create golden ages from which we have fallen. One example: old people. Sociologists, one of the few groups that have studied old people, if they have a historical framework at all assert that old people were honored in the past and have fallen into disfavor in a youth-oriented society. This is almost certainly wrong. Is there anything unsavory in a 55-year-old widow marrying a 60-year-old widower? In a pre-industrial village this could have been the occasion for massive, violent protests, at the least ridiculing the woman. Women were not supposed to be anything but passive grandmas after they were fifty or so. Gradually, against the common culture (many people still think, erroneously, that sex after 50 or so is evil), old people have hacked out a jazzier life, particularly of course in the middle class where funds are relatively adequate.

It has been argued that workers have declined with modern times from the artisan who produced his own whole product to the assembly line piece worker. But most workers in preindustrial times were pulling a plow or following the ox who did it. They were interesting people, they had a valuable culture. But can one be sure that, as agricultural labor has declined and varied urban work (not primarily factory labor, in point of fact) has replaced it, that there have not been gains? Otherwise why do people still leave the countryside? The golden age approach has been applied to women. They had great roles when they did productive work for the family, and now they are mere household toys. Against this, first, their preindustrial productive work was extremely strenuous. Second, they were having (if married) eight to ten pregnancies on the average, half of which would result in dead infants, as against the two or three common today, given the massive use of birth control. Third, their family role has in many ways improved, in terms of decision-making power and emotional equality (including sexual enjoyment). Obviously, all this tends toward the conclusion that modern western society, as it industrialized particularly, tended to make lives better. Not perfect, but better. This is a teleological view, and one might accept some of the facts and reject the teleology, saying that there is no improvement, just constant misery or even rising degradation through capitalists or males or some other exploitor. This approach, however, not only distorts history but also discourages efforts for further improvement by making us look backward and not forward. Those people who want to go back to peasant life and peasant virtues are, first, rarely of peasant stock; the peasants, at least after a generation of acclimation to the city, know better. And, second, they have not studied the psychic as well as material constraints of traditional agricultural life. But all of this is to indicate an opinion, which some might call bias, in favor of the direction of the modern world.

If the modern world has a direction, how far does it extend? We have tried to delineate western civilization geographically. For centuries it has included England, France, the Low Countries, Scandinavia, and West Germany. Italy has been central at key points, though the backward social structure of the South raises some problems. This is a narrow base, as we have pointed out. Other areas have shown elements of western civilization but not the whole culture. Prussia and Russia, for example, long followed western trends in government but not in social structure; which means ultimately not in government either, because governments could be formed that western people, so far at least, would not tolerate. And then there are the frontier lands—the U.S., Canada, and Australia. On the whole, there is clear sharing of western values in such areas, again with exceptions such as American slavery. We find similar forms of government, a shared intellectual community, and a shared popular culture. In the 1920s, Europe imported American movie stars; in the 1960s, the U.S. imported the Beatles. Clearly the same world. But there are peculiarities. Houston, an enterprising city, has more murders annually than the whole of England with a population less than 1/15 the size. The American divorce rate is four times that of Sweden. Are Americans at the forefront of modern western society? (British rates of violence and divorce rose in the 1960s, though to only about a fifth of ours, but the British may just be behind the times). Or did a distinctive frontier experience, unprecedented mixing of racial groups, create a variant—and not necessarily a pleasant variant—of the western tradition? Latin America poses an even more difficult interpretive problem, for western elements, mainly urbanized, have not fully penetrated Indian rural areas; and no Latin American country is fully industrialized yet.

How far, then, has the West spread its net? We have granted the obvious, that with industrialization western civilization itself changed greatly. There were, however, continuities with tradition. With industrialization will other areas come to resemble the new west? Will Russia develop more pressure for consumer goods and individual choice, and will this change the orientation of government? Studies of Russian families find them modernizing as in the West: lower birth rates, high personal aspirations for children and affection for them, marriage on the basis of love, a sense of considerable equality between the sexes and interest in sensual enjoyment. Japanese popular culture becomes increasingly identifiable in western terms. Even the unusually deferential Japanese workers are beginning to agitate for a better life as individual consumers and less dominance by paternalistic employers. None of this is to argue that we'll all homogenize in one peaceful, or dull, world; clearly distinctive cultural traditions will be retained, as remains the case in individual European countries. But increasing similarities, embodying values first displayed in the West, are developing. Dress, family structures, courting patterns—the list is long. The similarities are based on the common experience of industrialization combined with some direct copying of the West.

All this is at the level of popular culture. It leaves two unanswered questions. First, we must not assume that similar popular cultures will produce similar intellectual and political trends. The Russian family resembles its western counterpart. A Russian managerial class has arisen to train people very similar to western managers in personal goals and professional behavior. But the Russian government, though providing elaborate welfare facilities for the masses, is not a welfare state; it remains totalitarian, though we must not ignore continued police repression of intellectuals and dissidents in the West. The anomaly posed by similar lifestyles developing while different governmental traditions persist may not last forever, for governments may change or political pressures may force popular cultures further apart even at present, in terms of lifestyles. For though one may hope that political difference is compatible with peace, real political difference remains, and it reflects long standing historical divergence; it would be rash to predict growing assimilation here. Further, we must note that we do not assume that all areas of the world can or should industrialize. Some places may have population structures and cultural values that will make massive industrialization impossible. So we are not predicting one world. A key threat to the western world lies in the growing gap between impoverished countries whose leaders, at least, strive for independence and growth, and the highway-dotted, meat-guzzling west. Does this portend a new world division, particularly menacing to Europe which is not conveniently separated from key areas of the Third World by ocean frontiers? Again, the problem's potential can be stated, but forecast remains cloudy.

In fact, we are not definitely predicting anything. For the western world, the last thirty years have been good. Like all civilizations the West has gone up and down for a long time. There is no sign that western people will voluntarily change the present course of their societies. There are no new mass political movements or vast new trends in protest, no signs of major intellectual reorientation. But one of the new values the West, like all industrial areas, has incorporated, is change. Sometime, surely, the change will be great enough to create a new era, not just a new fad or a new phase of industrialization. What or when this will be we cannot know. What will be interesting, for those of us still around, is to see how much of the western form of civilization is retained amid change. For this has been a resilient culture, and even now that it is devoted to change it may bounce a good bit without losing its basic shape.

Suggested Readings

An interpretation of the twentieth century as a distinct period in European history is Geoffrey Barrsclough, *An Introduction to Contemporary History* (1967); predictive essays are Daniel Bell, *The Coming of Post-Industrial Society* (1973) and Alvin Toffler, *Future Shock* (1971). Studies of the postwar era are Maurice Crouzet, *The European Renaissance* (1970); George Lichtheim, *The New Europe Today—and Tomorrow* (1964); Stephen Graubard, ed., *A New Europe?* (1963); and Carl Degler, *Affluence and Anxiety: The United States since 1945* (1968). Critical interpretations of the modern world are Herbert Marcuse, *One Dimensional Man* (1964) and R.D. Lang, *The Politics of Experience* (1967).

On intellectual and cultural developments, E. Zimmer, *The Revolution in Physics* (1936); L. Barnett, *The Universe and Doctor Einstein* (1952); Benjamin Nelson, ed., *Freud and the 20th Century* (1958); Morton White, *Age of Analysis* (1955); H.E. Barnes, ed., *An Introduction to the History of Sociology* (1948); C.P. Snow, *The Two Cultures* (1970); A.H. Barr, Jr., *What is Modern Painting* (1968); and Carlo Cipolla, *Literacy and Development in the West* (1969).

The vital topic of the development of leisure is treated in Michael Marrus, *The Rise of Leisure* (1974) and R. W. Malcolmson, *Popular Recreations in English Society* (1973); see also Peter C. McIntosh, *Sport in Society* (1963).

On imperialism, Stewart Easton, *The Rise and Fall of Western Colonialism* (1964) and D.K. Fieldhouse, *The Colonial Empires* (1966). On a case of decolonization, John Strachey, *End of Empire* (1960).

For the coming of World War I, Laurence Lafore, *The Long Fuse* (1965); on World War II, Gordon Wright, *The Ordeal of Total War* (1968). For the Cold War, W. LaFeber, *America, Russia and the Cold War* (1968); David Sumler, *Europe and the Cold War* (1974); John Lukacs, *A New History of the Cold War* (1966). For the Common Market, Leon Lindberg, *The Political Dynamics of European Economic Integration* (1963).

Concerning the Russian Revolution, Daniel Brower, *Russia and the West: The Origins of the Russian Revolution* (1975); E.H. Carr, *History of Soviet Russia* (1950) and B.O. Wolfe, *Three Who Made a Revolution* (1964). Subsequent developments are treated in Carr, *The Soviet Impact on the Western World* (1947); M. Salvadori, *The Rise of Modern Communism* (1963); and Barrington Moore, *Soviet Politics: The Dilemma of Power* (1950).

On fascism and nazism, Stanley Payne, *Fascism and National*

Socialism (1975); F. L. Carsten, *The Rise of Fascism* (1967); David Schoen-baum, *Hitler's Social Revolution* (1966).

For socialism, Harvey Mitchell and Peter N. Stearns, *Workers and Protest* (1971); on western communism, Annie Kriegel, *The French Communist Party* (1973).

On economic trends, James Laux, *The Great Depression* (1975); Andrew Shonfield, *Modern Capitalism* (1967); and M.M. Postan, *An Economic History of Western Europe, 1945-1964* (1967).

Interwar social trends are entertainingly discussed in R. Graves and A. Hodge, *The Long Weekend* (1941). Changes in social structure are analyzed in Ralf Dahrendorf, *Class and Class Conflict in Industrial Society* (1958). On women, E. Sullerot, *Women, Society and Change* (1971) and R. Patai, ed., *Women in the Modern World* (1967). Two studies on the family by P. Willmott and M. Young are particularly important: *Family and Kinship in East London* (1957) and *The Symmetrical Family* (1973). On workers, Peter N. Stearns, *Lives of Labor* (1975) and J. H. Goldthorpe and others, *The Affluent Worker in the Class Structure* (1966). A new current of unrest is analyzed in H. Bourges, ed., *The Student Revolt* (1968); see also John Gillis, *Youth and History* (1974).